My Mother's Sons

My Mother's Sons

Managing Sexuality

in Islamic & Christian

Communities

Patrick Krayer

WILLIAM CAREY
LIBRARY

Published by William Carey Library
1605 E. Elizabeth Street
Pasadena, CA 91104 |www.missionbooks.org

Aidan Lewis, editor
Brad Koenig, copyeditor
Rose Lee-Norman, index
Alyssa E. Force, design

Cover photo: iStockphoto LP

William Carey Library is a ministry of the
U.S. Center for World Mission
Pasadena, CA | www.uscwm.org

Printed in the United States of America

17 16 15 14 13   5 4 3 2 1 BP1000

Library of Congress Cataloging-in-Publication Data

Krayer, Patrick.
    My mother's sons : managing sexuality in Islamic and Christian communities /
Patrick Krayer.
        pages cm
    Includes bibliographical references.
    ISBN 978-0-87808-625-2
    1. Sex--Religious aspects--Christianity. 2. Sex--Religious aspects--Islam.
    I. Title.
    BT708.K735 2013
    306.7088'297--dc23
                                                            2013004856

*To all who cross ethnic, cultural, and religious boundaries
in order to be faithful representatives of Christ.*

TABLE OF CONTENTS

Part I
Sexuality and Its Management in an Islamic Community

Part II
Sexuality and Its Management in Christian Communities

Part III
The Pashtuns and Paul: Sexuality, Culture, and Transformational Involvement

INTRODUCTION

Daughters of Jerusalem!
I am dark, but I am beautiful,
like the tents of Kedar,
like the curtains of Solomon.
So don't stare at me because my skin is dark;
it's because the sun has stared at me.
My mother's sons were angry with me,
they made me tend the vineyards;
but my own vineyard I tended not.

SONG OF SONGS 1:5,6[1]

THE FEMALE LOVER in this song distances herself from her brothers by referring to them as her mother's sons. Why? They did not treat her like brothers should. They mistreated her. Due to their anger, they put a workload on her that caused her to neglect herself. So she suffered at their hands. No reason is given for their anger. The poem is constructed so that we side with the lover, assuming that her brothers' anger was unjustified.

If we back up from the text and think about the cultural context, these verses were written in a time and place where beauty was in part probably determined by the lightness of one's skin. (I have lived in several contemporary cultures that determine beauty this way.) Thus the female lover had become "ugly" due to her heavy workload in the vineyards and her overexposure to the sun. Though her circumstances negatively impacted her appearance, they clearly did not diminish her self-esteem. Her positive self-image refreshingly bursts forth in the first couplet (v. 5). Her beauty did not depend on the color of her skin.

These verses were written in a patriarchal setting, where males generally held the dominant position in family and society. The society had given the brothers the ability to control their sister's movements and determine her responsibilities. From the lover's vantage point, her brothers abused their position. Since we are inclined to side with the lover as we read, the text is subversive, subtly rebuking the misuse of male position and power.

Our own cultural assumptions and values impact the way we read Scripture and how we view other social systems. Those of us in Western cultures who have grown to value egalitarian social systems have developed a proclivity to devalue patriarchal social systems. Due to this, we are inclined to interpret the lover's rebuke as a diatribe against patriarchy. However, her subtle rebuke does not malign the patriarchal system. It only rebukes the misuse of power within that system.

This distinction is important, especially for those of us who live and work interculturally. Some of us are inclined to malign male-preferring, hierarchical social systems wherever we encounter them. We blur the distinction between hierarchical social systems and the abuse that occurs within these systems. It doesn't occur to us that many people live and work in such systems and support them. Contemporary Western readings of Scripture sacralize our perspective and strengthen our resolve to change these systems and make them egalitarian.

I have seen insiders resent attempts by Western outsiders who advocated for an egalitarian social model. These insiders felt that change was being imposed upon them, especially in an area that is so volatile as sexuality and its management. These attempts by outsiders for egalitarian change made the insiders feel like their society's moral foundations were under attack. Globalization and the consequent rapid social changes that have been taking place all over the world exacerbate the insiders' feelings.

I have interacted with many intercultural workers who were blind to these fears and tensions of insiders. The workers were appalled by the traditional ways the host society managed sexuality. Therefore they advocated for change. Though change was needed, the change these workers called for was constructed and imposed from the outside. Besides this, the workers had no idea of what impact their advocacy was having upon the society. Their advocacy provided fuel to those who opposed change. This advocacy also hindered the insiders who were sensitive to the need for change. These insiders wanted change, but they knew it had to occur at a much more gradual pace because they were sensitive to the apprehensions of their own people.

From my vantage point, these intercultural workers misused the social power they enjoyed due to their status, and they themselves inadvertently became like the lover's brothers, her mother's sons.

Purpose and Structure

This book is an attempt to help my fellow intercultural workers reflect on sexuality and its management from two different vantage points, Islam and Christianity. The goal in viewing sexuality and its management in this way is to become sensitive to the various cultural issues that are interconnected with gender management. This sensitivity is not meant to discourage advocacy and working for change; it is meant to help workers direct their energies in constructive ways so that their advocacy is culturally appropriate and can accomplish what they truly intend while ensuring that the host community does not feel under attack.

To pursue this goal, this book is divided into three parts. The first part looks at how sexuality is perceived and managed in a particular Islamic culture. The Islamic culture I chose for this is the culture of the middle-class Pashtuns of Peshawar, Pakistan. The reason I chose this ethnic group is because my family and I lived in the Peshawari Pashtun culture for many years and fluently speak their language. People manage sexuality according to the religio-cultural assumptions and values that they hold about sexuality. Therefore I describe not only the ways these Pashtuns manage sexuality but also the reasons why this style of management exists (ch. 1). I proceed to show how this system of management impacts engagement and marriage (ch. 2). I conclude this part by showing how Islamic sacred literature (i.e., the Qur'an and Hadith[2]) provides the basic rationale and framework for Pashtuns in how they perceive and manage sexuality (ch. 3).

Islamic cultures are not monolithic. Nonetheless, what makes this study beneficial is that, though Muslim cultures differ in the particulars, they share the sacred literature of Islam. This sacred literature creates a level of consistency and conformity across the differing cultures. Therefore this specific description of the Peshawari Pashtuns and the overview of Islamic sacred writ provide a baseline of information by which workers can more sensitively reflect on the dynamics surrounding sexuality and its management in their specific contexts.

The second part of the book looks at how sexuality and its management are viewed in Christian cultures. Just as Muslim communities shape their lives by their understanding of their sacred texts, so Christian communities have used the biblical texts to shape their lives. By studying the key biblical passages on sexuality and its management we gain insight into how Christian communities think about and manage human sexuality.

Sexuality and its management in Western, evangelical Christian cultures are shaped by two interpretive readings of Scripture: egalitarian and complementarian. As a Westerner, I find the egalitarian reading more appealing than the complementarian. Nonetheless, as an intercultural worker I view the egalitarian reading as being too culturally bounded, overly shaped by Western egalitarian ideals. Therefore this model can be destabilizing rather than constructive in non-Western, traditional cultures. Though the complementarian reading can be adapted to traditional cultures, it does not intentionally reform traditional structures. The complementarian school draws too much from historical, patriarchal readings and misses the reformational intent of Scripture. Since I view both schools as inadequate for intercultural work, I present an alternative reading of the biblical texts.[3] I affirm the reformational intent of Scripture, and I contend that God offers human cultures much more freedom of movement in expression than the egalitarian school tends to allow.

To provide a foundational level of content to help intercultural workers think about Christian cultures, I identify how Paul addressed issues of sexuality and its management in his first-century Greco-Roman context. To accomplish this I divide Part 2 into a series of manageable steps. First, I describe the first-century Roman approach to gender and its management (ch. 4). Describing Roman society is fraught with limitations, primarily because we are predominantly given the viewpoint of a limited number of Roman aristocrats who happened to be almost exclusively male. Nonetheless there is an agreement that with careful analysis it is possible to reconstruct a reliable portrait of gender management in the first-century world (see Cohick 2009, 20).

Second, I make an in-depth analysis of Genesis 1–3 (chs. 5–7).[4] The reason for this is that Paul refers to the creation account directly or indirectly in these texts about sexuality and its management: 1 Corinthians 11:2–16; Galatians 3:28;[5] Ephesians 5:22–33; and 1 Timothy 2:9–15.[6] The creation narrative apparently provided Paul with his cognitive framework.

Third, I proceed to work though the key Pauline texts to show that Paul harmonized his understanding of sexuality and its management as presented in the creation narrative with the on-the-ground realities of his cultural context (chs. 8–12). I assert that, since Paul lived and operated in his first-century world, he accepted and operated within the framework of his society. For example, Paul did not advocate for the abolition of slavery. He probably could not imagine a world free of the institution. Nonetheless, though Paul may have accepted and operated within first-century social structures, Paul did not accept the values and assumptions behind those structures. Paul spoke his countercultural values into his world, subverting that world. Following the example of the female lover in the Song of Solomon, Paul sought to elevate the dignity of each person and transform the way power was used in relationships.

Finally, in Part 3 I summarize and synthesize the material (ch. 13) and I provide suggestions as to how to engage our host cultures as we seek to encourage transformational change (ch. 14).

The Need for Emotional Distance

Talking about sexuality and its management can stir up a hornet's nest of controversy. We naturally attach strong emotions to our beliefs and values, whether we are fundamentalist, conservative, or liberal. These emotional attachments develop as we live out our lives in our communities. Our beliefs and values are connected to memories of significant events, and these connections only increase the intensity of our feelings.

The problem is that these emotional attachments can be detrimental. If our beliefs or values are contradicted, our emotions kick in and shut down our thinking processes. When it comes to the topic of sexuality and its management, it seems that our emotions respond at hyperspeed.

The generic topic of sexuality is not so volatile, because we are all sexual beings. However, when we talk about managing sexuality, then the artillery comes out. The word "manage" can instantly conjure up images of control and oppression. For others the word may have the opposite effect. Managing sexuality might be perceived as essential, protecting the very foundation of moral order from erosion.

When we add Islamic and Christian beliefs to the discussion of sexuality, the topic can become explosive. Images of women covered in black with only their eyes showing can evoke strong negative reactions in Western communities. In contrast, images of women in tight-fitting tank tops and short shorts evoke strong negative reactions in conservative Islamic communities.

Whether we realize it or not, all communities and societies manage sexuality. I suggest that a positive way forward for those who work interculturally is to view the way any given society goes about managing sexuality as different, not necessarily wrong. God loves diversity: ethnic and cultural. As God's representatives we should look for ways to affirm culture, not just identify the ways that it does not measure up to God's standards. Also, as intercultural workers we should acknowledge that cultures are ever changing. This should give us hope and flexibility. We can adapt to the present because we know that the ways in which any given society structures itself can change. As values change, structures within the society can change.

Conclusion

This study examines the cultural systems (assumptions, beliefs, folklore, and values) about maleness and femaleness in both Islamic and Christian contexts and how sexuality is managed in the light of these systems.[7] Since these contexts vary in space and time, we are able to hear from a variety of communities, ancient and modern. This hearing increases our capacity to critically reflect on what we believe and why we do the things we do. In this way we are empowered to consider if our beliefs, assumptions, and values are valid; and we are empowered to judge if our corresponding behaviors are truly appropriate for our cultural context as well as other cultural contexts.

This is a topic about which people have very strong feelings. Due to this I try to respect every position as I interact with the material. I present the material in a coherent and documented manner in order to make each point compelling. Yet I expect disagreement with portions of my analysis and conclusions. In this light, I do not ask for agreement; I only ask for critical reflection. When critical reflection occurs, the possibilities become alive for transformation.

– Patrick Krayer

---

1   The biblical and Qur'anic translations in the Introduction and in chapters 1-7 are mine and the biblical quotations in chapters 8-14 are from the Revised Standard Version (RSV) unless otherwise noted.

2   The Hadith are compilations of the sayings of the Prophet of Islam.

3   I could assert that my position is more "biblical" than the others. However, I find such an assertion anachronistic.

4   The assumption behind the exegetical method I employ is that the Bible contains contextualized universal truths. The goal of the study of the Scriptures is to understand the original languages of the Scripture

and the social, cultural, gender, religious, economic, literary, and narrative worlds of the authors and authorial audiences in order to unwrap these universal truths. This method stands in contrast to the method that assumes Scripture contains ahistorical/acultural articulations of universal truths.

5 In this verse Paul breaks with the linguistic pattern of the first two clauses when he refers to males and females: *There is not Jew nor Greek; there is not bondman nor free; there is not male and female.* This break in pattern in the third clause indicates Paul is quoting from Genesis 1:27 (see Scholer 1998, 7; Snodgrass 1986, 171; Stendahl 1966, 32).

6 This is in contrast to scholars who assert that Paul's interpretive *locus classicus* for gender is Galatians 3:28. Richard Hess recognizes the significance of the creation narrative. He states, "The accounts of creation, the Garden of Eden, and the Fall in Genesis 1–3 may contain more doctrinal teaching concerning the nature of humanity as male and female, as well as the state of the fallen world, than any other single text in the Bible" (Hess 2005, 79). This also stands in opposition to those who use 1 Timothy 2:9–15 as an interpretive lens for the other Pauline passages.

7 See Appendix A for an explanation of cultural and social systems.

Part I

Sexuality and Its Management in an Islamic Community

Tell the believing men to lower their gaze and be modest. This is purer for them. Look, Allah is aware of what they do.

Tell the believing women to lower their gaze and be modest, and to display of their attire only that which is obvious, and to draw their veils over their chests, and to reveal their attire only to their husbands, fathers, husbands' fathers, their sons, their husbands' sons, their brothers, their brothers' sons, their sisters' sons, their women, their slaves, their eunuchs, or to children who know nothing about women's nakedness. And, they should not stamp their feet, revealing what they are concealing of their attire.

Sura an-Nur [24]:30,31
The Noble Qur'an

1

Purdah: A Means of Understanding and Managing Sexuality

MUSTAFA WAS OPEN-MINDED and he wanted to learn about the Christian faith. He had heard about it but never had much exposure to it. He also wanted his new bride to learn about it. To do this he thought about visiting a Christian pastor whom he had met. The pastor lived in a city only a few hours away from Mustafa. Mustafa wrote a letter to the pastor asking if he and his church practiced purdah (the practice of separating nonrelated men and women). The pastor wrote back and said they did. As a result, my friend felt comfortable taking his wife to visit the pastor and attend his church. Everything was fine at the pastor's home, because the pastor was an older man and only he and his wife lived in the house. After the meal, the pastor invited the young couple to attend the church service. When the couple walked into the service, they found the men sitting on one side of the room and the women sitting on the other side. The man sat his wife down at the back of the women's section, and they stayed through the service.

The experience at the church was horrific for Mustafa's wife. She left feeling as if she had been raped. It took her months to get over her feeling of defilement.

What went wrong?

Purdah[1] is much more than the practice of covering one's head or body. Purdah is a cultural system comprised of sacred stories, folklore, beliefs, assumptions, and values about male and female sexuality. Out of this cultural system a series of shared schemas arise by which Pashtuns understand and interpret male and female sexuality. Purdah is also a corresponding social system that structures and manages sexuality and intergender interaction.

One of the driving desires behind the system is to create moral and social order. I think this is a desire that all humans have. One of the ways Pashtuns seek to fulfill this desire is through this system of purdah.

It is understood that without purdah a destructive force would be created that would attack the society. One person described it this way: "Without purdah the society would become confused. But the thought of Islam is that confusion should not be created."

As one would expect, the assumptions and values embedded within the shared schemas reinforce the need for the practice of purdah. In addition, many of these assumptions and values are also found in the sacred literature of Islam. Thus they enjoy special sanction. Since these assumptions and values are in the sacred literature, they are shared throughout the Muslim world and influence the way sexuality is perceived and managed in each location.

In this chapter I will describe the key beliefs, folklore, assumptions, and values embedded within the schematic world of the Pashtuns and describe how Pashtuns live out purdah as a social system.

Purdah Means "Curtain"

The word *purdah* literally means "curtain."[2] A curtain symbolizes the ethos of the system: separation. Separation is what everyone experiences when they arrive in the city of Peshawar. Seven- to eight-foot walls line the streets, blocking the passerby's view of each house and yard. The walls butt up right against the street.

When I first went to Peshawar in 1984, I did not like the walls. I was used to living in American suburbs where everything was open and I could see the nicely manicured lawns. In contrast, the Peshawari walls had no aesthetic beauty. They only added more shades of brown to what I perceived as an already drab landscape. I had no idea how integral these walls were to purdah.

Years later, while I was in the US, I picked up an Afghan couple from their house in the middle of the afternoon. When I arrived at their house I noticed that they had all the drapes drawn in the windows in the front of their house. Since they did not have walls surrounding their yard, their drapes served the same purpose. Purdah in their house had returned to its literal meaning.

Purdah: Separating the World into Public and Domestic Space

The system of purdah separates the world into two separate spheres for human activity: the public and the domestic. The public sphere is given primarily to men, and the domestic sphere is given primarily to women.

In this world of separated space, men have free and unlimited access to the public sphere, while women are given limited access. Conversely, women are given free and unlimited access to the domestic sphere, while men are given limited access.

This separation seems sexist and restrictive from a Western point of view. Those who are not used to dichotomizing space in this way tend to react negatively to it. They wonder how a society could restrict a woman's access to the public sphere. However, Pashtuns view purdah in a positive light. One Pashtun described purdah like this: "Islam has given women the right to move about elegantly inside the house, and the man is given the honor to move about outside with men."

Though this man's description might irritate Western sensibilities, it does not adequately describe how this separation of space works. Since men have free access to the public sphere, the newcomer to purdah is prone to assume that men have no restrictions. This is because Westerners see purdah's public space as the realm with the most possibilities for personal and professional development. Thus men get all the benefit and women are restricted. However, men also face restrictions. Even though men can move about freely in public, they encounter restrictions the moment they enter domestic space. These restrictions in domestic spaces indicate to the man that he is an outsider. In a culture that is communal in nature, not individualistic, being an outsider has negative implications. In a converse manner, though women have restricted access to the public sphere, women are free to move about in their own houses and (theoretically) in every house they enter. Thus women are ascribed the honor of insiders.

Purdah: Separating People into Insiders and Outsiders

As the purdah world separates space into two categories, public and private, it also separates people into two categories: insiders and outsiders.[3] The outsider is a nonrelationally connected male; that is, neither a relative nor a close friend. Since the outsider is not relationally connected, no social constraints exist to keep him from acting in self-interest.

Part of that self-interest is to gratify one's sexual desires. One Pashtun described it this way: "When men want sex, there are only two ways to get it. One is through male-to-male interaction. The other is by illegal means, where a man can get with a woman. Well, he wants to have sex with her. He will try with her. He will talk with her in order to connect."

Therefore, in the purdah world the outsider is inherently suspect, a potential sexual predator, and he must be kept at a distance. One Pashtun summed up this suspicious view of the outsider when he said, "I think that people do more purdah here [in Peshawar], because when [my wife or sisters] go out they come face to face with people we don't know. They can do anything."

This assumption stands in marked contrast to fundamental assumptions about outsiders that exist in Northern Europe and in North America. We do not inherently have misgivings about males who are not relationally connected to us. This is because Northern European and North American cultures are considered to be "high trust" cultures.[4] However, the purdah world is a "low trust" world.[5] The relational characteristics by which outsiders and insiders are defined are clear. The outsider has to be kept at bay until he has earned trust.

This underlying level of suspicion of the outsider provides the first foundation stone for purdah. Purdah cannot be understood apart from it. The second foundation stone is *hayá*.

Purdah: Shaped by Hayá

Hayá is the overarching moral principle within the system of purdah. *Hayá* is an Arabic word which literally means "modesty." As a moral principle, hayá encompasses males and females. In the minds of Pashtuns, hayá is foundational for a healthy, moral society. Without hayá the society would collapse into moral and social confusion. As I mentioned previously, one of the main desires of the Pashtun, and one of the chief goals of the system of purdah, is to create moral and social order. Hayá and maintaining proper separation are primary steps in achieving this moral and social order.

One Pashtun described a man's hayá this way: "A man's hayá is to keep your gaze down. Don't look at wrong things. If you see a woman, don't look at her with a wrong intention. Don't look lustfully. For a man, hayá is of the eyes." However, hayá embraces much more than self-controlled sexual behavior. It also encompasses all moral conduct, such as keeping promises, respecting elders, and being moderate in one's behavior. A man can be perceived as immodest (*be-hayá*) if he laughs too loudly or excessively. One can gain no respect or standing in the community if one is considered *be-hayá*.

Therefore there is a bit of incongruity within the schemas of purdah. On one hand, a male is supposed to internally control himself and be modest. However, no one assumes that outside males will internalize the need for hayá and act appropriately.[6] Since there are those who do not, one needs to separate the outsider from the insider's family in order to safeguard the moral order. However, one does not only need to protect the female members of the family from outsiders, one also needs to protect females from their own weaknesses. To these weaknesses we now turn.

Purdah: Assumptions about Females

A compelling desire for social and moral order, the inherent suspicion of the outsider, and the moral value of hayá provide a significant part of the cognitive framework for the system of purdah. Three assumptions Pashtuns have about women and about female sexuality are also integral to this framework. The term "woman" refers to any postpubescent female. Two of these assumptions are part of the collective consciousness, shared by women and men. The third appears to be solely within the male schematic world.

The first assumption is illustrated by the coarse proverb "If a woman didn't have a nose, she would eat s--t." This proverb overtly means that a woman's eyes are not adequate to let her know what is bad for her. She needs extra help. It indicates that even though a woman can be very intelligent, she is limited in terms of her common sense. Some would say this limitation exists because a woman's intelligence is inherently inferior to a man's. They justify this with a quote from the Prophet of Islam: "*Naqis ul aqal wa naqis ul iman*" ("deficient in intelligence and deficient in faith").[7] In their view, even an ignorant man has a perceived advantage over an educated woman. Others disagree with this and say women are naive because they get very little exposure to what men in the public sphere are really like. This limitation, for whatever reason, exists in Pashtun schemas. Due to this, women need protection because they are prone to being deceived by cunning, sexually charged outside males.

A second assumption is that a woman's heart is somewhat inclined to stray from her husband. Subsequently, women are inherently untrustworthy. A common proverb articulates this sentiment: "Three things are untrustworthy: money, guns, and wives." The idea is that as long as these three are in your own hand, they are yours. However, if they get into another's hand, they become theirs. Therefore, one has to ensure that the woman does not stray and get into someone else's hands.

A third assumption is completely sexual in nature. It is assumed that a woman's sex drive is ten times greater than a man's.[8] Pashtun women do not appear to know that this assumption exists. It is not based in any sacred text; however, it is deeply embedded in the collective male consciousness.

These assumptions about females hinder the construction of intimacy in the marriage relationship. Men are inclined to mistrust their wives. One acquaintance told me that every man had some level of mistrust toward his wife. Time sometimes diminishes this mistrust and sometimes does not. One friend of mine said that a relative, in his later sixties, still mistrusted his wife, even though she too was in her sixties. A friend mistrusted his wife at different times throughout their first ten years of marriage. Waves of mistrust would come over him. In those times he would not let his wife go to the bathroom alone. One of his sons had to accompany her and wait outside the door while she was inside. If she ever went out of his immediate sight in the house while he was experiencing those waves (the house was very small), he would scream at her to find out where she was.

This mistrust causes men to monitor their wives' behaviors and movements outside the home. Some men prefer to live as exogamous, extended families[9] because their relatives (primarily the husband's mother and sisters) can keep a watchful eye on their wives. It is standard practice for a wife to keep her husband and his family fully aware of her movements in public space. This means that a woman has to get permission from her husband if she wants to leave her house. Women who have the permission to work are on a timed schedule. Relatives in the house know how much time it takes the women to get home after work. These women work hard to ensure they are never late in getting home or else they will get in trouble.

Though these assumptions are deeply embedded within the Pashtun schematic world, they are assumptions in transition. Women who gladly lived within the limitations placed upon them have been able to build trust with their husbands and their husbands' kin. Abiding by the limits is translated into their being virtuous. Their virtuous lives allow their husbands to relax some of the limitations they place on their wives. These women's behavior has also built trust within the community so that their communities have been relaxing some of the restrictions placed on other women. Some men assert that they trust their wives, though I only knew of two men who did not place limits or monitor their wives' movements. Also, the assumption about female erotic desire is losing currency among the educated. Some of the married men immediately dismiss this as erroneous (though single men I talked to never did). These changes demonstrate that the assumptions are in transition. This transitional nature of the assumptions is also demonstrated by the diverse ways in which purdah is practiced.

Purdah: Boundaries in Domestic Space

The assumptions about the predatorial nature of nonrelated males and the weak female nature make sense of why purdah separates space into two spheres, public and domestic. These spheres are needed to create and maintain social and moral order. Besides creating separate spatial spheres, purdah manages and safeguards these spheres by creating a series of boundaries within the spheres. The series of boundaries that protect the domestic sphere are walls, *betak*, and sound.

The Boundaries of Walls and Betak
The first of these boundaries is the high walls and gate that surround each and every house. These walls and gate effectively create the first boundary marker between the public and domestic spaces. For a culture that is primarily communal and social, not individualistic, this boundary has a significant, negative implication. The walls communicate to the man in the public sphere that those behind the walls view him as an outsider.

Over my years in Peshawar, I noticed that when visitors came to people's compounds, some would be led inside the gate while others were kept outside. The appropriate man of the house would come out and interact with the guest outside. The inherent mistrust of the outsider explains this behavior. The gate to the compound serves as a relational boundary. If the visitor is relationally not connected to the males of the house, and the interaction is strictly transactional, the visitor will remain outside and the transaction will be completed. An outsider will only be invited inside beyond the gate once he has a relationship with an insider and a significant level of trust has developed between them.

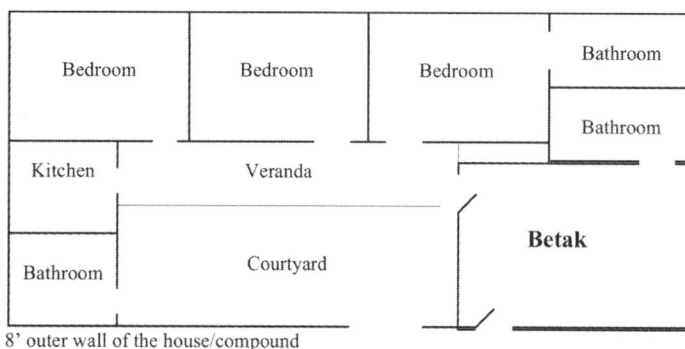

8' outer wall of the house/compound

Fig. 1. Traditional Style House with Betak

The invitation to move inside signifies that a significant level of trust exists between the two and that the insider feels secure in making the invitation. It is a privilege to be invited into someone's home. I enjoyed this privilege for many years without realizing it.

If a man is permitted to move inside these walls through the gate, he encounters another boundary, the boundary of the separate sitting room. This room is called the *betak* in Pashtu.

The betak is traditionally a room with its own entrance to the street (see fig. 1). It can also be a separate room inside the compound, but one that restricts the visitor's access to the rest of the house (see fig. 2). The betak often has an attached bathroom so there is no need for an outside male to enter any other portion of the house.

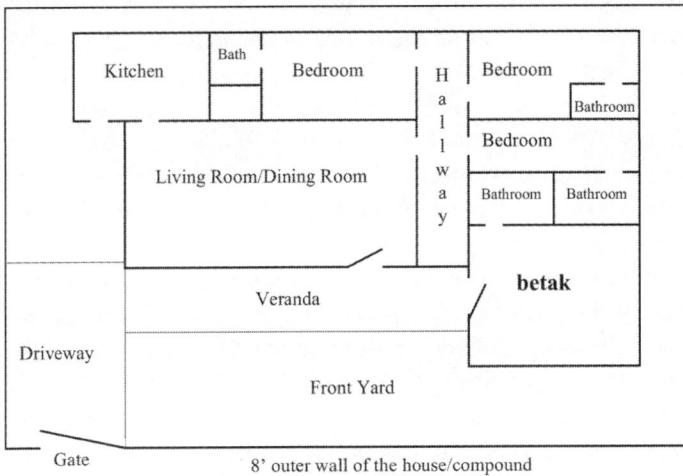

Fig. 2. Contemporary Style House with Betak

The betak enables the men of the house to allow guests inside the compound while effectively blocking access to the communal areas of the house, where the women and children are located. Through the use of the betak the men of the house can allow outside guests into the compound and satisfy the social requirements of their relationships while keeping their domestic space free from outsiders. Thus they can bring guests inside the house without really bringing them inside. The females of the house do not enter the betak while male outsiders are in it. The drinks and snacks are prepared by the women of the house but brought into the room by the men or the children of the house.

The betak does more than simply restrict the outsider's access to the house. The betak enables the men to protect the *namus* (sanctity) of the women of the house. *Namus* is a powerful word in Pashtu. If refers to the sanctity of one's homeland and one's women. Protecting the sanctity of the women of the house is a fundamental moral obligation.

The Pashtun classification of the outsider is not static (see fig. 3). A person can move along a relational continuum from outsider to insider in order to strengthen the relational bonds. One friend of mine told me that his father had developed such a close relationship with a friend that the family removed the boundaries of the walls and betak for him. Another acquaintance told me that he and a friend removed these boundaries between them and they interacted as couples.

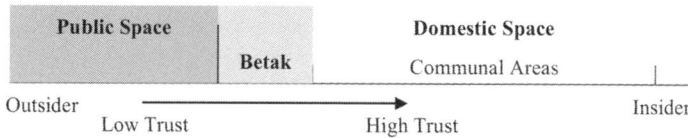

Public Space		Domestic Space	
	Betak	Communal Areas	
Outsider			Insider
Low Trust		High Trust	

Fig. 3. The Outsider-Insider Continuum

I experienced this removal as well. A conservative family that my wife and I had known for years was over at our house for dinner. I had set up the evening according to the boundary of betak. I had the males of the family in one room along with a Swedish acquaintance of mine while the women of the family were in another room with my wife. The head of the Pashtun family asked me to have my Swedish guest leave the room. After my guest stepped outside, the Pashtun man went and brought his new bride into the room to introduce her to me. He did this to strengthen our ties of friendship.[10]

I have observed that even though the betak boundary is removed, the boundaries of personal space and limited interaction arise. There is an implicit understanding that the "outsider brought in" will maintain appropriate spatial distance between himself and the females of the house and that his interaction with them will be limited in words, glances, and eye contact.

To the contrary, when a woman enters a house as a guest, she bypasses the betak and enters the private, communal areas. She has full access to all the women and the children. As I mentioned previously, a woman's restrictions exist in the public sphere, not in the domestic.

The Boundary of Sound

Men are technically not supposed to hear the sound of a nonrelated woman. One man put it this way: "A woman should not speak loud enough that a man can hear her. We are not supposed to hear a woman's voice." A friend told me that he was having problems living in his present location. He did not have a way to keep guests from hearing the women's voices, so he could not invite his friends into his compound.

This boundary of sound also extends into the public sphere. When women are out and about in public, they are usually reserved in manner. If they talk with one another, they do so in subdued voices.

In conclusion, purdah is a system that denotes separation. Pashtuns separate their communities into insiders and outsiders. Outsiders are nonrelationally connected males. Pashtuns also separate space into public and domestic space. With purdah Pashtuns are able to separate insiders from outsiders, protecting the insiders and their domestic space from the potentially malevolent outsiders. Purdah accomplishes this protection by creating a series of boundaries: walls, betak, and sound.

Purdah: Boundaries in Public Space

Women have unrestricted access to and movement within domestic spaces. However, female access and movement is restricted in public space. Women are permitted to enter public space when there is a justifiable need. This permission is based upon one of the sayings of the Prophet of Islam.[11]

Defining need is where Peshawari Pashtuns differ. For the ultraconservative, there is no need justifiable for a woman to leave her house, even if sick. One Pashtu saying illustrates this extreme view: "*Aya kor de, aya ghor de*" ("It's either the house or the grave"). However, this is considered to be an extreme view. Though I knew no one in the city who held this view, I knew one educated man from the village who leaned in this direction. His wife became pregnant and he would not take her to a clinic for antenatal care. I tried to reason with him about the need for antenatal care, but he would not listen. His wife sadly was unable to give birth in the home and had to be taken to a clinic after many hours of labor. She had a caesarian operation, but it was too late. The trauma of extended labor caused the baby to suffer severe brain damage. This probably would have been avoidable had he been willing to take his wife out of the home for regular medical checkups.

Though there may be disagreement over what constitutes need, Pashtuns agree that there are justifiable needs that release women to enter public space. Therefore it is their obligation to accommodate the woman who enters this space. To enable this, a series of boundaries exists to facilitate women's movement in the public sphere. These boundaries are cloth, companion, and specially designated female space.

The Boundary of Cloth

On one level, the cloth boundaries delineate what is proper covering for men and women. The cloth covering demonstrates a person's hayá (modesty). At another level the boundary of cloth creates a sense of separation between the sexes.

With regard to modesty, a man is supposed to cover himself from the shoulders to the arms and legs. Due to this, I cannot remember seeing any Pashtun in short-sleeve shirts, even in the blazing hot summers. Short sleeves were not appropriate. Professionals (upper-level bureaucrats, doctors, professors, and salesmen) wore nice Western trousers and long-sleeve shirts, indicating their employment status. However, the average person typically wore traditional Pashtun attire: the *shalwar-chamise* (baggy trousers and a baggy shirt that extends below the knees).

The uniformity in the expression of the boundary of cloth for males is striking. However, there is considerable variety in how the boundary of cloth is expressed by females. Women exclusively wear the traditional *shalwar-chamise.* On top of the *shalwar-chamise,* at one end of the spectrum, there are the rare few who wear a *jilbab* (black overcoat), black shoes, black gloves, and a *niqab* (black scarf that leaves only the eyes exposed). At the other end of the spectrum, a few women wear a simple shawl over their heads. Women from the lower economic spectrum typically wear a *burqa* (shuttlecock-style covering that has a cloth mesh in front of the eyes). The most typical covering over the *shalwar-chamise* for women is a *chaddar* (shawl of varying colors that covers the woman's head down to anywhere from the upper thigh to lower calf, leaving the face, hands, and feet exposed).

Though women cover in diverse ways, there is a consistency in one detail: women uniformly have an additional cloth covering besides the *shalwar-chamise.*

This cloth boundary serves a very important purpose: it enables women to enter public space without being fully present. Even though a woman has a right to enter public space, she has a responsibility to purdah and to society to not be fully present. One man described this expectation this way: "The meaning of purdah is to hide yourself. It is good that a woman be shapely and she not show it to a male; so what is in the man's heart, like a bad thought, will not arise." By not being fully present, the covered woman communicates that she has hayá (modesty), and she protects men from being overcome by their sexual desires.

The Boundary of Companion

When a woman goes out in public, she should not only be covered, but she should also be accompanied by a companion. The companion demonstrates to those in public that the woman is relationally connected and properly covered by her unseen family. A small child is sufficient to function as the companion.

An unaccompanied woman in public space communicates to others in that space that she is not relationally covered by her family, and therefore is potentially sexually permissive. The unaccompanied woman may be perceived as be-hayá (without modesty) and be exposed to sexual harassment.

The Boundary of Special Space

Since women have a right within limitations to the public sphere, Pashtuns adjust to this right by creating special public spaces for them. Busses and other public transport vehicles have women-only sections in the front of the vehicles where women can sit separate from the men. Men will not stand alongside nonrelated women on the road as they wait for the bus. They stand separate. Males are also expected to not look in the direction of the women. If men line up at the post office or the bank, women are not expected to stand in line. Women are expected to go to the front of the line. They are to be immediately served, and promptly leave.

Purdah: Boundaries in Academic Space

One of the justifiable needs women have that permit them to leave their domestic space is education. Almost every Peshawari Pashtun supports female education.[12] A Pashtun man summed up the reason like this: "When the mother is educated, the boy will become educated. If the mother is uneducated—well then—the son, he cannot progress." Over the years the resistance to educating females has subsided. It is only the extremist Taliban that disallow female education. The Pashtun schemas changed as they saw that educated women take better care of their children and are able to help them with their schoolwork when they come home, facilitating the children's success.

The disagreement arises over the amount of education that a woman needs. Some feel that a woman can study up to any level. Conservatives prefer to limit the woman's education at the tenth class. In their view, if a woman is better educated, she will be prone to compete with her husband and not be submissive. In addition, the better educated a woman is, the more empowered she will be to become independent. If independent, she may leave her husband. Though not frequent, this happens. One man told me of an acquaintance who went to Australia with his wife for further education. The wife was well-educated. When the family emigrated to Australia, she left her husband and their children. She was able to make it on her own and she took the opportunity when it came.

Coeducation is a contentious issue, because it strikes at the heart of purdah, which is separation. Most oppose it. However, a few favor coeducation, because in their view it empowers women to be able to compete with men in the marketplace. Women entering the workforce is a contentious issue, and to that we now turn.

Purdah: Boundaries in the Workplace

Employment is another potentially justifiable need for women. Those who favor women working see this as another valid reason for women to enter public space.

The majority of Pashtun men are not in favor of women working. Men who make enough money on their own are inclined to view their wives' desire to work as a desire to get out and mingle with other men. One man expressed his thoughts this way: "Why would she want to work? I provide all the money she needs. If she were to reply to me and say, 'No, I want to work,' then mistrust would arise." He felt that if she wanted to work, that had to mean that she was upset in the house. He said, "If the wife has money and love, then what is she doing outside with strange men?"

The more conservative men feel that if women are to work, they should only engage in jobs that they can do from their homes.

Yet there are those who feel that women can and should work outside the home. There are limits within which women's employment can be seen as acceptable. One Pashtun said, "Purdah is necessary. Giving women some freedom is necessary. They can go to work within limits, but not beyond the limits, the cultural limits, the Islamic limits."

The limits to which this man was referring were that their work should be restricted to teaching, medicine, or dentistry. In addition, women should be in offices or schools where gender separation is maintained. Teaching is acceptable because female education is a need and women should also teach the girls and women in the higher grades. Also, in the Pashtun schema women know how to handle children better than men, so the best primary school teachers are women. Women should become doctors because other women need women doctors. Nursing is not an acceptable job for women because it demands that the nurse interact with nonrelated men.

Even though there are more and more who are willing to admit that women can and should work, there is still a significant amount of social pressure to keep women from working. One Pashtun said, "If a man allows his wife to work, his cousins will taunt him and say, 'Ha, your wife shows her face there!'" Nonetheless, one sees more and more women working in the city. This in and of itself indicates that this is a boundary in transition.

Purdah: Crossing Boundaries

Ensuring that the boundaries of purdah be maintained in an urban setting where women have some freedom of movement is difficult. It is well acknowledged that breaches of purdah's boundaries happen. Cognizant of this fact, one mother told her son, "Purdah is of the heart." If people want to do purdah, they will. If they don't, they will find ways to cross the boundaries.

Nonrelated single men and women do cross the boundaries and develop relationships. They may meet at school, at work, or just by walking down the street. Interaction has been facilitated by text messaging on mobile phones and instant messaging on the Internet. Though it was virtually unheard of in the 1980s, now it is common to see a few dating couples interacting in parks in the upscale neighborhoods.

Marriages that result from dating relationships are called love marriages. The Pashtun community generally frowns upon love marriages because it is inappropriate for a man and a woman to choose their own partner without the parents' involvement. (It is also assumed that the couple had sex before marriage.) Nonetheless, love marriages happen. When parents object, there are ways to maneuver around the objection. Upon hearing his father's refusal to let him marry the girl he wanted, one man went into his room, brought out a pistol, held it up to his head, and said that if his father did not grant immediate approval to the marriage he would kill himself. His father capitulated.

A friend of my wife was dating a man. She was slowly working on her family to get permission to marry him. Hers was a conservative family, yet they were not angry with her for dating the man. She was in her late twenties and was working. Her age and financial contribution to the family gave her more liberty of movement. The family did not like the idea of her choosing her own husband. Even more, they did not like the fact that he did not have a very good job. She had the better education and job. They felt that she would end up supporting him rather than he supporting her. It took a few years, but she was able to get their approval. She was the only one of her sisters to have a love marriage.

How do Peshawari Pashtuns adapt to these changes in society and this incongruity of crossing the boundaries that maintain separation?

Some have been inflexible to those who crossed the boundaries, while others have adapted. Families can murder any woman who crosses the boundaries.[13] Although honor killings happen, they are not common. Disowning is a much more common initial response. One father disowned his oldest son for marrying a girl while studying abroad. However, the younger brother in the family was able to reconcile his father to his older brother after a few years. He agreed to marry any girl that the father and mother chose for him without ever seeing a picture of the girl before they married. Due to this concession to tradition, the father agreed to forgive the prodigal older brother.

Abusing the new daughter-in-law is also a common occurrence. One man's parents eventually approved of his love marriage, but they could not adjust themselves to it. The father-in-law refused to attend the wedding. After the marriage the wife's mother-in-law abused her for a number of years. Eventually they came to accept her after a few children were born.

One would expect that dating behavior would only reinforce the assumption that women are untrustworthy and cause the Peshawari Pashtuns to object to female education and employment. However, this crossing of the boundaries has had no impact on female education. The Peshawari Pashtun community has deemed female education essential. Although the society has been slow to accept female employment, some middle-class families have deemed employment necessary due to their need for more income. It appears that the boundaries and the limits that have been created to adjust for these changes are considered secure enough to marginalize any confusion that can happen.

Conclusion

Purdah is the means by which the Pashtun society understands and manages sexuality. It is driven by a desire to create and maintain social and moral order. Purdah creates this order by the internal value of hayá (modesty) and by following an elaborate system of separation. Without hayá and separation, there can be no moral order.

This is why Mustafa's wife felt so defiled when she went to the Christian service. Even though there was a separation that was adequate for the Christian community (men and women sitting in separate sections), it was not adequate for Mustafa's wife. These men were sitting in the same room. These were all outsiders. Through this lack of clear separation, Mustafa's wife had become be-hayá, defiled by being in their presence.

The purdah world is clearly different from the Western world. The purdah system sees the world as somewhat malevolent, working against creating and maintaining moral order. The purdah world's default position is one of suspicion and mistrust with regard to outside males and women. With regard to male outsiders, once a meaningful relationship is established with an outsider, the outsider can begin to move along the outsider-insider continuum and is able to earn increasingly higher levels of trust.

Four assumptions provide the framework for this paradigm. First, Peshawaris perceive the male outsider as a potential sexual predator. This appears to be an unquestioned assumption. Second, women are less intelligent than men and prone to be naive, making them susceptible to the predatorial schemes of the outsider. Third, women are fundamentally untrustworthy. Fourth, a woman's sex drive is ten times stronger than a man's. That these assumptions are operational is seen in the ongoing need for the boundaries of purdah and the monitored movement of females. The second, third, and fourth assumptions are in various stages of transition.

This pessimistically inclined trust paradigm is reinforced by the culture's myths, stories, folklore, architecture, allotment of public space, and daily rituals of intensification. The boundaries of walls, betak, sound, covering, and companion can all be interpreted as defensive in nature due to the lack of trust in or mistrust of the outsider and woman. They exist to protect the husband, the wife, the family, and the society from potential disaster.

Since this trust paradigm is oriented toward managing male outsiders in the public and domestic spheres, one would expect that as trust is built between males and families the need for the boundaries should diminish and boundaries should be removed. This is exactly what occurs. As two male friends and as a family with a male outsider establish meaningful trust, the boundaries of wall and betak are removed. One interviewee said that his friend wanted him to marry a relative of the friend in order that his friend and he could be bound tighter together in personal relationship. Thus the outsider through marriage became a complete insider.

Integral to purdah is the paradigm of limits. Limits set the parameters of women's movement in the public sphere in order to judge a woman's respectability. Though the edges of those limits are not clearly delineated, there is consensus as to what the limits are.

The baseline limit is necessity. A woman can leave a domestic sphere and study or work in those fields that are considered necessary for the benefit of society. Thus teaching and medicine are approved vocations. In line with the purpose of purdah, another limit is that women should move in spheres where outside men are at a minimum. Therefore girls' colleges or primary schools are preferred, because these are areas where there are few males. Female doctors should have female patients. Offices should be segregated by gender as well. Social pressure against wives working continues, indicating that working as a married woman is a value in transition. Two other limits are restricted movement and monitored movement.

Though the daily rituals of purdah vary in expression, purdah is the means by which the community defines propriety in male-female relationships. The variety of ways that women abide by these boundaries is a result of the independence that classes, subcultures, and individual families have in shaping the expression of the boundaries. Yet even with the diversity in expression, a uniformity exists within the diversity. Walls are everywhere. Women practice some form of covering. Distance is kept in the public sphere between the sexes. In every house I visited where I had not moved sufficiently along the outsider-insider continuum, I encountered the boundary of the betak. It appeared that almost all women experienced limits in movement whether or not there was any actual monitoring taking place.

The community expects the boundaries and the limits of purdah to be demonstrable, because purdah is the means by which the society creates a sense of security. Consequently, every family expects them to be upheld. Those who violate the norms do so at their own risk. While some individuals are inflexible toward those who cross the boundaries, other Peshawaris adjust to and absorb those who cross the boundaries.

One would expect that since females are crossing the boundaries, the dissonance would compel Peshawaris to object to female education and employment. Yet they do not.

Islam is also an integral aspect of the Pashtun identity. Most Peshawaris see Islam and Pashtun culture as an integrated whole. They refer to Islam to justify their particular expressions of purdah. As I compare the assumptions that lie behind the practice of purdah along with the boundaries, I can see that Islamic sacred texts exert a defining influence on Peshawaris' understanding of the purpose of purdah, its boundaries and limits, and on Peshawari assumptions about men and women. I will take up the influence of Islamic sacred writ upon purdah in chapter 3.

However, the next step is to look at how purdah influences the manner in which marriages are formed and expressed.

---

1   In South Asia the word *purdah* is used in this respect. In Arabic the equivalent word is *hijab*.

2   The Arabic equivalent, *hijab*, literally means "curtain" as well.

3   The purdah world has a *bounded set* perspective of reality. This bounded set perspective clearly delineates what comprises an insider and an outsider.

4   With regard to high and low trust cultures, see Francis Fukayama's *Trust: The Social Virtues and the Creation of Prosperity* (1996).

5   A number of contemporary societies that are historically agrarian (also called peasant societies) can be classified as low trust societies. For an overview of these societies and the relational dynamics within them, see Potter, Diaz, and Foster's *Peasant Society: A Reader* (1967) and Rosen's *Peasant Society in a Changing Economy* (1975).

6   Within the city one encounters males who act contrary to the norms of hayá. Some uncomfortably stare at women, and some inappropriately touch women as they pass them on the street. Some young men will congregate on the streets outside female educational institutions and watch the girls as they leave.

7   This saying is derived from a hadith in the *Sahih al-Bukhari* (1:304).

8   Even though the following quote was not written by a Pashtun, it demonstrates how embedded this assumption is in male schemas in South Asia: "Sexually she [the wife] is far more profound than he and is physically and psychologically more intensely inclined to it" (Siddiqi 1992, 23).

9   The extended family system is this: a man, his wife, and his children share a house/compound with his parents, his brothers, and his brothers' wives and their children. Almost everyone lived in the extended family system when I lived in Peshawar. However, living as nuclear family units was becoming more desirable and acceptable as the economic conditions improved.

10   Another reason for setting aside the boundary may be more transactional in nature. I have known people to set aside these boundaries for foreign doctors because they considered the relationship with the doctor to be an invaluable asset for the family. Therefore the betak boundary was quickly removed.

11   "You [women] have been allowed to go out for your needs" (*Sahih al-Bukhari* 6:4795).

12   This represents a radical shift in values. One man said that, when he was young, it was just beginning to be acceptable for males to attend school. A common verse at the time was: *The maddrassa lesson studies he, only for money studies he, no place in heaven will his be, like an arrow shot to hell shall he be.* Resistance to education has been eroding for some time, but it is still being resisted by the radically conservative in the tribal areas. A newspaper article dated August 25, 2006, reported that an extremist group in Bajaur Agency ordered "Bajaur residents to stop sending their daughters and sisters to middle and high schools" (Yusufzai 2006).

13   The high-profile case of Samia Sarwar exemplifies this danger. Samia was shot to death on April 6, 1999, in her lawyer's office, in the presence of her mother by her mother's companion. Samia wanted to divorce her abusive husband for another man (BBC News 2000).

2

Purdah and Marriage

MUSTAFA HAD CHOSEN his own wife. After looking around for a potential mate, he decided to marry his first cousin, Hamida.

Mustafa had been staying with Hamida's parents when she was born. His father at that time had recently died. His stepmother had been incredibly abusive and Mustafa could bear the abuse no longer. Using the privilege as the oldest son, he moved out. His aunt and uncle were sympathetic and let him come and stay with them.

After Mustafa had been working for a few years, he decided it was time to get married. Hamida was the perfect choice. Since she had grown up before him, there would never be another girl whom he knew as well as Hamida.

Prior to the wedding Mustafa had been counseled by some elders on how to start the marriage relationship well. So Mustafa followed their advice. When they were getting ready for bed, Mustafa asked Hamida for a drink of water. She obediently brought it to him. He took one sip and threw the rest of the water on the floor, yelling at her for bringing him lukewarm water. Shortly after this, he asked her to come and unstrap his sandals. He had strapped them on so tightly he could hardly undo them himself. When Hamida could not undo the straps, he contemptuously slapped her and asked why she couldn't do such a simple task.

Why was Hamida the perfect choice for Mustafa? Why was Mustafa advised to be so overbearing on his wedding night?

In chapter 1 we identified the cognitive framework for the system of purdah. Purdah is a sociocultural system that seeks to create and maintain social and moral order. It creates this order by separating space into public and domestic spheres, and then it provides means for people to access those spheres in ways that safeguard the individual, the family, the community, and society. The means of protection is through an elaborate system of boundaries and limits.

However, purdah does more than manage public and domestic spheres. Purdah also influences and shapes the conjugal relationship. In this chapter I describe the husband-wife marriage relationship, beginning with the process of engagement and tracking the husband-wife relationship as it moves into marriage and beyond into family life. In doing so I draw attention to the assumptions and the values that impact the relationship between the husband and wife.

The Arrangement-Engagement

Peshawari Pashtuns follow the principle of keeping purdah with all *ghermahram* (marriageable males). One man said, "In Islam, it is our rule that purdah is essential with those you can marry." Since endogamy (i.e., marrying within one's own group) is the traditional custom among Pashtuns, females technically need to be cloistered from all marriageable cousins in addition to the male outsiders. Since only a minority are willing to cross the boundaries of purdah and develop a long-term relationship with the opposite sex, most have their marriages arranged.

The traditional route for arranging marriages is to have the parents choose the girl they want for their son, and then present her to their son on the day of his wedding. My professor at the University of Peshawar was married this way. His mother had died when he was sixteen. His father told him he wanted to get a bride for him to comfort him on the loss of his mother. My professor refused, asserting he was only sixteen. Nevertheless, his father went out and chose a girl for him. He did not want to get married, but he had no choice. He did not meet his bride until the day of his wedding.

The traditional route is often not followed anymore. Parents usually first get the son's permission to arrange a marriage, and then they begin to search for a suitable woman. In some cases when the parents live in the village and the son is in the city, a close friend of the son makes the initial arrangements. Even though the parents or friend are making the arrangements, they share information about the girl and her family's background with the marriageable male. This type of arrangement aligns nicely with traditional boundaries because the marriageable male does not see the woman that the parents (or friend) have chosen prior to the wedding.

Though not as common, it increasingly happens among the middle class that the son sees a woman that he is interested in and asks the parents to go and arrange the marriage. This breaks cultural norms because it is typically not appropriate for a son to talk to his parents about a woman in whom he is interested. Such conversations are simply not meant to take place. However, those who are educated are crossing traditional boundaries and are emboldened to get their parents to pursue the girl they want.

Though we in the West would shudder at arranged marriages, many of the people I talked to expressed complete confidence in the decision-making ability of their families.

Criteria for Selection

It is typical for the man to have completed his education and have a job before he is eligible for marriage. Therefore the male is typically marriageable when he is twenty-four or older. The ideal age for the bride is eighteen years old, which would place the bride at about six-plus years younger than her husband. However, it appears that there is often a discrepancy between the ideal and what really happens. The difference in age is quite fluid, ranging from thirteen years younger to even a few years older.

The key factors in eligibility for the girl are her background and education. Exogamous marriages happen with greater frequency in the city. For some conservatives, endogamy is preferred due to the low-trust relational paradigm. Relatives are known entities. There is nothing hidden in their lives. Since a man has watched his relatives grow up, he knows their background and character. This knowledge brings security. One man asserted that if you go outside the family, then "how can you know about the girl?" Mustafa chose his cousin because she grew up right before him. He knew she was a safe woman to marry.

A lack of knowledge about the girl's background is something that can be manipulated. A friend of mine was married to a girl outside his extended family. A few weeks after his wedding he came to my house absolutely distraught. He had received a note saying that his wife had a boyfriend and that she was not to be trusted. Someone was getting sordid pleasure out of his lack of knowledge of her background by trying to ignite mistrust and destroy his relationship with his bride. We sat down and tried to think who would gain from manipulating him. In these initial weeks of the marriage he realized that he had been showing favoritism to his wife in the household. It appeared likely that one of his sisters had written the note out of jealousy.

Besides background, the potential bride's being educated is important. The vast majority, if not all, of Peshawari Pashtuns acknowledge that it is best that the wife have at least a tenth grade education. Having an education enables the wife to provide the proper care for her children and enable them to succeed in school. However, a college level education is not considered essential for a wife. In fact, this could be a negative factor. Some men feel that if a wife is too educated she might not want to submit to him and eventually be tempted to break away from the relationship and become independent.

Peshawari Pashtuns generally live virilocally (i.e., men live with their parents and their unmarried sisters, their brothers, their brothers' wives, and their brothers' children). Due to this custom, the parents look for a woman who will adjust well to their extended family context and will care for them when they get older. Thus they seek to find a woman who has traditional values.

Contact between Engagement and Marriage

Since most marriages are arranged, the potential bride and groom know nothing about each other. The couple traditionally has no contact prior to the marriage. However, this is changing slowly. With mobile phones couples are able to talk with each other and try to develop an "understanding" about who they are and what their aspirations are for the future. One man told me that all his friends of his economic status communicated with their fiancées. They all wanted to get to know each other. Nonetheless, even with connecting by phone, something that is easy to do, many are still reluctant to do so.

Male Dominance in the Marriage

It is assumed that within the marriage the husband exercises the dominant role in the husband-wife relationship. This relational hierarchy is supported by divine fiat. One man said, "In Islam, a man is always to be dominant over his wife." Another said that God in Islam had given men a status over women so that the men could consider themselves superior.

This dominance and authority manifests itself in different ways. In one example, a friend of my wife was visiting her family in Peshawar. She lived with her husband and his family in Karachi. My wife, Joan, was in one room with the women, and I was in another with the men. Joan's friend needed to pass through the room where I was sitting in order to get to another room. When she hesitated, her stepmother told her to go through the room because her husband had previously broken purdah with me. So she entered the room. Later on that afternoon, Joan's friend was about to leave the house and she put on a *chaddar* (sheet-type covering). Her stepmother and sisters objected to her *chaddar* because they considered it immodestly short and sheer. She looked at it again and decided it was fine. After all, her husband had approved it. Therefore the rest of the family had no say in the matter.

Though many Peshawari Pashtuns would say that the husband's superior position and authority should not lead to domination, it can often lead to that. One woman described her experience in this way:

> I was thinking that if there is love, when the marriage happens, my husband will be with me. Well, practical life is different. My husband's priorities changed when we married. He wanted me to adjust to his environment. He told me to do whatever his mother and father said. It was my thinking that my husband would be with me a lot; but his friends, his own priorities, his job—well, I felt very lonely. I was very alone.

Though this is a common experience, it is not the complete picture. For one man, after his marriage when his mother entered the room to talk about the wife's new responsibilities, he spoke up and said, "She will do none of that. She will do her education. She will study. She will go outside.… Leave her alone to do what she wants." Though this is a rare occurrence, it is part of the picture of what happens in the culture. Since the husband was understood to have authority over his wife, he had the power to dictate what the wife would and would not do. Others in the extended family were expected to adjust to his dictates.

Roles and the Division of Labor

A clear division of labor exists in the conjugal relationship. Men are to work outside the home. Women's duties are primarily domestic. One friend said, "I have the job. I make the money." He expected his wife to keep the house. As she fulfilled her domestic role she would get everything she needed.

If a woman is given permission to work outside the home, she still is expected to take full care of her duties to her husband and her children. Pashtuns understand that Islam teaches that it is bad for a woman to disregard the care of her husband and children. It is wrong for a woman to go out to work and come home late at night. If she can manage her job, her house, and her children, then there is no harm in her working. I had one Pashtun friend whose wife was a teacher. They had five sons. Since they were sons the husband did not think they should help her around the house. So the wife had to go to work, and then come home and take full care of her husband and her five sons.

This division of labor in the conjugal relationship reinforces the male dominance in the relationship. It clearly separates between male and female roles, and it exists to maintain that separation. However, it appears that this separation of roles works in the woman's favor, compelling her husband to delegate to her more and more authority, which eventually enables the wife to control her domain.

However, delegating authority does not release the wife from being under her husband's ultimate authority. To illustrate this, I wanted to interview a principal of one of the women's colleges in the city. The principal was a woman and she was fifty years old. After receiving my call for an appointment, she took a few days to get back to me. The reason for the delay was that she had to get her husband's permission to be interviewed by me, a nonrelated, foreign male.

The Impact of Living as an Extended Family

Most Peshawari Pashtuns live in a virilocal, extended family arrangement. This means that the household might have the husband's living parents, single sisters, brothers, and the brother's wives and children. This joint family living impacts the husband-wife relationship. The new wife has to adjust not only to her husband, but to the extended family as well.

There are advantages in the joint family system. The first is economic. Pooling resources enables each family to have more infrastructure in the house than if they were living alone. The joint family can afford expensive household appliances like a refrigerator and washing machine.

By living together there is always someone at home. Therefore they can protect their possessions from thieves. For men at work, the joint family system ensures that someone is always available in case of an emergency. They do not have to leave work if an accident happens. Also, since someone is always home, the family is always able to fulfill important social obligations. For example, if a man's friend came to the house while the man was at work, the man's brother could host the guest and send him away without the man having to leave work.

In contrast, there are disadvantages in living together in the joint family system. First, in joint family living one cannot show favoritism to one's nuclear family. Disparity of any kind causes problems. If a man wants to buy a gift for his child, he has to buy a gift for all the other children in the household. If he wants to buy a gift for his wife, he has to buy a gift for his mother and for all the other women in the house. For example, I had a friend who was recently married. He wanted to be a good husband, so he brought some perfume home as a gift for his wife. The other women and men in the household found out about it and were livid. It was like a volcano had erupted in the household. Treating everyone equally gives no room for jealousy and maintains harmony in the household.

Second, the joint family system offers no opportunity for becoming financially independent. The husband's father or mother controls the purse for the household. Therefore neither the husband nor the wife can put money away to buy the things they want for their children. The wife cannot put anything aside to buy gifts for her own family.

If one of the men has a very good job and earns a lot of money and his brothers do not make much money or are unemployed, this financial interdependence creates tensions. The man's wife ends up resenting the others in the family, because she knows that if she and her husband lived separately they would have much more for themselves than they do by living jointly. Whereas the husband may have a sense of loyalty to the others in his family, all his wife can see is that her husband's income is being eaten up by the others in his family.

Third, parents cannot raise their children as they would like. Since there are other families in the compound, one's children can be negatively influenced by one's brothers or by the other children if they do not have good character.

Finally, when there are a lot of people in a household, there is a lot of opportunity for interpersonal conflict. One of the areas of conflict is over the shouldering of new responsibilities in the joint family setting. A husband may want his new wife to perform for his parents by getting up early and getting breakfast ready for them. The wife may be young and not used to preparing meals, especially for so many people.

Another area of conflict is between the new wife and the women of the house. The greatest enemy a wife may ever encounter in her life is her mother-in-law. The mother-in-law may be jealous that her son's attention is being shifted away from her to his wife. She may also become manipulative and create problems between the husband and wife in order to get her son's attention to return to her. A mother-in-law might malign the wife so that her son lashes out at the wife and abuses her.

Thus there are positives and negatives about living as an extended family. As people are becoming more and more economically able to live on their own, there are those who are moving away from the joint family system. The system was deemed valuable due to limited economic resources, but as people are becoming more and more financially independent, they are slowly deciding that the difficulties in living as an extended family outweigh the advantages.

Constructing a Marriage Relationship

Given the difficulties a new wife faces in moving into a house full of people, how do the husband and wife develop a meaningful relationship? The wife is moving in with a man with whom she has had no, or extremely little, personal contact. She is also moving into a situation where there is little personal privacy. The only privacy a couple generally has is their bedroom.

Peshawari Pashtuns use two words to describe this phase of relationship-building between the couple: understanding and compromise. The expectation is that the wife and husband will gradually grow to understand each other and make compromises so that they can get along. Since the husband and the new wife come from different homes, they naturally enter the relationship with different sets of expectations as to what the relationship should look like.

Many wives enter the relationship with the expectation that their husbands will love and care for them. However, what these wives do not realize is that they were chosen for their family background, their intelligence, and their commitment to traditional values. The husband enters the relationship looking for a companion who will perform a number of services for him and for his household. The wife is to abide by the limitations he sets for her, help with the housework, provide sexual satisfaction, and bear and raise children.

Developing harmony and mutuality in the conjugal relationship with these different and unspoken expectations is naturally difficult. What complicates this is that the wife not only marries a husband, she also marries his family. While he goes to work in the morning and comes home in the evening, she remains with all the other women of the household. Therefore, besides learning what her husband is like, she has to learn what all her in-laws are like.

Due to all this, it is natural for the initial phase of the marriage relationship to degenerate into a season of conflict with each one of the power players in the household maneuvering for control. The odds are stacked against the wife in this power game. What eventually happens is that she has to adjust to the others in order to make the marriage and the living situation tolerable. In Pashtun society divorce is not really an option. One woman put it this way: "Among Pashtuns there is only one husband." The wife knows that she has to make her marriage work.

Even though the wife is expected to adjust to her new living situation, this does not mean that the husband is not required to make any compromises. He is expected to make some as well in order to make the marriage work. However, the average man does not enter the marriage relationship predisposed to listen to his wife to learn what she desires or to be sensitive to her feelings. Men are enculturated to be dominant. Therefore, though many men may make some compromises along the way to minimize some of the conflict, they expect their wives to understand their limits and make the best of their new living situation.

The result of the differing expectations and living conditions is that many husbands and wives find their marriage relationship unfulfilling. However, there are marriages in which the husband and wife are satisfied. Those who live separately, being spared the difficulties of the joint family system, have a greater likelihood of being content.[1] While the joint family system has its inherent problems, it is possible to build a successful marriage while living in the extended family context. As one Pashtun told me, the key is to make proper use of the bedroom. The bedroom is the one place where the couple is alone and can talk freely. The wise husband learns that this is the place where he must affirm his devotion to his wife while making her understand that when he leaves the bedroom he has to obey his mother and make it appear as if she is first in his heart. If he does not, he will unleash a tigress in his mother who will eventually devour the wife. Just as the wife has to come to terms with all the limitations that joint family living creates, so too does the husband. Through their private discussions they can learn how to positively negotiate through all their relationships so they can enjoy each other and keep the peace in the household. It may not be easy, but it can be done.

Conclusion

Purdah as a system of managing sexuality influences the way the conjugal relationship begins and the shape the relationship takes. Due to how purdah restricts intergender interaction, most marriages are arranged. Even when there is a possibility of the couple interacting after the engagement and prior to the wedding, the woman is often reluctant to interact. It appears that only those females in the upper-middle-class range are willing to cross that boundary. Due to this, the average couple has virtually no meaningful interaction prior to the wedding.

The negotiations for the arrangement are carried out by the young man's family or a very close and influential friend. Peshawari Pashtuns are moving away from the traditional custom of arranging the marriage where the young man had no voice in the choice of his bride. This is because many of the arranged marriages failed and the young man blamed his family for the choice. With the new custom, even though the bride has virtually no personal relationship with the young man, she knows that he chose her above others as his bride. This knowledge helps to set the marriage off on a positive note.

The joint family living situation, the dominant position of the male in the conjugal relationship, and the inherent lack of trust in the new woman in the household potentially create a difficult living environment for the wife. For those women who have strong husbands who set the boundaries for their wives' activities in the house, purdah fosters an atmosphere of empowerment. The woman can study or work if her husband wants her to, and there is nothing directly the others in the house can do to object.

However, most men are unwilling or unable to contradict the wishes of their parents. For example, I was renting an apartment, and the landlord and his wife came to visit my wife and me. They were in their fifties and they were living with his parents in the village. To get his wife permission to travel with him to Peshawar to meet me, he had to tell his mother that his wife was ill and she needed to see a doctor in Peshawar. If he had not done this, his mother would not have given her permission to travel with him.

Though there is a longing within many men and women for intimacy in the conjugal relationship, the enculturation of the male to take a dominant position in the relationship hinders this intimacy. Many men are not enculturated to listen and learn about the desires or wishes of their wives and expect them to happily fulfill their expected roles as wives. They are enculturated to get the wife under control so she learns to fit into the household. (This is why Mustafa was so overbearing on his wedding night.) The wife's role is to live within the limitations the husband sets, help with the housework (the duties of which are often determined by his mother), provide him with sexual satisfaction, and bear, raise, and help the children succeed in their studies. If she does these things well, she will gradually earn his trust and find him placing more and more confidence in her. However, some men are unable to move beyond their inherent lack of trust in women and spend their lives suspicious of their wife's fidelity. The assumptions and values about women's inherent nature and the mistrust of the outsider are so deeply embedded within the society that they exert an influence that is difficult to contradict.

One of the reasons that purdah, as a system of understanding and managing sexuality, enjoys such durability in the modern, globalized world, is that the sacred writings of Islam provide and undergird its cognitive and social framework. Therefore it is imperative that we understand what these writings teach. It is to these writings that we turn in the next chapter.

---

1   None of the women my wife interviewed enjoyed living with their in-laws.

3

The Sacred Foundations of Purdah

PASHTUNS USE THE SACRED WRITINGS of Islam to shape their beliefs and practices of purdah. The sacred writings are the Qur'an and the Hadith.[1] The Qur'an is the book revealed to the Prophet of Islam. The Hadith are the compilations of his sayings. The Hadith do not share the same status of the Qur'an as being sent from heaven. Nevertheless, since the Prophet of Islam is viewed as having been divinely directed, the guidance that comes through his sayings is considered to be equally authoritative.

In this chapter we will look at the sacred history[2] of and the assumptions and values inherent within the system of purdah.

The Beginning of Hijab[3]

Purdah finds its *raison d'être* within the Islamic tradition of *hijab* (veil). In the Islamic literature, hijab began with Sura al-Ahzab [33]:53.

> Oh believers! Do not enter the Prophet's dwellings for a meal early unless you are given permission. When you are invited, enter. When your meal is over, leave. Do not linger for conversation. This would annoy the Prophet and he is shy to ask you to go. But Allah is not shy of the truth. And when you ask the wives of the Prophet anything, ask them from behind a curtain. This is purer for your hearts and for their hearts. And you should not annoy the messenger of Allah, nor should you marry his wives after him. This would be a grave sin in Allah's sight.

The tradition apparently began due to some untoward incidents that occurred during the marriage feast of the Prophet of Islam with Zainab.

Some of the influential guests at the wedding feast had been teasing him that they would marry some of his wives after he died (Mernissi

1991, 92). To add insult to injury, 'Umar's hand accidentally touched A'isha's hand (the Prophet's favorite wife) while they were eating from the same dish (L. Ahmed 1992, 54; Sherif 1987, 155). The Prophet saw this and it upset him. When the feast was over, some of the guests were not inclined to leave. The Prophet was embarrassed to tell them to go. He hinted that he wanted them to leave by retiring toward his room and then returning. He left and came back three times before the guests got the hint and left. Finally, Anas, the Prophet's fifteen-year-old servant, accompanied the Prophet as he went to retire with his new bride. The Prophet lowered a curtain between himself and Anas as he entered the room. With this act the tradition of seclusion and the veiling of women began (*Sahih al-Bukhari* 7:5166).[4]

Sura al-Ahzab [33]:33 is a pivotal verse in the development of the tradition because it exhorts women to stay in their houses:

Stay in your houses. Do not display the displays of the time of ignorance. Establish *salah*, pay *zakah*, and obey Allah and his messenger. Allah's wish is only to remove uncleanness far from you, O members of the household, and cleanse you with a thorough cleansing.

This discourse sacralizes the division of the world into public and domestic space. Women are to live and work in the domestic realm. The *Sahih al-Bukhari* modifies this injunction. It states, "You (women) have been allowed to go out for your needs" (6:4795). Due to this modification, women are allowed to enter public space. The question over how much access women would have to public space still had to be negotiated.

The Meccan Influence

This negotiation process was important, because there appear to have been two conflicting approaches to women entering public space. The men of Mecca had a more separationalist approach to sexuality and its management that the Medinans. The Meccans wanted the women veiled and restricted in their access to public space. The Meccan male attitudes are in part exemplified by the Prophet's brother-in-law and the second Caliph, 'Umar.

In the *Sahih al-Bukhari* 'Umar entreats the Prophet to begin the tradition of segregation and veiling. 'Umar is recorded as saying, "Oh, Allah's Messenger! I wish you ordered your wives to cover themselves from the men, because good and bad men talk to them" (1:402). 'Umar bolstered his appeal for women veiling one night when he recognized one of the Prophet's wives going outside to the bathroom. 'Umar called out to her and said, "Oh, Sauda! By Allah, you cannot hide yourself from us, so think of a way by which you should not be recognized on going out" (6:4795). Due to 'Umar's repeated requests and the disconcerting events at Zainab's wedding, the verses for hijab came to be revealed (1:146; 8:6240).

Veiling women was just one step in this process of sexual management. The Meccan men also wanted to significantly restrict women's access to the public sphere (El Fadl 2001, 223). This is developed through a story over a clash about women attending prayers at a mosque (*Sahih al-Bukhari* 2:900). 'Umar did not like women attending the mosque for prayers. However, the Prophet of Islam appeared to be uncomfortable with the strict Meccan position. Being a negotiator, the Prophet conceded to both parties. The Prophet gave the women the right to attend the mosques for prayer (2:900), even at night (2:899), while stipulating that the women had to obtain permission from their husbands before going (7:5238). He also stipulated that the husband should not refuse her request (1:873).

The hadith in the *Sunan Abu Dawud* indicates that the Prophet's permission for women to go to the mosque did not appease the Meccan-influenced dislike of women in the public sphere. The hadith begins in a somewhat conciliatory fashion to women praying in the mosque, but the hadith's rhetorical flow encourages men to restrict women's movement.

First, the hadith acknowledges that women are permitted to attend the mosque for prayers, but they should not wear perfume (1:565). Second, even with this permission, women are encouraged to pray in their houses (1:567). Third, Abdullah ibn 'Umar and his son, Bilal, argue about women praying in the mosque. Bilal does not want women to attend the mosque because the women will "defraud." This undefined but clearly pejorative meaning of "defraud" is an integral part of the rhetorical flow. The reader's imagination is supposed to fill in the details as to what "defraud" entails. Bilal's father rebukes him for taking a stance that contradicts the instructions of the Prophet (1:568). Fourth, the tone turns pointedly against women being in the public sphere with a quotation from A'isha, the Prophet's favorite wife. A'isha is reported as saying, "If the Apostle of Allah (may peace be upon him) had seen what the women have invented, he would have prevented them from visiting the mosque (for praying), as the women of the children of Israel were prevented" (1:569).[5]

The reader is given no direct information as to what the women were doing. The literary impact of this nebulousness, of the intensity of Bilal's complaint, and of A'isha's insistence that the Prophet would have been appalled by the women's behavior motivates the reader to be as vexed as A'isha and renege on the Prophet's permission.

The next hadith climaxes with the intended result of the flow of the text. Women are encouraged to remain cloistered at home. "It is more excellent for a woman to pray inside her house than in her courtyard, and more excellent for her to pray in her private chamber than in her house" (1:570).

However, the Prophet did give women permission to pray in the mosque. So, as an addendum, this series of hadith concludes with Ibn 'Umar being conciliatory to the Prophet's dictum by appointing one door in the mosque for use by women. However, the hadith injects, "Ibn 'Umar did not enter through it (the door) till he died" (1:571). Ibn 'Umar's refusal to use the door reinforces the climax of the sequence of the hadith, casting a negative light on women praying in the mosque.

The Meccan influence and values ended up exerting the dominant influence over the shape Islam took.

Protection from Harassment

Social conditions in Medina at the time of the Prophet enabled the Meccan values to exercise a more dominating influence in the shaping of Islamic values. Fatima Mernissi points out that there were many slaves in Medina at the time and many slaves were used for prostitution (1991, 181).[6] Consequently, single men were on the streets propositioning any woman who happened to be on the streets. In order for these men to distinguish between the available slave women and the nonavailable free women, the free women were ordered to cover themselves (ibid., 183).[7] Sura al-Ahzab [33]:59 states, "O Prophet! Tell your wives and their daughters and the women of the believers to draw their coats close around them (when they go outside). This will be better so that they will be recognized and not be annoyed." Thus by this decree free women were able to go out on the streets and not be harassed. However, they had to be veiled.

Protection from Temptation

Another area of protection within the system of hijab was through the establishment of boundaries governing with whom women and men could interact. Sura al-Ahzab [33]:55 states:

> It is not a sin for your wives to interact with their fathers, or their sons, or their brothers, or their brothers' sons, of their sisters' sons, or with their own women, or their slaves. O women! Keep your duty to Allah. Allah is the witness of all things.

Women are to restrict their interaction to other women, children, and those males within their extended family with whom they cannot marry. The Islamic classification for males that a woman cannot marry is *mahram* (*Sahih Muslim* 3B:2171). Any marriageable male is classified as *gher-mahram*.

The reason for this restriction appears to be that the sexual drives of men and woman are of such a nature that without the establishment of proper boundaries between them immorality will result.[8] This is due to two reasons. First, men and women are naturally weak with regard to resisting temptation.[9] Second, this weakness is exacerbated by the devil, who actively works in human beings to encourage immorality.[10] The Prophet of Islam admitted to suffering from this weakness, but he declared that Allah protected him from succumbing to it.[11]

It is due to this human proclivity toward immorality and its exploitation by Satan that the Qur'an charges both sexes to lower their gaze and protect their modesty:

> Tell the believing men to lower their gaze and be modest. This is purer for them. Look, Allah is aware of what they do.

> Tell the believing women to lower their gaze and be modest, and to display of their clothing only that which is obvious, and to draw their veils over their chests, and to reveal their clothing only to their husbands, fathers, husbands' fathers, their sons, their husbands' sons, their brothers, their brothers' sons, their sisters' sons, their women, their slaves, their eunuchs, or to children who know nothing about women's nakedness. And, they should not stamp their feet, revealing what they are concealing of their clothing. (Sura an-Nur [24]:30,31)[12]

This injunction falls on both sexes because in Islam both have equal moral responsibility before God.[13] This shared responsibility indicates that when the community works together in following Allah they will succeed in fulfilling their moral duty. However, in order to minimize temptation, an additional command is given to women to conceal their beauty and not walk in an alluring manner.[14]

This passage adds definition to the parameters of hijab. First, women are told they can relax with regard to dress in front of children, other women, eunuchs, and males they cannot marry. This injunction reinforces the definition of the *gher-mahram*. Second, women are told they can leave uncovered "that which is obvious." The *Sunan Abu Dawud* defines the area that can remain uncovered as being the face and the hands (3:4092). However, the *Sahih al-Bukhari* contradicts this and in its commentary on this verse states that the face and hands should be covered (6:4758–59). Third, the covering of women and their careful gait in public is necessary to protect men from being tempted. Though men are commanded to lower their gaze, when a woman leaves her residence the devil is in the public sphere seeking to harass those men who can see her.[15] Therefore, a woman's restriction from being in the public sphere and her covering of everything but the obvious is meant to protect men from being attacked by the devil.

The sacred passages create a system of hijab which is meant to protect men and women from one another. To achieve this protection, it removes women from the public sphere except in circumstances of need. This creates a safe zone for the men. Whenever women do appear in public, they are not to fully appear. They are to be covered and restrained. Hijab also creates a safe zone for women, the domestic sphere. Men are not allowed free access into this sphere unless they fall into the *mahram* category that grants them permission.[16]

Gender and Power

Islamic sacred narratives also seek to create order in intergender relationships through a sacrosanct, patriarchal social order, subordinating women under male authority.[17]

Some of the most powerful stories establishing this sacred order for intergender relationships concern the Prophet's own examples of polygyny. Though polygyny had been practiced in Arabia prior to the time of the Prophet, the Prophet sacralized the polygyny, making it a religious institution.[18] The Prophet also transformed the practice. Montgomery Watt points out that, prior to the Prophet, wives generally lived in separate locations. In contrast, the Prophet kept his wives in the same compound (1956, 277). Living together led to numerous altercations among his wives. At one point the infighting had become so irritating that the Prophet left his wives alone for one month (*Sahih al-Bukhari* 7:5191). At the end of the month he gave them a choice to submit to him or be divorced.[19]

These sacred discourses about the Prophet's life serve to marginalize a woman's power in the conjugal relationship. Since the Prophet's wives were to submit, all wives are to submit. However, should wives find this difficult to do and assert themselves instead and become obnoxious to their husbands, the husbands are empowered to manage them in order to keep them in line.

This dimension of power between husbands and wives is expressed in Sura an-Nisa' [4]:34:

> Men are the managers over women. God has caused one of them to excel over the other because they spend from their wealth. So the good workers are devout, guarding in secret that which God has guarded. And if husbands fear their ill-conduct, then admonish/warn them and separate from them, putting them in the resting places, and beat them. If they obey you, then do not seek a way against them. Truly, God is the most exalted, the greatest.

The reason given in the above passage for the wife's subordination is that the husband is the one who works in the public sphere and gains the income for the survival of the family. The wife receives that support. The appropriate response by a pious woman is to be grateful for the sacrifices of the husband, be obedient to him, and ensure her sexual fidelity to him (this is the meaning of "guard in secret"). Such a response would facilitate the growth of the love and companionship that God had intended in the conjugal relationship.[20]

In addition, this sacred passage places a significant level of social power in the hands of the husband. He is not only a manager, he is also a disciplinarian.[21] If the woman acts in a way that is inappropriate to the husband, she can be spanked like a child.[22] However, the spanking should not turn into an excessive beating.[23]

The patriarchal division of power in the conjugal relationship is reinforced by the final speech of the Prophet:

> Consequently O men, you have a right over your women, and they have a right over you. You have this right over them, that they trample not on your carpet beds in any way that you find detestable, and that they not commit flagrant immorality. If they do, then God permits that you separate yourselves from them, putting them where

you sleep, and freely beat them without severely hurting them. If they restrain themselves, then you are to amicably give them their daily food and their clothing. Also, you are to charge the women in doing good. They are in your possession as child-bearers; they do not have control over themselves in any way. You have taken them by the blessing of God, and they are your permitted pleasure by the words of God. You understand, O men, my word. I have certainly informed you, and certainly I leave with you that to which you are to hold fast and by doing so never err, a clear command: the book of God and the practice of his Prophet. (Ibn Hisham 1936, 251)[24]

In his speech, the allocation of power within the relationship is clearly delineated. The Prophet places the husband above the wife. He is to manage and, if necessary, discipline her. However, the Prophet encourages the husband to amicably manage and treat his wife.[25]

Another way that power is allocated in the conjugal relationship in the sacred discourses is through the narrative recipients of the discourses. The speaker in the discourses is talking to men.

In addition, the content within the discourses demonstrates that men enjoy a favored status with God in contrast to women. In Sura al-Baqara [2]:187 the men are told that they can go to their wives at night for sex during the month of fasting. Sura an-Nahl [16]:72 shows that God has gifted women (as well as sons, grandsons, and the good provisions of life) to men. Sura al-Baqara [2]:223 tells a man he can have sex with his wife any way he likes. This verse through its use of metaphor reduces the status of the wife to being one of the husband's possessions: his cultivatable field.[26] The rhetorical effect of these speeches demonstrates a divine preference for the man. This divine favoritism strengthens the positional authority of the man.[27]

Even though the woman is to be subservient to her husband, the woman's position of subservience does not mean that she is left without any standing in the relationship. The woman has been fully empowered to operate within the domestic sphere. It is the woman's primary duty to care for the home. The *Sahih al-Bukhari* states, "A man is the guardian of his family and [is] responsible (for them); a wife is a guardian of her husband's home and she is responsible (for it)" (7:5188).

The allocation of power between the husband and wife is also manifested through the way divorce happens. In Islamic writ marriage is not an unbreakable covenant between the partners made before God. Marriage is a contract. Contracts can be broken, therefore divorce is permissible.

The primary holder of power to divorce is the husband, though the woman has certain grounds upon which to seek a divorce (Esposito and DeLong-Bas 2001, 28–34). A man simply needs to state three consecutive times that he divorces his wife in order for the divorce to become valid.

The threat of divorce can elicit fear within a woman if she has no independent means of supporting herself. The Qur'an recognizes this and encourages her to make peace with her husband (see Sura an-Nisa' [4]:127,128). The Hadith suggest that when facing the possibility of divorce a woman should give up her rights to the relationship; that is, her right to his presence, sex, and clothing, in order to be kept on as a wife (*Sahih al-Bukhari* 3:2450; 6:4601; 7:5206).[28]

In conclusion, husbands and wives have been allocated a measure of social power within the relationship. Women are empowered to function within their domestic spheres. However, they are to submit to their husbands, for the husbands enjoy a superior position, one that is created and acknowledged by God.

Rights, Differences, and Inequality

The Qur'an teaches that males and females were created with an equal moral responsibility[29] to carry out their duties and fulfill the rights of the other. These gender-oriented rights reinforce the perception of difference between the genders. Part of this is due to the different spheres in which men and woman have roles. These spheres require different obligations, and these different obligations cause inequality to exist between the sexes (see Chaudhry 1991, 160). "Different" in this regard has negative implications for the woman.

The sacred discourses define equality as this: the husband and wife are equally obliged to meet the other's gender-specific rights. For example, men have the right to sexual satisfaction[30] and the right to more than one wife. Husbands are commanded to love their wives equally. However, this love does not refer to the special, inner attraction and affection that a husband may feel toward one of his wives.[31] Wives in a polygynous household share a right to equal time with the husband (*Sunan Abu Dawud* 2:2128–33), and they have a right to adequate maintenance in terms of food and clothing (ibid., 2:2137).[32] However, it is understood that a husband cannot feel the same level of affection toward each one of his wives. The Prophet of Islam had a special affection toward his youngest wife, A'isha. Though this was a constant source of friction among his wives, his special affection toward A'isha was not wrong.

Gender and Nature

Though the woman was created equal in terms of moral responsibility, the sacred texts indicate the woman's nature is flawed. The *Sahih al-Bukhari* records this interaction between the Prophet of Islam and a group of women:

> "O women! Give alms, as I have seen that the majority of the dwellers of Hell-fire were you (women)." They asked, "Why is it so, O Allah's Apostle?" He replied, "You curse frequently and are ungrateful to your husbands. I have not seen anyone more deficient in intelligence and religion than you. A cautious sensible man could be led astray by some of you." The women asked, "O Allah's Apostle! What is deficient in our intelligence and religion?" He said, "Is not the evidence of two women equal to the witness of one man?" They replied in the affirmative. He said, "This is the deficiency in her intelligence. Isn't it true that a woman can neither pray nor fast during her menses?" The women replied in the affirmative. He said, "This is the deficiency in her religion." (1:304)

This discourse portrays women as being intellectually and constitutionally impaired. Their impairment is evidenced by their behavior. The religious laws have been adapted to compensate for this impairment. Women are less intelligent and reliable than men, so more women are needed as witnesses in a legal issue than men.[33] Women's menstrual periods (their biology) stigmatize them and make them deficient in the practice of their religion.

The impact of this discourse is that women need to respect and uphold the divinely ordained hierarchy for the home. They are not inclined to do so, and this is why the majority of them are going to hell.[34] The hadith adds that the impaired woman could lead a sensible man astray from the right path. In Sura at-Taghabun [64]:14 a husband is warned to watch out for the wiles of his wife: "Believers! Among your wives and your children are enemies. Therefore, beware of them."

This view of women's nature is affirmed elsewhere in the sacred texts. Woman is seen as a possible source of *fitna* (i.e., a source of sexual temptation as well as a source of trials, misfortunes, discord, or societal confusion). The *Sahih al-Bukhari* quotes the Prophet as saying, "I have not left any [f]itnah (trial and affliction) more harmful to men than women" (7:5096; see also *Sahih Muslim* 4B:2740–42).

One sacred discourse grounds the woman's impaired nature in her being created from the man's rib:

> And I command you to take care of the women in a good manner, for they are created from a rib and the most crooked portion of the rib is the upper part; if you try to straighten it, you will break it, and if you leave it, it will remain crooked, so I command you to take care of the women in a good manner. (*Sahih al-Bukhari* 7:5186)[35]

Though the sacred discourses warn believing men about the difficulties women bring, and their need for management and even discipline, the sacred narratives consistently appeal to men to treat their wives gracefully and amicably in spite of this.[36]

Conclusion

The Islamic sacred discourses teach that women and men are made equally as moral beings. Thus they are able and obliged to obey God's commands. Woman is fully human, therefore the potential exists for a husband and wife to have a meaningful and satisfying relationship. The Prophet demonstrated the possibility of this through his relationship with A'isha, his favorite wife.[37]

The definition of equality between the sexes is modified by the delineation of rights within the husband-wife relationship. The wife has a right to be sheltered, fed, clothed, and sexually satisfied. The husband has a right to his wife's fidelity, his sexual satisfaction, and her care of his children and belongings.

The sacred stories cast a shadow over the husband-wife relationship by diminishing trust. Other men can be a man's friends, and even his brothers, but they also can be predatorial.[38] Complicating this, since men and women are susceptible to sexual temptation, a husband needs to protect himself and his wife from such temptations.

The discourses direct the community to create two safe spaces to assist in providing protection: the public and the domestic. Public space is meant to be safe for the men. Women are not to appear in public space unless there is a necessity that compels them to enter that space. When women must appear in public space, they are not to fully appear. They are to be covered and restrained. Domestic space is meant to be safe for the women. In that space only those men who fall within specific relational boundaries are permitted to appear. Beyond those boundaries, only men who have received permission by the husband can appear.

An additional complication impacting the potential for a meaningful relationship is the flawed nature of the woman. Her impairments require that the husband manage her and, if necessary, discipline her. However, the husband is guided to treat her graciously, because God is able to produce a sizeable blessing for the husband through his ongoing relationship with his wife.

Finally, the marriage is a contract that can be terminated. The wife can be sent off if she does not adequately serve her purpose. To a lesser extent, a wife can divorce her husband if he does not fulfill his responsibilities. This contractual nature of the marriage injects a level of insecurity into the relationship. It would seem that the woman's weaker position in her family and in society with regard to movement and employment would exacerbate her feeling of insecurity.[39]

Understanding this Islamic perception of sexuality and its management facilitates understanding of how sexuality is perceived and managed in Peshawari society. One can see that purdah is connected to a sacred schematic world that integrates deeply embedded assumptions and values about men and women as human and sexual beings with the social practices of that schematic world. This being the case, one has to be very careful as one considers advocating for social change. The Pashtun system is not simply a cultural phenomenon that can easily be modified. It is also a religious system. In advocating for change, one should try to ensure that the fears and the apprehensions of the conservative religious community are not ignited.

The Apostle Paul fortunately provides a model by which advocacy can be pursued without challenging actual practices and disrupting the social order. It is to Paul and his first-century world that we now turn.

---

1 The authoritative sacred writings of Islam are the noble Qur'an and the *Sihah Sittah* (*Authentic Six*). The *Sihah Sittah* are the six most prestigious compilations of hadith, which are the sayings and practices of the Prophet of Islam. Though the noble Qur'an enjoys special status within the Islamic sacred corpus as being divinely revealed, the hadith compilations practically carry as much authority as the noble Qur'an. These six compilations are: the *Sahih al-Bukhari*, the *Sahih Muslim*, the *Sunan at-Tirmidhi*, the *Sunan Abu Dawud*, the *Sunan ibn Majah*, and the *Sunan an-Nasai'*. Of these six, the *Sahih al-Bukhari* and the *Sahih Muslim*

enjoy a special status above the other four. In addition, I draw from *Al-Muwatta of Imam Malik ibn Anas*, which many feel should be given the same authority as the last four of the *Sihah Sittah*.

2   Most of the information we have about early Islam is through the sacred literature of Islam. Due to this the question arises: Is this history an actual record of what transpired or is it a sacred history, constructed to reflect Islam as it had become? For further reading on this topic, see Brown's *A New Introduction to Islam* (2009, 49–51, 76–77). For detailed analyses on questions of origin, see Wansbrough's *Quranic Studies* (1977) and *The Sectarian Milieu* (1978), and Juynboll's *Muslim Tradition* (2008).

3   There is no single interpretation of the passages that speak of hijab. Pashtuns, in forming their traditions, appear to have relied upon classical interpretations of the Qur'anic and Hadith materials. However, there are Muslims who advocate for *ijtehad* (new readings and applications of the sacred texts) rather than *taqlid* (submitting to traditional interpretations). Khaled Abou El Fadl advocates for a system of *ijtehad* called "proportional inquiry," which takes into consideration issues of substance, transmission, historical context, as well as the social consequences of any proposed application of the Qur'an and Sunnah (2001, 217–18). There are feminist scholars who emphasize exegeting the Qur'anic text within its historical context while minimizing the influence of the Hadith and the interpretations of the classical jurists (see Barlas 2002; Wadud 1999; Karmi 1996; L. Ahmed 1992). In contrast to these feminist scholars, Pakistani Aiysha Madani takes exception to disregarding the significance of the Hadith (2005, 114). Syed Muzaffar-ud-Din claims orthodoxy demands keeping the Hadith central in matters of faith and practice (2000, 37–44). Fazlul Karim is representative of those who advocate for a "moderate" practice of purdah by glossing over or ignoring passages that seem to favor a classical interpretation (1998, 650–58).

4   For more commentary on Al-Ahzab [33]:53 see *Sahih al-Bukhari* 6:4790–95; 8:6240. In referencing the Hadith, I will give the name of the collection followed by the volume number and the number of the hadith. The quotations from the *Sunan at-Tirmidhi* will only include the hadith number.

5   This comment of A'isha is also included in the *Sahih al-Bukhari* (1:869) and *Al-Muwatta of Imam Malik ibn Anas* (14.5.15)

6   In Sura an-Nur [24]:33 the Prophet recognizes that prostitution is occurring. In this verse he does not outlaw the practice, but he does

order the owners not to force their slave girls into prostitution if the girls want to keep their chastity. However, the girls are promised forgiveness if they are compelled to perform sex for pay (see *Sahih al-Bukhari* 3: ch. 20, p. 266). *Sahih al-Bukhari* 3:2283 states that the Prophet outlawed prostitution.

7 The *Sahih al-Bukhari* describes this practice of veiling as being a distinction between slave and free women. When the Prophet of Islam captured Khaibar and took Safiyya for himself, the onlookers were wondering whether he would keep her as a slave or make her his wife. They knew she was to become his wife when the Prophet covered her with a veil (5:4213; 7:5085).

8 It appears that this assumption caused a heightened level of mistrust among men. 'Umar's complaint that the Prophet's wives talked to both good and bad men helped set the stage for the instituting of hijab (*Sahih al-Bukhari* 1:402). Embedded in 'Umar's complaint is that there are untrustworthy men. The Qur'an admits this in Sura al-Azhab [33]:32: "And be not soft of speech lest he in whose heart is a disease aspire you." This suspicion appears to have radically and negatively impacted how men viewed each other's behavior. This mistrust is exemplified in the *Sahih Muslim* where the Prophet is seen walking home with one of his wives at night by some passersby. The Prophet intentionally identifies the woman as his wife to them in order to eliminate any suspicions they might have had about what he was doing (3B:2174–75). This level of mistrust had developed to the extent that a husband was advised not to trust his own brother in being alone with his wife (3B:2172).

9 Sura an-Nisa' [4]:28b states, "And humankind was created weak."

10 "Whenever a man is alone with a woman the Devil makes a third" (*Sunan at-Tirmidhi* 930).

11 "The Prophet (peace be upon him) said: 'Do not visit women whose husbands are away from home, for the Devil circulates in you like your blood.' He was asked if this applied to him also and said, 'To me also, but Allah has helped me against him so that I may be safe'" (*Sunan at-Tirmidhi* 931). The *Sahih Muslim* gives an example of the temptability of the Prophet: "Jabir reported that Allah's messenger saw a woman, and so he came to his wife, Zainab, as she was tanning a leather and had sexual intercourse with her. He then went to his Companions and told them: The woman advances and returns in the shape of a devil, so when

one of you sees a woman, he should come to his wife, for that will repel what he feels in his heart" (2B:1403; see also *Sunan Abu Dawud* 2:2146).

12   Injunctions to guard one's modesty are also given in Sura al-Ahzab [33]:35 and Sura al-Mu'minun [23]:1–7.

13   Sura an-Nahl [16]:97 says, "Whosoever does right, whether male or female, and is a believer, truly we shall quicken him with a good life, and we shall pay them a recompense in proportion to the best of what they used to do." See also Sura al-Ahzab [33]:73; Sura al-Hadid [57]:11–15.

14   Though women are singled out to dress modestly in Sura an-Nur [24]:30–31, men are commanded in the Hadith to control their gaze toward women: "Jarir said: 'I asked the Apostle of Allah (may peace be upon him) about an accidental glance (on a woman).' He said: 'Turn your eyes away'" (*Sunan Abu Dawud* 2:2143; see also 2:2144). In one incident, a beautiful woman approached the Prophet while he was standing with al-Fadl. The Prophet noticed him staring, so he grabbed his beard and turned his face away so he would not stare at the woman (*Sahih al-Bukhari* 8:6228).

15   The *Sunan at-Tirmidhi* states, "When a woman goes out the devil looks at her" (928). This has been explained as, "The devil prompts men to enjoy looking at her get-up, appearance, beauty and dress" (Shahri 2001, 7).

16   In addition, a wife is not allowed to let a man in her house without the prior permission of her husband (*Sahih al-Bukhari* 7:5195).

17   This subordination is to include the home and the polity. "Never will succeed such a nation as makes a woman their ruler" (*Sahih al-Bukhari* 9:7099).

18   Due to the Prophet's example, polygyny is encouraged (Sura an-Nisa' [4]:3; see also Watt 1956, 274). Its practice earns one merit with God (Hirshfelder and Rahmaan 2003, 23).

19   See Sura al-Ahzab [33]:28,29.

20   "He created for you from yourselves companions that you may be at rest with them, and he put between you love and compassion" (Sura ar-Rum [30]:21).

21   Barbara Stowasser asserts that presentations of the sacred material like mine are rooted in medieval Islamic interpretations (1994, 21–24), and she asserts that even contemporary Islamists would read the texts differently (ibid., 36). However, in a later article she disagrees with herself, showing how even Islamists concur with the traditional interpretations (1998, 37–38). In this vein, in a BBC Internet article on March 3, 2006, regarding Hamas' win in the election and what impact that would have on women, Lama Hourani indicated that the pressure was growing upon women to conform to more conservative standards. Ms. Hourani said, "This is the main issue: they don't look at men and women as equal—when they educate women they always say that she has to obey the male in the family" (Johnston 2006).

22   Ghada Karmi takes exception to this aspect within Islamic writ and says that the end result for the woman is that she is infantilized (1996, 79). With regard to a wife's discipline and the potential for beating/spanking, see *Sunan Abu Dawud* 2:2140–42. *Sunan Abu Dawud* 2:2137 states that a man should not strike his wife on the face.

23   "None of you should flog his wife as he flogs a slave and then have sexual intercourse with her in the last part of the day" (*Sahih al-Bukhari* 7:5204).

24   This translation is mine. The *Sunan at-Tirmidhi* presents this speech in a similar form (104).

25   Sura an-Nisa' [4]:34 commands the husband to forgive and forget an issue if his wife responds positively to his discipline. This enjoining for husbands to amicably treat their wives is reiterated in Sura al-Baqara [2]:228. In Sura an-Nisa' [4]:19 the man is encouraged to look for the good in his wife and relate with her in a kind manner, even if he dislikes her. On the other hand, though men are permitted to spank their wives, the sacred stories never portray the Prophet as one who laid a hand on his wives when he was not getting along with them.

26   "Your wives are your fields, so go into your fields whichever way you like." With regard to Sura al-'Imran [3]:14, Bamyeh observes that women and offspring are offered no intrinsic value. Their value is integrated with terms of commerce (1999, 23). *Al-Muwatta of Imam Malik ibn Anas* classifies marriage with a woman in the same category as purchasing a slave or a camel (28.22.52).

27   "If I were to command anyone to make prostration before an-other, I would command women to prostrate themselves before their husbands, because of the special right over them given to husbands by Allah" (*Sunan Abu Dawud* 2:2135).

28   The *Sunan Abu Dawud* states that Sauda, one of the Prophet's wives, feared he would divorce her when she got too old. In order to remain a wife she gave her right of time with the Prophet to A'isha (2:2130). *Al-Muwatta of Imam Malik ibn Anas* gives the example of Rafi' ibn Khadji, who worked out a term of peace with his wife (58.22.57, 220).

29   For example, Sura an-Nahl [16]:97; Al-Ahzab [33]:73; Al-Hadid [57]:11–17.

30   See *Sahih al-Bukhari* 7:5193–94; *Sunan Abu Dawud* 2:2136. In contrast, Abdelwahab Bouhdiba asserts that within boundaries Islam is a celebration of carnal desire, and sexual satisfaction is meant for both sexes (1998, 88–92).

31   See Sura an-Nisa' [4]:129. See also *Sunan Abu Dawud* 2:2129 and footnote.

32   See also the footnote for *Sunan Abu Dawud* 2:2137.

33   See also Sura al-Baqara [2]:282.

34   See also *Sahih al-Bukhari* 7:5196 and *Sahih Muslim* 4B:2736–38.

35   See also *Sahih al-Bukhari* 7:5184, 5187.

36   As another example of this appeal to amicableness, Sura al-Baqara [2]:228 states, "And their husbands are more just in restoring them in that case if the husbands want reconciliation, and to the women is a simi-lar right; and the men who are over the women in kindness have a degree of honor over them. Allah is Mighty and Wise." For alternate transla-tions of this verse, see Sale (Wherry 1975, 372) and Bell (1937, 32). For translations from a feminist hermeneutical perspective, see Barlas (2002, 194–96) and Wadud (1999, 66–69).

37   The narrative of A'isha also brings a cloud upon the marriage re-lationship. While the Prophet and his army were returning from battle, she was accidentally left behind as she had strayed from the camp as they were leaving. She was picked up by a young soldier who also had gotten separated from the group. They returned together to the city. It was initially assumed that they had an affair. She denied having any

illicit relationship with the man. The Prophet separated from A'isha for a month, probably to see if she had her period. After the month was over, he received a word from God that A'isha had been faithful and they were restored.

38 The level of mistrust had developed to the extent that a husband was advised not to trust his own brothers in being alone with his wife (*Sahih Muslim* 3B:2172).

39 Women's reaction to the tenuous nature of marriage appears absent in the Islamic sacred literature.

Part II

Sexuality and Its Management in Christian Communities

So God created the human in his image,
in the image of God he created him,
male and female he created them.

GEN. 1:27

And Yahweh Elohim said, "It is not good that the man be alone. I will make an appropriate helper for him.... So Yahweh Elohim had a deep sleep fall on the man, and he slept; then he took one of his ribs and replaced it with flesh. And Yahweh Elohim constructed woman from the rib that he had taken from the man.

He brought her to the man and the man said:
This at last is bone from my bones,
and flesh from my flesh.
This shall be called woman
because from man was taken this.

This is the reason why a man leaves his father and his mother, clings to his woman, and they become one flesh.

And the two were naked, the man and his woman, and they were not ashamed.

GEN. 2:18,21–25

4

The Greco-Roman Approach to Sexuality
and Its Management

THE GRECO-ROMAN WORLD had demeaning assumptions and values about women. These assumptions and values influenced the shape the social systems took within that world. Being aware of this context enables us to make sense of the key Pauline texts on sexuality. It is easier to identify how culture had shaped and impacted the husband-wife relationship. It is also easier to see how Paul subverted the assumptions and values of the Greco-Roman cultural system.

Stratification in Society

The Greco-Roman social world was very class- and status-conscious. They had numerous ways to stratify their society, separating one group from another in order to create inequality (Alföldy 1988, 106–9). A series of boundaries developed within this world to create and enhance this stratification. A person was an aristocrat or not, a landowner or not, a Roman citizen or not. A person was either rich or poor; free, freed, or slave. Each classification was meant to have its own level of prestige and power. The Greco-Roman world created and maintained a large social distance, a large power distance, between those who had prestige and power and those who had little or none.

Power distance is a social construct that was developed and popularized by Geert Hofstede (Hofstede and Hofstede 2005, 39–72). Hofstede studied corporate cultures in a number of countries and watched how people approached leadership and power. He classified what he observed along a continuum between large and small power distance (see table 1). The characteristics of stratification that existed in the Greco-Roman world (and the understanding and the means of sexual management that exist in the Peshawari Pashtun community as well as those reflected in the Islamic sacred writings) reflect the characteristics of large power distance.

TABLE 1 Characteristics of Power Distance in Society

Small Power Distance	Large Power Distance
All should be interdependent.	A few should be independent; most should be dependent.
Inequality in society should be minimized.	There should be an order of inequality in this world in which everyone has his/her rightful place; high and low are protected by this order.
Hierarchy means inequality of roles, established for convenience.	Hierarchy means existential inequality.
Subordinates are people like me.	Superiors consider subordinates as being of a different kind.
The use of power should be legitimate and is subject to the judgment between good and evil.	Power is a basic fact of society that antedates good or evil; its legitimacy is irrelevant.
All should have equal rights.	Power holders are entitled to privileges.
Stress on reward, legitimate and expert power.	Stress on coercive and referent power.
The system is to blame.	The underdog is to blame.
The way to change a social system is by redistributing power.	The way to change a social system is by destroying those in power.
Latent harmony exists between the powerful and the powerless.	Latent conflict exists between the powerful and the powerless.
Older people neither respected nor feared.	Older people respected and feared.

(Hofstede 2001, 98)

Since the Greco-Roman world was a large power distance world, inequality existed among the different classes within the society (see fig. 4). One of the ways that inequality manifested itself was in the use of social power and the application of law. Those with power were able to act according to the principle "Might makes right."[1] In the Greco-Roman context the elite were able to use their power to enhance and secure their own status and income. Those in the highest seats of power exemplified this principle, and those in lower seats of power followed their example.

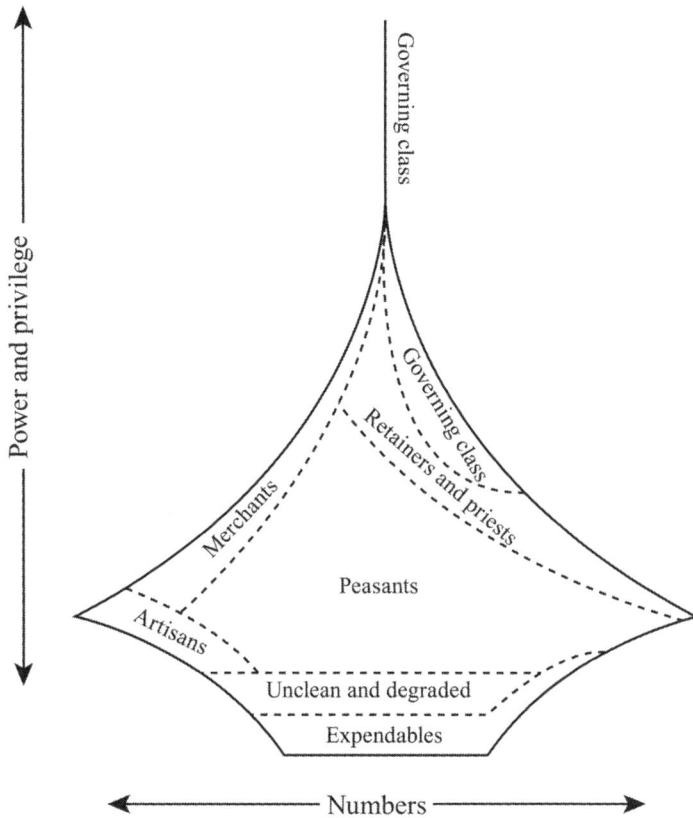

Fig. 4. Social Stratification in Greco-Roman Society
(Lenski 1984, 284)

Antony is one of those who misused power. He had Cicero killed be-cause Cicero opposed his coming to power (Velleius Paterculus 1995, 2.66.2). The emperor Augustus provided numerous examples of the misuse of position and power. He had Pinarius executed at an assembly simply because Augustus suspected he was a spy (Suetonius Tranquillus 1960, 2.27.3). Suspicious of Quintus Gallius' loyalty, Augustus person-ally pulled out Gallius' eyes before he had Gallius tortured and executed (ibid., 22.27.4). When Augustus wanted to marry Livia Drusilla, he took her from her husband, Tiberius Nero, even though she was pregnant with Nero's child (ibid., 2.63). At one dinner engagement Augustus had the audacity to take the wife of an ex-consul, before the ex-consul's very eyes, into a bedroom and sleep with her (ibid., 2.69).

Nero also felt free to misuse his power for personal gain. He had his stepbrother, Britannicus, poisoned in order to eliminate him as an heir to the throne (Tacitus 1943, *The Annals* 13.14–16). Nero also committed incest with his mother and later had her murdered.

Since people with power were excused from the rule of law, corruption was endemic in the Greco-Roman world. Juvenal alludes to the pervasiveness of corruption in his third satire: "What can I do at Rome? I don't know how to tell lies.... Is there anyone these days who inspires affection unless he's an accomplice?" (Juvenalis 2004, 3.41–50).

Stratification in the Family

Roman tradition set the living male patriarch in charge of his children and grandchildren. This tradition dated back prior to the beginning of the republic. The authority and power allotted to the patriarch was called *potestas*. The *Digest of Justinian* describes the principle of *potestas*:

> When a grandfather dies, his grandchildren through his son normally fall within the power of that son, that is, of their own father; in the same way also, great grandchildren and so on either come into the power of that son, if he is alive and has remained within the family, or they come into the power of that ancestor who is above them within the *potestas*. (Justinianus 1985, 1.6.5)

The patriarch/father ideally exercised total authority over the children in his household (ibid., 1.6.3; Dionysius of Halicarnassus 1948, 2.26–27). This meant that the father had the power of life or death over his children. The father was the one who would decide whether or not to expose a newborn child (Corbier 2001, 58, 71). It appears that the practice was widespread throughout the empire.[2] Exposure could have happened for a few reasons: if the family was too poor to feed another mouth, if the child was deformed, or if the father was uncertain of the paternity of the child.[3] Some Roman aristocrats exposed children so there would be fewer children to share the inheritance (G. Clark 1996, 37). Beyond exposure, the *paterfamilias* also had the right to beat, sell, and even kill his children. According to Dionysius, a father could sell his son three times (1948, 2.27.2).

The design of the Roman house was meant to project the *potestas* of the patriarch (Wallace-Hadrill 1996, 114). From the street the *atrium* and the *tablinum* were visible. The *atrium* was the place where the patriarch received his guests and clients (Hales 2003, 113), and "the *atrium* symbolized Roman patronal practice and social hierarchy" (Wallace-Hadrill 1996, 106). In the *atrium* the busts of the notable ancestors of the family were positioned.[4] Those busts created an aura of power and status for the patriarch by linking him with his power-filled ancestral history. This visible connection with his past further legitimized and enhanced his prestige.

Beyond the *atrium*, at the symbolic heart of the house, was the *tablinum*, the patriarch's office. Initially it had been the master bedroom, symbolizing the union of the master of the house and his wife (Hales 2003, 107). The *tablinum* was elevated above all other rooms, placing the patriarch in a physically superior position to all others in the house (Osiek and Balch 1997, 25).

The institution of *patria potestas* (the authority of the father/patriarch) within the family was reinforced by the Roman government, because the government modeled itself after the family (see Lacey 1986, 123; Rawson 2001, 38). Augustus' title as emperor was *pater patriae* (father of fathers). Thus this stratified relational paradigm of large power distance impacted the way both government and families functioned.[5]

Stratification and Assumptions about Sexuality

Stratification in the Greco-Roman world included the way sexuality was perceived and managed. Women were assumed to be the inferior sex, the *infirmitas sexus*. Due to their inferior nature they were seen as less rational and more emotional than men.[6] Men, being ontologically superior to women, naturally enjoyed a higher status. However, this status granted by being male was modified by one's status within the society: free women had inherently more status than freed men or male slaves.

Due to their weaker nature, women needed management and protection.[7] The Greco-Roman response to this was to place men in charge of women. The Twelve Tables, an early codification of Roman law (possibly 450 BC), required that each woman have a guardian throughout her lifetime because of her fickle disposition (Warmington 1967, 445).[8]

Stratification in Marriage Due to Age

This stratification in gender was reinforced by the difference in the ages of the couple when they married. The ideal age for the first marriage within the Roman aristocracy was fifteen for the female and twenty-five for the male. For the masses it was twenty for the woman and thirty for the man (Saller 1994, 41). Thus the average age difference between the couple was about ten years in their first marriage. This did not rule out wider age spans. Cicero was sixty years old when he married Publilia; she was about fifteen. One epitaph records that a woman had married her husband when she was seven years old.[9]

The prime age for marrying a girl was between fifteen and twenty because this was the time when females were physiologically at the peak of their fertility. Bearing children in the Greco-Roman world was the primary purpose of marriage.

This age span contributed to the stratification of the relationship between a husband and wife. With the husband being older, more experienced and already engaged in an occupation, and the wife just coming of age, it is easy to see that the husband saw himself as fulfilling the role of master (*dominus*), and the wife would have been expected to come under his management rather than enter the relationship in a more egalitarian way.[10] Pliny describes the conjugal relationship as one where the husband "fashions and forms" the wife's good habits (Plinius 1969, *Panegyricus* 83.8). Cato the Elder provides an example of large power distance between husband and wife in his instructions to a farm manager on how to manage his wife: "See that the housekeeper performs all her duties. If the master has given her to you as a wife, keep yourself only to her. Make her stand in awe of you. Restrain her from extravagance" (Cato and Verro 1954, *On Agriculture* 143.1). Pliny and Cato's advice reflects an infantilizing of the woman, expecting her to be treated more as a child than as a responsible adult. The relationship between the husband and wife in the Roman marriage is "analogous to that between a father and child, or a tutor and ward" (Bradley 1991, 7).

Stratification Due to *Concordia* and Partnership

The ideal marriage for the Romans appeared to be where the couple demonstrated *concordia* (harmony) and partnership (Dixon 1992, 105). These values were supposed to develop naturally in the stratified conjugal relationship.

The couple would achieve *concordia* through the wife's submission.[11] The husband was to be viewed as the elder in the relationship due to his position, age, and experience. Gracious acquiescence was her pathway to honor (Plinius 1969, *Panegyricus* 83.6–7). A young woman would have understood this, because from birth she would have been enculturated to submit herself and to serve the head of her household (G. Clark 1996 116), first to her father, and then to her *dominus* (husband/master).

Likewise the couple would achieve partnership when the wife made her husband's aspirations her aspirations. The wife was expected to have as her ambition to serve her husband well (Treggiari 1991, 202–3). Serving the husband did not mean that the wife became a nonentity in the household. It was expected that she would assume her partnership by assuming the domestic role that was laid out for her. She was required to run the affairs of the household. The husband's many obligations demanded he turn his attentions outward, to the issues of the wider community. Besides attending mandatory public functions, he had to host clients and guests in his house, as well as visit those with whom he needed to maintain close relationships. The household was a beehive of activity, a place that needed continual oversight. With the husband preoccupied with his obligations and pursuits, it was the wife's duty to provide oversight for the household (*domus*) (Rei 1998, 104). Her effective oversight kept proper order and enabled the husband's life to operate smoothly.

One other factor affecting partnership in Roman marriage was that the wife brought to the marriage relationship a dowry. That dowry was often needed to enable the household to be financially solvent. Plutarch indicates that there were times when the wife's dowry was even more substantial than the possessions of the husband. This being the case, it is understandable why her financial partnership would have been essential in maintaining *concordia* and releasing the household to increase its wealth.[12]

Stratification Modified

Marriage implies that a relationship exists between two individuals. However, the conditions surrounding these two individuals will impact how their relationship finds expression. Though the Greco-Roman world envisioned in its values and assumptions a stratified marriage relationship, the society had created a dissonant set of mores that in some cases undermined the power a husband could exercise over his wife. The husbands' power in the Greco-Roman world was impacted by how marriages were legally constructed, how families perceived the purpose of marriage, and how intimate the marriage relationships became.

Marriage *sine Manu*

In the early days of the republic, the Roman legal model for marriage was *cum manu* (with hand) (Pomeroy 1975, 152). This meant that the wife went out from under her father's authority and came under the hand/authority of her husband (Treggiari 1991, 29). Over time this tradition changed and women married but remained under the authority of their father until he died. This model for this marriage was called *sine manu* (without hand) (G. Clark 1996, 46). When the woman's father died she became independent (*sui iuris*): a free person who was able to own property. Nevertheless, the woman was legally required to remain under the tutelage of a guardian (Cantarella 1987, 139). However, the guardian probably did not exercise much oversight.

A woman entered the marriage with a dowry, which could have been quite substantial. Though the husband could take the dowry and use it for the benefit of the household, there were times when the wife managed the dowry.

In addition, the divorce laws also changed in that the woman was empowered to sue for a divorce. If she sued for a divorce without reasonable cause, she was liable to lose her dowry. If her husband divorced her, he was obligated to give her the dowry.[13]

The Extended Family

In a marriage *cum manu*, a woman's allegiance would naturally shift to her husband's family, because she was brought into the family like a daughter. In contrast, in a marriage *sine manu* a woman was entering the husband's family as one who could provide children. She remained legally under the authority of her family. Her allegiance, therefore, potentially remained with her family.

In Roman society the extended family (*familias*) was essential for the survival of the clan. The circumstances of life were too unstable for a nuclear family to adequately cope on its own.[14] This sense of insecurity fostered a tighter bond between relatives, causing people to act collectively rather than individually. Individuals understood that their partnership was essential to enable the extended family to meet its collective needs. Included in the strategy for survival were marriages, because marriages were contracted to advance the needs of the extended family and the clan.

Plutarch provides a number of examples of how marriages were used by powerful men to meet the needs of the extended family. The dictator

Sulla admired Pompey and wanted to form an alliance with Pompey to further develop his administration (Plutarchus 1955, *Pompey* 9.1). Sulla persuaded Pompey to divorce his first wife, Antisitia, so that he could marry Aemilia, Sulla's stepdaughter (ibid., *Pompey* 9.2). Aemilia was pregnant at the time with her first child from Manius Glabrio (Plutarchus 1950, *Sulla* 33.3). Unfortunately, Pompey's marriage to Aemilia was a short one, because Aemilia died in childbirth (1950, *Sulla* 33.4; 1955, *Pompey* 9.4). Pompey then married Mucia, who was part of the Metellan clan, thus forging a powerful alliance with another powerful Roman family. After seventeen years and three children, Pompey divorced Mucia (1955, *Pompey* 42.7), probably for the sake of political expediency. Later Julius Caesar gave his daughter Julia to Pompey in order to forge a political alliance (1955, *Pompey* 47.6), an alliance that lasted until Julia's death (1955, *Pompey* 53.4–6).

Plutarch also records the story of Quintus Hortensius, which is one of the extreme examples of the use of women to form beneficial alliances. Hortensius was a prestigious man and he wanted a closer relationship with Cato the Younger. Therefore Hortensius asked Cato for Cato's daughter's hand in marriage. Cato's daughter, Porcia, was already married and pregnant at the time, and her husband was devoted to her. Hortensius suggested he marry Porcia just long enough to have one child by her, and then she could return to her husband. Cato was unwilling to grant his request. Hortensius was determined to cement a relational bond with Cato, and so he proceeded to ask Cato for his young wife, Marcia, who in turn was pregnant with Cato's child. Cato replied that he could not do such a thing without her father's consent. Amazingly, Marcia's father consented. Consequently, Cato gave Marcia to Hortensius in marriage. After Hortensius died, Cato remarried Marcia (Plutarchus 1959, *Cato the Younger* 25).

It could be argued that the literary examples of using women to advance personal or familial standing reflect the behavior of the aristocracy, not the commoner. However, if the desire to create stability or advance oneself or one's family were significant factors in how aristocrats made their choices, these same desires would have motivated the common person as well. Instability caused by death, disease, or misfortune plagued everyone. The nature of some of the misfortunes between the aristocrats and the poor may have varied significantly. The poor would have been prey to petty injustices whereas the aristocrats would have suffered from the detrimental repercussions of shifts in political power. However, in both contexts injustice could permanently mar their lives. In the global context of instability and lack of control over the circumstances of life, marriages were probably arranged at all strata of society with the goal of creating some level of stability for the extended family.[15]

The impact of this approach to marriage arrangements was that a wife's ultimate allegiance could remain with her side of the extended family. If she brought a sizeable dowry into the household, this would have resulted in minimizing the power of the husband over her and decreased the power distance between her and her husband.

Juvenal in a tongue-in-cheek manner speaks of the problems that could arise when a woman did not transfer her allegiance to her husband. The wife could assert that her lineage was better than his (Juvenalis 2004, *Sixth Satire* 174–77). Also, if she was attractive and from a noble family, she could be arrogant, making peaceful coexistence difficult (ibid., 161–70).

Female Fidelity

Though some aristocratic women may have felt empowered to act independently, one of the values that would have marginalized independent action was the value of the fidelity of the wife within the society (Treggiari 1991, 234). For a first marriage, the bride was to have been a virgin, while the husband probably had been sexually active. After marriage, it was expected that a woman would remain faithful to her husband,[16] while a husband may have reserved the right to amorously liaise on occasion.[17]

This double standard had the potential to impair the marriage relationship. It likely created distress for the wife,[18] and it could have increased a husband's inclination to objectify his wife, potentially seeing her as just another one of his possessions within his household (Veyne 1987, 38–39).[19]

Stratification in Space and Cloth

This sexually oriented stratification found expression in the manner in which the Greco-Roman world perceived space. The world was divided into public and household space. Thucydides, as quoted by Plutarch, spoke of this division of space: "The best woman is she about whom there is the least talk among persons outside regarding either censure or recommendation, feeling that the name of the good woman, like her person, ought to be shut up indoors and never go out" (Plutarchus 1931, *Moralia* 3.Bravery of Women.Preface).[20] It was not as if women did not go out. They did. However, when they went out, they went out wearing a *palla* (veil).

A married woman always wore a head covering. Veiling was an integral part of becoming and being married. Susan Treggiari points out: "The verb used of the woman marrying, *nubo*, is related to *nubes*, a cloud, and means literally 'I veil myself.' From this come *nupta*, a married woman, *nova nuptia*, a bride, and *nuptiae*, the wedding" (1991, 163). The married woman wore a woolen *stola* over her tunic and a woolen *palla* "which was used to veil her head when she went out in public" (Sebesta 2001, 48). No respectable woman would have left her house without covering her head with the *palla* (Croom 2000, 87). This head covering was a symbolic representation of the woman's position and status within her household.

Conclusion

Stratification, status, and inequality characterized Greco-Roman societies. Thus the social systems in the Greco-Roman world functioned along a large power distance paradigm and impacted people's approach toward sexuality and its management.

This stratification and inequality shaped the needs of the extended family, and these needs in turn impacted the Greco-Roman couple. The patriarch and the males in the family were concerned with maintaining their status in society or their advancement. Women were utilized to enable the family to meet these needs. If marrying a daughter to someone would secure a better position for the family, the daughter was expected to marry that person.

Daughters would have learned that they were ontologically inferior to men. In this enculturation process, they would have also learned that they were required to be subservient to their husbands and develop the values of harmony (concordia) and partnership. In her first marriage, a girl would likely have married a man about ten years older than she, placing her in an inferior position in the relationship. She was supposed to gain honor by serving her husband well, being sexually faithful, running the household, making him appear successful, and bearing children for him.

However, the inferior position the woman held within her household in Paul's time was modified by the development of the sine manu marriage arrangement and by how wealthy a woman was. Within the sine manu marriage, the wife remained under the authority of her father or the head of her family. Therefore it was possible for a family to influence a woman to divorce her husband and marry another man if it would benefit her family.

When the woman married she brought a dowry with her. If the wife came from a more wealthy family than the husband, the size of the dowry could have diminished the amount of domination the husband exercised in their hierarchical relationship. The large dowry could have made the husband indebted to his wife and given her leverage in negotiating through disagreements.

Nevertheless, there were symbolic ways to reinforce the system that women were subordinates in a hierarchical world. The Greco-Roman world divided space into two: public and domestic. Women were to be reserved when in public space, and married women covered their heads with a long, woolen cloth called a palla.

It was into this hierarchical, urban Greco-Roman world that Paul wrote his letters.

---

1   The *Digest of Justinian* declared that the code of law was meant to bring order to the Roman society by placing everyone under law (Justinianus 1985, 1.2). However, the rule of law was for those under the law, not necessarily for those who created it (Garnsey and Saller 1987, 109).

2   Saller interprets Strabo and Tacitus' surprise that the Egyptians and Jews did not practice exposure to indicate that it was a widespread practice in the empire (Saller 1987, 69; see Strabo 1949, *Geography* 17.2.5; Tacitus 1943, *Histories* 5.5).

3   Seneca in his *Moral Essays* wrote, "Unnatural progeny we destroy, we drown even children who at birth are weakly and abnormal" (1928, *De Ira* 1.15.2)

4   However, Wallace-Hadrill points out that no ancestral images have been found at the archaeological finds of Pompeii that match the descriptions in the literature (1996, 109).

5   Such stratification, along with the notion of absolute power in the hands of the father, conjures up images of paternal tyranny. Dionysius recognized the potential tyrannical dimension to this custom (1948, 2.27.1). Stories—like the one of Verginius, in which he slew his daughter to save her from violation (Justinianus 1985, *Digesta* 1.2.24); of Brutus, who had his sons brutally executed because they revolted against the new

republic (Livius 1957, *Livy* 2.5.5–9); of Cassius, who executed his son for treason; of Torquatus, who disowned his son because of corruption and showed no remorse over his son's subsequent suicide (Maximus 2000, 5.8.2–3)—illustrate the breadth of a father's power as well as a father's potential severity. However true these stories may have been, it is unlikely that they represented what life was really like for the average Roman family during the empire. Suzanne Dixon claims that any inclination toward severity by a patriarch was significantly mollified by social ethics and family pressure (1992, 78; see also Eyben 1991, 122; Rei 1998, 99; Saller 1994, 131). These stories probably played a more mythic function within the society, buttressing idealized values by which the society sought to define itself. Eyben points out that "almost all known cases of a father killing a son involved offences against the early Republic" (1991, 122). Saller points out that "Romans traditionally perpetuated their moral values through retelling such *exempla* (rather than through systematic moral philosophy or sacred texts)" (1994, 109).

Though the Greco-Roman families were stratified, stratification did not always result in tyranny. Susan Treggiari suggested that one factor that might have limited tyranny in the home was the *consilium*, a family council (1991, 265). It was the custom that fathers were not supposed to make decisions that would affect the extended family without consulting other members of the family. However, there was a caveat. If a *consilium* decided against the father's wishes, the father could not be hindered from acting unilaterally (Lacey 1986, 124; Treggiari 1991, 266).

6   Livy's rendition of the debate between Cato and Lucius Valerius over the repeal of the Oppian Law revolves around the assumption of women's weaker nature in both Cato's speech (Livius 1953, 34.1–4)— Cato favored keeping the law—as well as in the response from Lucius Valerius, who favored repealing the law. Justifying the women's public response to the law, Valerius says, "A thing like this would hurt the feelings even of men: what do you think is its effect upon weak women, whom even little things disturb?" (ibid., 34.7.7). Valerius Maximus somewhat excused Roman women for their obsession for extravagant adornment because of their mental infirmity (2000, 9.1.3). Women were also seen as having less control over their sexual appetites. The reversal of these assumptions about women and men creates much of the humor in the ribald play *Lysistrata* (see Aristophanes 2000).

7   Regarding women's management, see Plutarch (Plutarchus 1998, *Moralia* 2.Advice to the Bride and Groom.48).

8   An example of this management is the *Senatusconsultum Velleianum*, which was passed sometime between AD 45 and 61. It demonstrated a somewhat benevolent protection of women in that it restricted them from becoming the guarantor of a man's debt (Crook 1986, 86–87).

9   The epitaph reads: "In life I was named Aurelia Philematium, a woman chaste and modest, knowing not the crowd, faithful to her man. My man was a fellow-freedman; he was also in very truth over and above a father to me; and alas, I have lost him. Seven years old was I when he, even he, took me in his bosom; forty years old—and I am in the power of violent death. He through my constant loving duties flourished at all seasons" (Warmington 1967, 53). Marrying a girl that young in age was permissible by law; however, the *Digest* indicates that the social expectation was that the marriage would not be consummated until she was older. The *Digest* proscribed: "A girl who was less than twelve years old when she married will not be a lawful wife until she reaches that age while living with her husband" (Justinianus 1985, 23.2.4).

10   Cantarella writes, "How did men view the relationship between the sexes? What did they expect from women? Though they never scaled the heights of Greek misogyny, the Romans had a very precise idea of the role of women and a fairly bleak vision of the conjugal relationship. Like the Greeks, the Romans wanted their women under their thumbs" (1987, 143).

11   Lucretius expected the woman to adjust and be clean and submissive. He didn't guarantee the unattractive wife would ever be loved, but he intimated that this was the only way that her husband would grow to love her (1997, *On the Nature of the Universe* 4.1277–87). Plutarch wrote, "Whenever two notes are sounded in accord the tune is carried by the bass; and in like manner every activity in a virtuous household is carried on by both parties in agreement, but discloses the husband's leadership and preferences" (Plutarchus 1998, 2.*Advice to Bride and Groom*.11).

12   This is the context behind Martial's verse, "You all ask why I don't want to marry a rich wife? I don't want to be my wife's wife. The matron, Priscus, should be below her husband. That's the only way man and woman can be equal" (Martialis 1993, 8.12).

13   It appears that few women independently initiated their divorces (Treggiari 1991, 444). In the highly unstable context of the Greco-Roman agrarian society, this is what one would expect. People were heavily

dependent on familial ties. One relied upon one's extended family to create a sense of stability for oneself. Few would be confident enough to act independently of their family.

14   Having little or no control over the circumstances of one's life is a common feeling in agrarian/peasant societies (Foster 1967b, 8), whether modern or ancient.

15   Evidence, though sparse, indicates that craftsmen married daughters of their fellow craftsmen (Hanson 1999, 32). These marriages were probably arranged to solidify relationships in their business world and create some stability in their unstable world.

16   Regarding the importance of virginity and fidelity, see Cantarella (1987, 130). See also Maximus (2000, 2.1.3).

17   Plutarch acknowledges this in his *Advice to Bride and Groom* (Plutarchus 1998, 16). Musonius Rufus, though speaking against sleeping with a maidservant, acknowledges that some regard it as acceptable (Treggiari 1991, 222, 301). Valerius Maximus gives Tertia Aemilia as a noble example of a woman because she overlooked her husband's infidelity with one of her slave girls (2000, 6.7.1).

18   The age span between husbands and wives and the low age expectancy may have dampened the expectations regarding intimacy between the husband and wife going into marriage. It is difficult to know if they expected to be married to one person throughout their life when they married, but the statistics indicate that each person who survived long enough would have had two spouses in a lifetime (Bradley 1991b, 85).

19   The poets Horace, Ovid, and Propertius define love more in terms of the erotic than of a relationship (see Horatius Flaccus 2004, *Odes* 2.4; *Epode* 11; Ovidius Naso 1962, *The Art of Love* 1.41–66; Propertius 1952, 2.15). Martial could be included in this list. He unquestionably objectifies women in his verses; however, his purpose appears to be bawdy, not to describe romance (1993). Horace's *Epodes* 8 and 12 are clear examples of objectification and of misogyny. Propertius is autobiographical. He describes in detail his tempestuous relationship with his lover, Cynthia (1952, 4.8). Plautus' *Casina* and Virgil's *Aeneid* continue this tendency toward reification and objectification of romance. In *Casina*, Lysidamus is simply overwhelmed by Casina's youthful beauty. Any desire to develop a communicative relationship with her is absent (Plautus 1966, 468–69, 830–50).

20   However, it appears that Plutarch did not mind women being in public; he simply did not like them talking in public (Plutarchus 1998, *Moralia* 2.Advice to the Bride and Groom.31). It was the women's brash presence in public that set Cato off in his speech in favor of the Oppian Law. He also made ample use of the assumption of women's infirmed ontology and their need for proper management (Livius 1953, 34.2.8– 14). Lucius Valerius acknowledged that women's presence in public was limited (1953, 34.5.7). Seneca in his *Moral Essays* stated that women were restricted in the public sphere. He also drew from the assumption of women's deficient ontology; in this case, their *muliebri impotentia*, which means a woman's lack of self-restraint (*To Helvia on Consolation* 14.2).

5

Creating the World of Sexuality:
Genesis 1:1–2:4

WHAT WERE PAUL'S ASSUMPTIONS and values about sexuality? Did he share those of the Greco-Roman world? If not, what were his assumptions and values, and upon what did he base them?

Since Paul refers directly or indirectly to Genesis 1–3 when speaking of issues related to sexuality—in 1 Corinthians 11:2–16; Galatians 3:28;[1] Ephesians 5:22–33; and 1 Timothy 2:9–15—it appears that Paul based his assumptions and values about sexuality on Genesis 1–3.[2] In addition, Paul's thoughts, though radically transformed by the Christ-Spirit event (this being inclusive of Jesus' life, death, resurrection, ascension, and the giving of the gift of the Spirit at Pentecost), were completely rooted in the Old Testament. Paul did not quote from the Genesis text to support novel and discontinuous ideas; he quoted it because he understood himself and the other people of God to be living out the narrative themes of that text within his present day (Witherington 1998, 230–31; N. Wright 2005, 9–13). Also, Paul understood the redemption of Christ to be the beginning of the renewal of creation (O'Donovan 1986, 13–14; N. Wright 2005, 21–39). In this light, there is ample reason to view the creation narrative as the pivotal interpretive text for Paul with regard to sexuality.

The creation narrative[3] begins with Genesis 1:1 and ends with Genesis 3:24, with two transitions. Verse 2:4 functions as a transitional verse, closing the first section of the creation narrative (Gen 1:1–2:4) while opening the second section (2:4–25). Genesis 2:25 also functions as a transitional verse, closing the second section while opening the third section.

Though we are not privy to the exact nature of the society of the recipients of the Pentateuch at the time of its compilation, I assume that the society viewed women in a manner similar to the Greco-Roman world. Thus I assume it was a society that reflected the characteristics of large power distance. These assumptions line up with the manner in which the text appears to have been shaped in the creation narrative. The narrative appears to have been intentionally crafted to inform and reform the worldview of the recipients of the narrative. The creation narrative asserts that the assumptions of male superiority, flawed female ontology, stratification, and the exercise of power by one over another are aberrations in the conjugal relationship as in all human relationships. While the creation narrative affirms the existence of hierarchy in social relationships, it portrays hierarchy in terms of small power distance.[4] Small power distance aptly describes the paradigm for relationships that Paul appears to have reflected in his writings.

Sexuality and Image

In the first section of the creation narrative the text shapes the receptor's[5] assumptions about humanity and sexuality. In this passage God's creative activity culminates with the creation of humankind in his image on the sixth and final day of his work. In verse 26 God declares his intent to make and commission *'adam*. Verse 27 records God's act of creation:

> So God created the human [*'adam*] in his image,
> in *the* image of God he created him;
> male and female he created them.[6]

Prior to verse 27, the narrative is in prose. However, in verse 27 the text changes genres and shifts to poetry. This shift in genre enables the use of parallelism in order to clarify and emphasize meaning (Gillingham 1994, 81).

Making this shift in genre is imperative, because *'adam* is a singular noun that literally means "man." Did God make only one man in his image? A receptor might be inclined initially to think this way. However, verses 26–27 go on to clarify that *'adam* cannot refer to a specific male as it does in chapter 2.[7] Verse 26 is written intentionally to demonstrate the collective nature of *'adam*. In this verse God says, "Let us make *'adam* in our image." Though *'adam* is singular, in the next clause God says, "and let them rule." The verb "rule" is in the masculine third person plural form. This shift from a singular noun (*'adam*) to a plural verb form shows that the intent in meaning is collective, not singular.

Having established the collective nature of *'adam* in verse 26, verse 27 clarifies and emphasizes that *'adam* does not refer only to males. The text does not leave the receptor to infer that *'adam* includes both males and females. One reason could stem from the nature of the Hebrew language. The word *'adam* is a masculine word, and the masculine plural ending is used in the verb in verse 26. Another reason could be the prevailing assumptions about women at the time. Women were likely viewed as inferior to men. The limitation caused by the masculine gender of *'adam*, combined with this false assumption about female ontology, may be the reason why the text specifies who was made in God's image.[8] So in the couplet the second clause ends with "he created him,"[9] and the third clause begins with "male and female." With this the intention in the use of poetic parallelism becomes clear. The text explicitly defines *'adam* as "male and female." The couplet's ending reinforces this: "he created them."

In this light, an accurate formal equivalent translation of the term *'adam* in contemporary English is "human" (or "human being," as per Soggin 1997, 22).[10]

"Image" is a key word in the first and second clauses of the couplet, yet the meaning of "image" is left undeveloped. Though the couplet clarifies that *'adam* was made in the image of God and that *'adam* includes the female and male sexes, the text does not describe what was meant by being made in the image of God. Even though being in the image of God is a defining characteristic of what it means to be human, the receptor is left to infer the meaning of this from the narrative.[11]

Therefore, through the use of poetic parallelism the author purposefully and artistically demonstrates that no ontological difference exists between the sexes.[12] Females and males comprise what it means to be human. Both are created in the image of God, which is another defining characteristic of what it means to be human.

Sexuality, Hierarchy, and Ontology

Having established the collective nature of the singular *'adam* and that it includes both sexes, highlighting the ontological sameness between women and men, the text narratively continues in this inclusive vein in verses 28–29. In these verses God authorizes both sexes to exercise a limited dominion over the earth. As God speaks he uses the plural "them" in verse 28 and the plural "you" in verse 29.

> God blessed them, and God said to them, "Be fruitful and multiply, and fill the earth and subdue it; and have dominion over the fish of the sea and over the birds of the air and over every living thing that moves upon the earth." God said, "See, I have given you every plant yielding seed." (Gen 1:28,29 NRSV)

However, in verses 26, 28, and 29 the writer uses masculine pronouns to refer to the collectiveness of 'adam. Does this usage of the masculine plural forms indicate a theological preference for the masculine sex?[13] Another item in the discourse that may appear to reinforce this perception is that the male is mentioned first in the sequence of male-female in the third phrase of verse 27. By listing the male first in this male-female phrase, does the author indicate a divinely sanctioned, sexually oriented hierarchy?

With regard to the second question, developing a gender-related hierarchy does not appear to be the author's focus in this section of the narrative (Page 1980, 77–78). The text treats both the male and female as a unit. God blesses them both and commands them to reproduce and exercise a limited dominion over the creatures in the air, in the sea, and on the land. In verse 29 God instructs both the female and the male as to what they are allowed to eat. The passage seems to place the pair on equal footing.

On the other hand, could placing the male first in the male-female phrase in verse 27 be a subtle indication of primogeniture,[14] indirectly affirming a male-dominated hierarchy? The notion of primogeniture appears to surface in the narrative themes in Genesis 2. The implication of word order is noted and will be referred to in the analysis of Genesis 2.

Returning to the first question, the use of the masculine plural forms in the pronouns in verses 28 and 29 reflects the plural usage in verse 26. It appears that due to the nature of the Hebrew language verse 27 exists in order to clarify that no ontological difference exists between males and females.[15] Both sexes are made in the image of God. The use of masculine pronouns is due to the relationship between the Hebrew patriarchal system at the time of the writing of the text and Hebrew discourse.[16] Thus the use of masculine pronouns reflects the impact of existing cultural paradigms upon language rather than being a statement of male-preferring biblical anthropology.

However, this first segment of the creation narrative demonstrates that hierarchy stemming from ontology exists. First, God is clearly portrayed as being ontologically and positionally above the creation. The repetition of the word bara (create) alludes to this, as well as God's commissioning different segments of the creation: the earth, the lights, the creatures in the seas and sky, and finally, the human race. Second, humankind is given an ontological and positional advantage over the rest of the material world (C. Wright 1995, 184). Humans enjoy a distinct status in the creation because they are made in God's image. They are given a limited dominion, and the earth exists in part to provide them with food (House 1998, 60).

The existence of a hierarchy based on ontology and position within the text appears to support the premise that hierarchy only forms among unequals (see Miller 1993, 9). If this premise were valid, it would indicate that God's leadership paradigm for the world is large power distance, where dominance and subordination characterize hierarchy, because hierarchy is the outward demonstration of ontological or existential inequality (Hofstede 2001, 98). However, the text appears to contradict this premise by demonstrating small power distance in spite of the vast ontological difference between God and his creation.

How is this? While the creation narrative seems to affirm in the commissioning of the humans that differences exist in divine, human, animal, and inanimate ontology, the text reshapes our understanding of hierarchy by demonstrating small power distance in God's relationship with his creation. Even though God is infinitely superior, God's relationality and loving character[17] contradict the characteristics of large power distance. First, though God is portrayed as royally ordering the creation into being, God personally makes specific parts of the creation.[18] Second, by creating male and female in his image God releases humanity to relate meaningfully to the Creator God (G. Klein 2001, 36).[19] Thus by emphasizing this similarity between God and humanity, in contrast to otherness, the text intentionally reduces the power distance between God and humankind. Third, in his communication with humanity, God blesses and authorizes humankind to function in leadership roles on the earth.[20] Though the submission of the male and female to this transcendent Creator God is implied in the nature of being created and commissioned, the text emphasizes God's release of humanity to be and to grow.[21] The commission of humanity indicates that it is also an elevation of human beings, enabling them in a finite way to empathize with God, as God and they jointly interact with the creation.[22] Fourth, God generously gives humankind the liberty to eat as much as they like. The pair is not treated as servants, slaves, or peasant farmers. In the ancient world, servants, slaves, and peasants generally were able to retain a reduced percentage of the produce of the land. A substantial portion of what was produced had to be given to those with power and authority. Contrary to these characteristics, God elevates the position of humanity and treats all of humanity as royalty (Bird 1981, 144; F. Martin 1993, 247) and with liberality.[23] In the ancient world this was a subversive text. It undermined the large power distance in the social order, where only the few were kings (and claimed to be divine representatives) and expected an inordinate share of all the land produced. Finally, there is an absence of tension or struggle in the divine-human relationship, whereas a constant level of subliminal animosity between subordinates and superiors characterizes large power distance social structures (Hofstede 2001, 98).

Thus, on the close of the sixth day, everything exists in a utopian harmony and is very good (Gen 1:31). Hierarchy related to ontology exists. However, the narrative effect of the text obscures the impact of this hierarchy in respect to God and humanity. God is the supreme Creator-King who has empowered and released humankind to be his vice-regents on the earth. Through his loving relationality God demonstrates small power distance in his actions. In addition, the absence of any disobedience and its consequences in the narrative serves to diminish the sense of this hierarchy.

Hierarchy, Task, and Context

Humankind has been given an objective: they are to populate and subdue the earth and exercise dominion. Just as God reveals himself in the narrative as a God at work (C. Wright 2004, 148), humanity is expected to work too.

Whenever there is a task to achieve and a group seeking to achieve it, some level of hierarchy will form among the group members.[24] This is the nature of social groups. Therefore, assuming that hierarchies only form among unequals is unwarranted. Inequality in hierarchy exists in large power distance settings, and in small power distance settings hierarchy serves a functional purpose.[25] Those positioned higher receive a measure of power and prestige in order to accomplish their tasks. Therefore, hierarchy exists in small power distance settings, but it is expected that those in power will take steps to reduce the distance between themselves and those below them.[26]

Since humankind is made in the image of God and the narrative reveals that God keeps the power distance small in his relationships, humankind should image God in the manner in which they construct and live out hierarchy. A fluid expression of hierarchy, influenced by the task and the sociocultural context in which the task is performed with a small power distance orientation, would suitably reflect what we have seen in the narrative. The seventh day of rest appears to reinforce this perception.

Hierarchy and the Seventh-Day Rest

The first segment of the creation narrative is crafted within a seven-day framework. God concludes his creative activity by grounding the task-based orientation of human beings in a relational framework by blessing and setting apart[27] the seventh day for rest (see Ex 20:11).

This setting apart of the seventh day is understood as having a global application, embracing all of humanity on the seventh day of each week, while also establishing a foundation for the development of a theology of the Sabbath[28] (Cassuto 1961, 63; Westermann 1984, 170–73).[29] The setting apart of the seventh day has a profound impact on all that humankind does, because it grounds all the works of humanity that will proceed in time and space in the completed work of God.[30]

The all-inclusive nature of the seventh-day rest directly impacts humanity's understanding of hierarchy. First, God's setting apart of the seventh day of each and every week for rest is another demonstration of his desire to elevate the position of humankind. God rests on the seventh day, and he releases all who are in his image to share in his rest (Hasel 1982, 26).

Second, the seventh day is a time when a person ceases from labor in order to lay aside a categorized identity derived from work, releasing each person to *be* (K. Barth 1958, 214). This rest enables humankind to understand that a person is much more than what a person does because God is more than a creator. Thus all of humanity is released to celebrate the person: God, one another, and one's own person.

This affects how hierarchy and power distance in interhuman relationships should be understood. On this day, as all rest, any hierarchy that has been created in order to achieve communal goals is removed. All are released to celebrate the person and the presence of God as well as the persons and the presence of one another.[31]

The seventh-day rest appears to be God's divine plan to provide a healthy framework for a task-orientated community to re-orientate itself and regard one another as equals and as significant.[32] Later in the Pentateuch God institutes rituals of intensification for the Sabbath day in order to make it one of the identifying characteristics of the community.[33]

Conclusion

God creates a divine-human community (K. Hall 2001, 62), with the human community enjoying a male-female sexual distinction. Females and males are made in God's image. Though the concept of image is not overtly defined, it appears from the narrative that relationality, the ability to carry out God's commission as royal representatives, and freedom are aspects of what being in God's image implies.

Though there is an ontological difference and a corresponding hierarchy that exists within and without the creation, and though that difference does connote preeminence and authority in terms of God and the creation and in terms of humanity and various realms on earth, superiority and dominance are inappropriate terms to describe the nature of this ontological and positional difference. God empowers the different spheres of the creation to have separate identities and appropriate levels of self-determination, with humankind enjoying the most significant level of self-determination possible.[34]

In the light of the task given to humankind, hierarchy should be properly understood as a social and functional construction that enables social units (family, group, community) to achieve shared goals and objectives. The shape of any hierarchy, then, is determined by the nature of the task and the context in which the task is being performed.

In the narrative, love subtly becomes the primary characteristic of God, modifying our understanding of relationality. God's love is demonstrated by elevating the position of the created human race. Based on God's example, hierarchy is not meant to be a structural support for the creation and maintenance of social inequality. God's example of hierarchy and leadership is other-centered, caring, responsible, and empowering.

This divine model of hierarchy is further developed in the second section of the creation narrative.

---

1   Paul breaks with the linguistic pattern of the first two clauses in Galatians 3:28 when he refers to male and female: "There is not Jew nor Greek; there is not bondman nor free; there is not male and female." This break in pattern in the third clause indicates Paul is quoting from Genesis 1:27 (Scholer 1998, 7; Snodgrass 1986, 171; Stendahl 1966, 32).

2   This is in contrast to those scholars who assert that Paul's interpretive *locus classicus* for gender is Galatians 3:28. Examples of scholars who hold this view are Gordon Fee (2005a), Robin Scroggs (1972), Krister Stendahl (1966, 31–35), and Anthony Thiselton (1978, 521). Richard Hess recognizes the significance of the creation narratives. Hess

states, "The accounts of creation, the Garden of Eden, and the Fall in Genesis 1–3 may contain more doctrinal teaching concerning the nature of humanity as male and female, as well as the state of the fallen world, than any other single text in the Bible" (2005, 79).

3   I am breaking with tradition as I refer to the creation narratives in the singular. Scholars have traditionally referred to them in the plural, considering Genesis 1:1–2:4a to be a single narrative (from P), distinct from the 2:4b–3:24 account (from J), following Kuenen and Wellhausen (Van Seters 1992; Vervenne 2001; von Rad 1961; Westermann 1984; contra Cassuto 1961). However, when source criticism is overemphasized, the biblical text can be reduced to a series of disjointed segments, with a receptor focusing on the creation of the text; that is, on compilation and redaction (Fox 1989, 31–32; Wenham 1987, xxxiv) rather than its meaning. Formalism is an alternative method that begins by viewing the text as a unified whole, a text that purposefully develops a set of shared themes in an artistic, literary manner (Alter 1981, 12–22). Stanley Grenz views "the two narratives as a mutually informing, composite story, rather than solely as isolated compilations of two independent redactors" (2001b, 269; see also Birch et al. 1999, 46; Sawyer 1992, 64–65).

4   Servant leadership functions within a small power distance paradigm.

5   The majority of people who encountered the biblical texts would have heard them read rather than have read them. However, there were those who did read the texts. Therefore I will generically refer to the potential reader-listener as the receptor.

6   The definite article (the) is in italics because it is implied in the Hebrew text.

7   See Van Wolde (1994, 16). The word *'adam* may also function as a title in Genesis 2, as Hess asserts (2005, 83); however, the narrative focus of Genesis 2 is on the person, *'adam*.

8   The repetition of male and female being made in the image of God—showing that both sexes are included in the meaning of *'adam* in Genesis 5:1,2—indicates how significant this point was to the author.

9   John Goldingay renders this third person pronominal suffix as "it" (2003, 99).

10   The NRSV translators chose to render 'adam as a collective noun: "humankind." However, since the Hebrew is a singular noun and Hebrew singular pronouns play a significant role in the development of the parallelism in the couplet, I have chosen the more formal equivalent, "human," which is inclusive in scope yet purposefully singular. This choice is also in contrast to Ortland, who feels that 'adam should be translated as "man" because 'adam anticipates the leadership role men are to take in the family, church, and society as revealed in Genesis 2:4–28 (1991, 98). The author's purpose in choosing 'adam appears better understood through the intertextual relationship between 'adam and 'adama (ground) (Beuken 1999, 13; see Gen 2:5–7; 3:19,23; 8:21).

11   Dumbrell suggests that the ancient receptors would have understood "image" to signify a royal representative (1989, 142; see also House 1998, 60–61). The narrative appears to include this as a dimension of what "image" means, as well as relationality. "Image" may have been left intentionally undefined because "image" can only be defined as 'adam understands this God in whose image 'adam is made. The content of that definition naturally will be shaped as humans deepen in their relationality with God. This is in contrast to Karl Barth, who says, "[Godlikeness] is not a quality of man. Hence there is no point in asking in which of man's peculiar attributes and attitudes it consists" (1958, 184). This is also in contrast to Raymond Ortland, who states that humanity was not made in God's image, but made with the potential to bear God's image (1991, 96).

12   This is in contrast with Phyllis Bird, who sees the mention of male-female in a strict reproductive sense with no broader social connotations (1981, 156). Bird perceives that the passage's mention of sexuality in humankind is meant to parallel the reproductive abilities of the animate creation. However, since the immediate context is highlighting humankind being made in God's image, there is room to assert that the author has more in mind than just a parallel between animate creation's and humankind's reproductive abilities as a possible polemic against Canaanite fertility cults.

13   Bird describes this tension created by Hebrew linguistic conventions: "What Genesis 1:27b affirms, 'male and female [God] created them'…is undermined linguistically and historically by the consistent representation of the species with male images and masculine terms" (1994, 522).

14   Primogeniture in this book refers to being the firstborn. In many cultures (ancient and modern) the firstborn male enjoys a privileged status over his other siblings. God undermines the conceptualizing of primogeniture as being a position of higher status within the family by adopting a servant posture in the creation narrative. The Book of Genesis also subverts this notion by the younger being blessed over and above the blessing of the firstborn (as in God's accepting of the younger Abel's sacrifice, the choice of Jacob over Esau, and the blessing of Ephraim over Manasseh).

15   This is not to assert that this ontological sameness was affirmed in Paul's first-century world. Philo was obviously misogynous in his writings as he felt the woman was equal to half of a man (*Questions and Answers on Genesis 1* (25)). See also Philo LV (156); *Questions and Answers on Genesis 1* (27), (29). Augustine appears to have had misogynous tendencies as well, though he lived centuries later. Augustine, in interpreting 1 Corinthians 11:7, writes, "[T]he woman together with her own husband is the image of God…but when she is referred separately to her quality of helpmeet, which regards the woman herself alone, then she is not the image of God; but as regards the man alone, he is the image of God as fully and completely as when the woman too is joined with him in one" (*On the Trinity* 12.7.10; see also *On Genesis* 3.22.34). The fact that the Genesis 1 text affirms ontological sameness is sufficient basis to assume that Paul potentially realized it, whether or not his contemporaries or subsequent theologians did.

16   This assertion is drawn from the ethnography of communication (see Bucholtz 2003, 43–64).

17   The word "love" does not appear in Genesis 1:1–2:4. However, that God loves can be inferred from the narrative (Brümmer 1993, 30).

18   See Genesis 1:7,16,21,25,27.

19   God's communication with the woman and man narratively demonstrates that relationality is an integral aspect of what it means to be made in God's image. With regard to the relationality of God and humankind, see Karl Barth (1958, 184–85), Grenz (2001), and Gunton (2003). With regard to the relationality of God and humankind as a central theme of the Pentateuch, see Sailhamer (1992, 80).

20   The Hebrew words for "subdue" and "rule" are quite strong (von Rad 1961, 146). The positive, relational context of the narrative suggests

that the humans' role on the earth would be caring and developmental, not domineering and exploitative (Birch et al. 1999, 50).

21 Brueggemann writes, "Yahweh's profound commitment to fidelity and compassion generates life-space for wondrous human freedom in the world, freedom to eat and drink and exult in a world of goodness" (1997, 457).

22 Abraham Heschel refers to this empathy as "theomorphic anthropology" (1962, 40).

23 This liberality is reinforced in the imagery of Genesis 2:8–14, where God creates a garden with every kind of tree that was good for food and pleasant to the eyes and with four massive rivers originating from it (Blocher 1984, 120). Brueggemann states, "God's movement toward creation is unceasing generosity" (1982, 28).

24 "Hierarchy is, of course, a universal feature of social structures" (Rogers 1980, 101).

25 See Bonhoeffer's cogent comments regarding this from his prewar, Nazi context (1965, 195).

26 This is the presupposition in the servant leadership model (Greenleaf 2003, 2–3). See also Hofstede (2001, 98).

27 Cassuto suggests that this setting apart implies the exaltation and distinctiveness of the seventh day (1961, 65; see also Hasel 1982, 25).

28 This rest being for all humankind is implicit in this passage, however it is elsewhere expressed in the Pentateuch (see Ex 23:12). Stating implicit themes may seem presumptuous at this stage in the text. Yet this is the time that the author is developing a set of narrative themes that will be further developed in the Pentateuch. For example, one narrative theme that is not developed here but finds development as the Pentateuch progresses is the theme of God's presence with his people. With regard to the development of this theme in the Pentateuch, see Sailhamer (1992); for its development in Exodus, see Durham (1987); in Leviticus, see Wenham (1979); in Deuteronomy, see I. Wilson (1995).

29 Karl Barth asserts, "So expressly and directly has the biblical witness linked the divine activity of the seventh day of creation with the institution of the Sabbath which man is to observe, that it is impossible to understand it otherwise than from this angle" (1958, 214).

30 With regard to the impact of this rest on humanity, Karl Barth writes, "Before and apart from all work and conflict, irrespective of any merits of his own, he is invited to cease from his own works, to rest, and therefore to enter into the freedom, rest and joy of God himself" (1958, 218). Also, this is the starting point of a theme which becomes the foundation of the ethical teaching of the Bible (see C. Wright 2004, 29).

31 Thus for Paul the seventh day could have indicated that there was to be neither Jew nor Greek, neither slave nor free, neither male and female; all are persons made in the image of God and all are to rest (compare Ex 20:10 with Gal 3:28). However, the suggestion that Galatians 3:28 implies that the elimination of divisions between humankind includes gender distinction and ethnic/cultural diversity (Litke 1995, 176; Stendahl 1966, 32) appears untenable because (a) God himself affirms the integrity and value of ethnic/cultural identity and diversity in Revelation 7:9,10; and (b) while Jesus states there will not be marriage in heaven, he does not imply that we will lose that aspect of our identity that we call female or male (Matt 22:30; see also Flemming 2005, 137–38; Ratzinger and Amato 2004, 2.12; Witherington 1981, 589–600). Stendahl links Galatians 3:28 to Genesis 1:27, viewing Genesis 1:27 in isolation, disregarding the immediate context of the creation narrative (its relationship with the Sabbath) and the larger context of the Pentateuch. Margaret Stewart Van Leeuwen states that "biblical equal regard does not require the endorsement of undifferentiated androgyny" (2004, 21). In addition, interpreting difference as division creates an unnecessary semantic shift from the valuable to the pejorative. Difference also does not mean dominance, though, as Mary Talbot has shown, it can be used to foster reified perceptions of gender differences (2003, 475).

32 See Brueggemann (1982, 35).

33 See Exodus 16:23–30; 31:12–17; 35:3; Leviticus 23:3; 24:1–9; Numbers 15:32–36.

34 See Welker (1991, 62–63). On the other hand, this viewpoint can be viewed as reductionistic. Unfortunately, the significance of the Sabbath gets lost in such a perception. As I wrote, "The setting apart of the seventh day has a profound impact on all that humankind does, because it grounds all the works of humanity that will proceed in time and space in the completed work of God." Any expression of freedom and self-determination within the creation depends upon God (Tracy 1994, 99–102). However, this dependence does not negate freedom, because God is the one who enables freedom.

6

Envisioning Sexuality and Its Management:
Genesis 2:4–25

THE FIRST SECTION of the creation narrative concludes with the seventh-day rest, the rest being a symbol of the intended intimacy within the newly established divine-human community. God reveals himself as the Creator who seeks communion with those in his image, calling them to partner with him in his work and in his rest.

In terms of hierarchy, the first section of the creation narrative portrays a task-oriented, divine-human community. The narrative creates the expectation in the receptor that the human side of this community, being task-oriented and made in God's image, would reflect God in the political dimension of their relationships, demonstrating small power distance. The seventh day would reinforce this small power distance because, regardless of status, position within the hierarchies, or sex, all humankind is to rest: women, men, slaves, free, masters, and servants.

The second section of the creation narrative (2:4–25) adds rich description to this newly formed, divine-human community. Shifting from the global perspective of the first section, the second section narrows its focus, developing a theme that the creation could reach its full potential through properly aligned and loving relationality.[1] The narrative continues to contradict the assumptions and values of Paul's Greco-Roman world.

Hierarchy, Partnership, and Incompleteness

Genesis 2:4 transitions the receptor from the first section of the creation narrative to the second (Cassuto 1961, 96–99; J. Collins 1999, 272–73): "These are the generations of the heavens and the earth in their having been created in the day Yahweh Elohim made earth and heavens."

The text immediately thereafter uses the theme of incompleteness to develop the story (Ross 1988, 125–26). The first mention of incompleteness is the barren earth (v. 5), a stark contrast to the fullness that characterizes the end of the previous section. Barrenness takes the receptor beyond the transition and draws attention to the necessary, cooperative relationship between God and humanity in the development of the earth (K. Hall 2001, 63; Fretheim 1994, 349). In Genesis 1:1–2:3 God empowers the different spheres of the creation to have separate identities and appropriate levels of self-determination, but here the author highlights the earth's dependence (Van Wolde 1994, 13). The earth cannot fulfill its purpose apart from the direct involvement of the one who causes rain (God) and the ones who till the ground (humankind). Only through the partnership of this divine-human community will the earth actualize its complete role in facilitating this community of love to express itself.[2]

Having depicted the necessity of the divine-human community in the development of the earth, the text also alludes to the hierarchical nature of the divine-human community.[3] God is mentioned first. The order of mention accentuates the preeminence God possesses in the community. As the Sovereign Creator, his involvement is essential in order for the earth to develop, because he is the one who controls the rain. By mentioning the human second, the text alludes to the subordinate position of humankind in this community. Humanity's subordinate position is reinforced by comparison and by wordplay. God makes the rain, but 'adam tills the ground ('adama).

Though the text draws the receptor's attention to the ontological disparity in the divine-human community through the tasks of the characters, the text also highlights the vital role humanity plays by stating that there was no human to work the ground (Birch et al. 1999, 50; Fretheim 1994, 349). This reminds the receptor of the commission humans are given to rule and reign in Genesis 1. The receptor knows that even though humans cannot compare with this Creator God, they are marvelously significant. The ensuing story continues to affirm their significance.

In verse 7 the text continues to weave into the narrative these two contrasting truths: first, the vast ontological difference between God and humanity, and second, the elevated status and value humanity enjoys. In this verse God tackles this incompleteness on the earth by making a man. The receptor ceases from viewing 'adam as a generic term; it now refers to a specific individual. This act of creation contrasts the man's humble origin of being from the dust from the ground with this all-powerful, self-existent divinity.

In spite of the ontological disparity, God is the one who gets his hands dirty. The use of the verbs "form" and "breathe" portrays God's intimate involvement in the creative event (ibid.). God forms 'adam and breathes into his nostrils the breath of life. The verb "form" conjures up the image of a potter working with a lump of clay.[4] Breathing into the man's nostrils continues the theme of God's close physical contact with the man. Through the word play of *'adam* and *'adama*, along with *'adam* receiving the breath of God, the author relationally connects humanity to both God and the earth. This anthropomorphic imagery effectively reduces the power distance in the divine-human hierarchical relationship.

Continuing to contradict the culturally dominant, large power distance paradigms of that age, the text demonstrates that this Creator God actively cares for the man. God is the one who plants and designs a well-watered and verdant garden.

The text continues to weave together the themes of ontological difference with small power distance. In the first section of the narrative, God gives humankind a command, but absent is any warning about disobedience and consequences. In contrast, in verses 16–17 God issues a command that the man must obey. Disobedience will result in sure death. Within this framework of other-centeredness, loving care, and empowerment, there is a clear expectation of obedience and fidelity in this divine-human relationship. God is the sovereign king and the man is the vassal. However, the command seems relatively easy to obey. The overall narrative effect is that this sovereign God has been truly magnanimous.

Hierarchy, Ontology, and Aloneness

Emphasizing the ontological disparity in the king-vassal/divine-human relationship is not the narrative's objective. Rather, the narrative portrays God as being other-centered and as expressing loving care, because God notices the incompleteness of the man's situation. The man is alone: "And Yahweh Elohim said *it is* not good *for* the man to be alone, I will make for him a helper like *and* corresponding to him" (Gen 2:18).

Ontology appears to impact the way relationships can find expression and fulfillment within this divine-human community. Due to the vast ontological difference between God and man, a state of aloneness exists that even the presence and active involvement of the all-powerful God cannot ameliorate. The man requires an *'ezer kenegdo*.

'Ezer is a term that causes considerable consternation. The English equivalent, "helper," implies someone assuming a subordinate position in the relationship.[5] The narrative does not permit this misperception, because "helper" describes the role of God in the story. God is the active agent in the story adopting the role of *'ezer*, working for the man's benefit.[6] Even though God assumes the role of *'ezer*, it is clear that God is not

the subordinate. Thus subordination cannot be an inherent characteristic of the term (contra Ortland 1991, 104).

The narrative creates hope in the receptor because the man's incompleteness can be resolved by an appropriate *'ezer*. Karl Barth argued that *'ezer* is best translated as "partner" (1958, 290). Since the narrative section opens with a comment on the partnership of God and man in enabling the earth to be fully productive, and since the man was commissioned to work the earth, and since the man is presently alone, "partner" appears to adequately convey the meaning of *'ezer* in this passage.

The Hebrew *kenegdo* is a difficult compound prepositional phrase to translate. First, *ke* is a preposition that means "like" or "as." Then *negd* is a preposition that can mean "before," "in front of," or "opposite."[7] Finally, *o* is the third person masculine singular pronoun "him." Semitic languages can display a remarkable semantic ambiguity within words, therefore context will have to determine the meaning of *kenegdo*.

God addresses this incomplete condition of the man by forming the animals from the ground and bringing them to the man to see what he would name them. The narrative linguistically connects *'adam* with the animals through the use of *'adama*, placing the man in a unique relationship with the animals.

It has been asserted that the naming of the animals by the man demonstrates his superiority over them (see Cassuto 1961, 130; Trible 1978, 92). However, demonstrating one's superiority through the use of power is incongruous with the narrative. God, the superior, notices the inadequate condition of *'adam*. God then takes on the form of a servant and does the work necessary to resolve the problem. According to ancient large power distance norms, *'adam* functions more like a king in this scene; that is, being the recipient of the labor of others and decreeing names upon those that come before him. In contrast, service, other-centeredness, loving care, and empowerment characterize the superior in the text.

Though it is clear from Genesis 1 that humankind possesses an ontological and positional superiority to the animals, the narrative emphasizes the relational connection humankind has with the animal kingdom. Therefore this process of naming describes the process of the man establishing a level of familiarity with the animals in order to find a suitable *'ezer* (Magonet 1992, 40–41). Therefore the purpose of the exercise and the way God is portrayed as superior does not allow us to interpret naming as a demonstration of superiority (contra Waltke 1975, 341).

As the receptor would expect, the animal kingdom does not offer the man the kind of relationship that can resolve his aloneness (K. Barth

1958, 292–93). Thus the text returns to the theme of incompleteness. Neither God nor the animals function adequately as an *'ezer kenegdo* for the man. This state of incompleteness is amplified by the fact that the animals are also formed from the land and are "living creatures" (Wenham 1987, 68).

God continues to serve and causes the man to sleep. God removes a rib (or side) and builds the woman from it.[8] God is as actively involved in the formation of the woman as he was involved in the formation of the man. This is one indication that there is an inherent equality between the sexes. Also, by recycling the theme of incompleteness, negating the previous possibilities for an *'ezer kenegdo*, the receptor is in a state of anticipation waiting for resolution to the problem.

Then God presents the woman to the man. The man's response removes any ambiguity as to the meaning of *'ezer kenegdo*. The text follows the pattern of Genesis 1 and changes genres to emphasize that the woman is ontologically the same as the man.

> This at last,
> *is* bone from my bones
> and flesh from my flesh,
> this shall be called woman
> because from man was taken this.
> Gen. 2:23[9]

The couplet[10] begins with the feminine singular demonstrative pronoun "this," repeats it at the beginning of the second clause, and closes the third parallel clause with it. The expressions "bone from my bones" and "flesh from my flesh" clarify the meaning of the term *kenegdo*. It refers to ontological sameness (Fretheim 1994, 353; Van Wolde 1994, 19).[11] This is reinforced by the final clause. Though the terms are derived from different roots, the word for woman, *isha*, sounds like the feminine form of "man," *ish*.[12] Since the woman (*isha*) was taken out of the man (*ish*), she is ontologically the same as he is.[13]

The man's interpretation of this event means that an equality of being exists between the woman and the man; the only difference between them is in their sexuality.[14]

Though the man had been made in God's image and though the animals were made from the ground as the man had been, an ontological disparity disqualified God and the animals from being an *'ezer kenegdo*. The aloneness of the man could only be alleviated by someone who was ontologically the same but a significant other. Woman so completely rectifies this condition of aloneness that the text interrupts the flow of the story, departs from the particularity of the creation event in time and space, and makes a universal application for all time (Cassuto 1961, 136; Wenham 1987, 70): "Therefore a man leaves his father and his mother and clings to his wife, and they become one flesh" (Gen 2:24 NRSV).

The definite article is not used with *ish* (man), and the verb "leave" is in the imperfect, denoting constant or continuing action (Soggin 1997, 26). Thus, this does not describe what the first man did; this describes what all men are expected to do. Throughout all time, men are expected to disengage themselves from their allegiance to their parents and align themselves to their wives.[15]

This interjection appears to accomplish two narrative purposes. First, it enables the narrative to create a sense of movement for the man. Up till now God had been the primary actor in the story, with the man primarily being a passive recipient of God's activity (Walsh 1977, 121). With this movement the man begins to act like God, moving toward his wife. Second, the text speaks prophetically into its original context, subverting the pattern of patriarchal, extended family systems where a man's allegiance would potentially remain with his parents.

Hierarchy, Action, and Image

The movement in these two verses is significant. Though the man does name the animals, the incident of naming is merely reported. The receptor does not see the man's active role in the process. God's activity is the primary focus (Westermann 1984, 191). However, as God presents the woman to the man, the man moves to the forefront and God seemingly disappears from the scene.[16] God does not reappear in the narrative until 3:8. Just as God had been the proactive one in the relationship up to this point, expressing action and movement toward the man, now the man is fulfilling his purpose as image bearer and acts like God as he now expresses movement and action toward the woman. The man speaks, he leaves his parents, and he clings to his wife. The movement is characterized by being other-centered and caring.

On the other hand, though the man is technically in the forefront in the scene as the speaker, the artistry of the narrative places the receptor's focus on the man and the woman. Though the man is speaking, the spotlight is on both of them. In addition, the spotlight remains on the two of them until the end of this segment of the narrative: "They were both naked,[17] the man and his wife, and they were not ashamed" (Gen 2:25) (see Cassuto 1961, 126).[18]

In verse 24 the man and the woman are referred to as "one flesh." The narrative identifies them as truly separate individuals, yet becoming one. The text creatively includes a reference to their sexuality, which only serves to deepen the expression of their companionship/partnership (Grenz 2001, 278).

The narrative effect of the failed attempts to find an *'ezer kenegdo*, the sheer delight of the man in response to meeting the woman, the interruption of the story in the text with movement and global application, and the consummation of the union being described as "one flesh"[19] indicate ontological sameness and relational harmony. These characteristics of the story obscure the notion of hierarchy in the conjugal relationship.[20] Terms like "dominance" and "subordination" appear inappropriate at this juncture in describing the kind of relationship that exists between the woman and the man.[21] In contrast, the narrative emphasizes that the man and the woman are completely for each other (see Gunton 2002, 44; Grenz 2001, 296–97).

However, does the narrative indicate that a hierarchy exists between the man and the woman? Hierarchy appears to exist within the passage.[22] First, there is the issue of order of creation, which could indicate some level of primogeniture for the man. The man is created first; the woman is second.[23] Second, though he plays a passive role through most of the section, the man enjoys a more dominant role in the story than the woman. Third, the man speaks in the section, not the woman. We do not hear from the woman until Genesis 3. Fourth, the man names the woman.[24] Finally, in verses 24–25 the woman is identified by her relationship to the man, as the man's wife.[25] Taken together, these could imply the existence of a hierarchy.

It appears that some level of primogeniture for the man exists in the narrative, simply because he is created first and enjoys the more dominant focus in the narrative. However, this does not indicate that a hierarchy exists in the conjugal relationship, because the relational movements within the narrative so modify hierarchy that it cannot be characterized by a paradigm of male dominance and female subordination.[26]

Why is this? God is the dominant person in the story. The receptor has been given no overt reason as to why Yahweh is doing any of his activity, yet the motion of Yahweh is other-focused and caring. It is evident that God does not derive personal benefit from the service of the man. The man's work benefits himself because he gets his food from the ground.

The only restriction the man has is to refrain from eating from one tree; everything else is at his disposal. This overt absence of personal benefit to God serves to obscure hierarchy and significantly reduces the power distance in the relationship. This absence of personal benefit also serves to heighten the relationality within the narrative.

God is also characterized by working to benefit the man. When the man finally becomes an active agent within the story, he begins to fulfill his role as being made in the image of God. The man is characterized both by delight (a characteristic of God in Gen 1:4,10,12,18,21,25,31) and by moving toward the woman and benefiting her. He leaves his parents and he clings to his wife. She becomes the recipient of his movement. The picture we have been given of God in Genesis 2 is one of God being positively absorbed with the man, of being for him. Likewise, the man reflects God in being positively absorbed with the woman, of his being for her, and of their becoming one.[27] In these ways hierarchy is lost in love and oneness.[28]

Conclusion

The second section of the creation narrative affirms the existence of an ontological difference between God and the human race. It further develops the content of that difference by emphasizing that God is the Creator-King and humankind is to submit to his authority and obey. However, the text reveals that the power distance between this Creator God and humankind is small. In addition, the text affirms the teaching of Genesis 1:27 that no existential or ontological difference exists between the male and female.

Ultimately, the passage affirms the conclusions of the first section while prescribing a model for one of the smallest units of social organization, the couple. The passage affirms that humankind is a task-oriented community, one that should image God and function with small power distance. The text appears to indicate that a level of primogeniture for the male exists in the conjugal relationship. However, this level of primogeniture does not warrant constructing a conjugal hierarchy described with the words "dominance" and "subordination." Primogeniture is to be characterized by the man's movement toward the woman. The man is to completely transfer his allegiance from his familial relationships to the woman. This transfer of allegiance is accompanied by the man's delight in the woman, resulting in a companionship/partnership defined by affection and love. Thus, though there is an element of primogeniture, it becomes obscured as the two become one, resulting in mutual regard for each other.

Keeping the context of Genesis 1 in mind, that the man and the woman are made in God's image, we can conclude that Yahweh Elohim is looking for an *'ezer kenegdo*, someone like God who is ontologically the same as the man, someone who could release the full potential of the relationality that is inherent in the man. This has to be a physical someone who could partner with the man, love, relate, care, understand, empower, and be capable of making a positive, constructive difference in his life.[29] Yahweh is also looking for someone for whom the man could image God by his movement, by his being loyal, other-centered, serving, caring, and empowering. Yahweh makes the woman-wife for these purposes (see Bird 1981, 158).[30]

This narrative section closes with the relationships in this divine-human community properly aligned and properly motivated. The third section of the narrative explains how these relationships became distorted.[31]

---

1   Walsh points out that there are seven scenes in the Genesis 2:4b–3:24 narrative, each scene dealing with relationships (1977, 170). See also Van Wolde (1994, 16).

2   Juxtaposing independence with dependence, along with barrenness and fullness, shows how the author uses narrative to develop theology.

3   Matthews points out how this portion of the text is intimately related to the consequences of sin in 3:8–24 (1996, 194–95). Thus, the preeminent position of God in this divine-human community is an integral component of this text.

4   Compare with Isaiah 29:16; 45:9; Jeremiah 18:1–6.

5   Stitzinger asserts that the use of the term "helper" signifies that the woman holds an inferior position in the male-female hierarchy (1981, 34). Phyllis Trible rightly argues that the word does not specify position within relationships (1973, 36; 1978, 90; see also Webb 2001, 128). Van Wolde concurs with Trible, pointing out that the word does not indicate either superiority or inferiority. The use of *kenegdo* clarifies that equality is the author's point (1994, 18). See also Grenz (2001, 274–75).

6 'ezer is a term used for God in Moses' blessing of Israel at the end of the Pentateuch (Deut 33:7,26). See Harman for other usages of the word for God as helper in the Old Testament (1997).

7 See Cassuto 1961, 127; Wenham 1987, 68; Wevers 1993, 31.

8 There are diverse approaches to what the rib signifies (see Rashi 1985, 12; Van Wolde 1994, 18; Webb 2001, 128; Westermann 1984, 230). Modern perceptions are quite different from the ancient. The early Syrian church fathers accepted Philo's interpretation that the woman was half a person because she was formed from only one side of the man (Levine 1951, 77). The *Sahih al-Bukhari*, apparently influenced by Jewish and Christian thought, concluded that the rib signified that the woman's nature was inherently crooked and could never be straightened (7:5184, 5186). Such creativity and diversity over time and across cultures suggest that we allow *'adam* to interpret the meaning of the rib and cease from speculation.

9 Wevers points out that the Septuagint loses the wordplay of *ish* and *isha*. He writes, "Gen's interpretation ties this verse more closely to v. 24 where marriage is described as the union of man and wife" (1993, 34).

10 Parallelism, chiasmus, assonance, wordplay, and repetition are used in this short poem (Wenham 1987, 70). This concentrated use of literary devices, and this being the second time the author has shifted from prose to poetry with the subject matter being concerned with the nature of woman, should alert the receptor that the event in chapter 3 and humankind's subsequent history represent a distortion of what was originally intended in intergender relationships.

11 See also Cassuto (1961, 135–36).

12 The *Etz Hayim* Torah and Commentary provides this comment: "The power of naming implies authority and the text here reflects the social reality of the ancient Near East. Yet the man gives her not a personal name, but a generic name (*isha*), one that sounds like his own (*ish*), although derived from a different root. This implies that he acknowledges woman to be his equal" (Lieber 2001, 17; see also Cassuto 1961, 136).

13 There is nothing within the text to assume that since the woman was built from material taken from the man, the man suffered a loss or became less than he was initially (contra K. Barth 1958, 296; Fretheim 1994, 353). That conclusion appears imposed upon the text. Rather, the

text indicates that the man's condition was incomplete before the appearance of the woman. With her appearance his condition becomes complete.

14   Phyllis Trible suggests that until the creation of woman *ish* was non-gendered, and at this point, with the use of *ish* and *isha*, male and female sexuality begins (1973, 37; 1978, 80). The text states, "from *ish* was taken this." This indicates that the rib was taken from *'adam/ish* when *'adam* was male. However, Trible seems to have some Midrashic support (see Rashi 1985, 7).

15   The verb "cling" is in the perfect tense.

16   God's disappearance is important as it implies freedom of action for the human couple (see Brueggemann 1982, 28)

17   Drawing on the use of nakedness elsewhere in the OT, Magonet points out that nakedness does not necessarily imply sexuality, though here it does because procreation is implied. In Genesis 3 it refers to "a state of defenselessness and helplessness, without possessions or power" (1992, 43). In that light, here it could simply imply the couple's dependence on God.

18   Wevers comments, "Our oldest Greek sources attach [v. 25] to ch. 3 in contrast to editions of the Hebrew text in which it is numbered 2:25 to end ch. 2" (1993, 36). Speiser, in his translation of Genesis, places 2:25 at the beginning of the next section (1964, 21).

19   Maggie Gallagher writes, "Spend enough time pondering how two can become one, and…you are drawn away, automatically, from discussions of household power relations" (2004, 113).

20   The text addresses only the conjugal relationship. It does not describe or proscribe parameters for the innumerable kinds of male-female relationships that can occur within a task-oriented group. To generalize from the conjugal particularity of the text to include all other kinds of intergender relationships would be to go beyond the scope of the narrative. Also, such a generalized application cannot reflect the conjugal intimacy that the text highlights.

21   This is in contrast to Longenecker, who suggests that Genesis 2 subtly supports submission and subordination (1986, 67). This is also in contrast to Walsh, who sees order in relationships as one of the integral themes of this narrative (1977, 174–77). Though I do not deny that order

exists in the passage, what is remarkable is how it is secondary to everything else happening in the narrative, especially since this was written at a
time when elevating those with authority above all others was the general
paradigm for maintaining social order.

22   Egalitarians do not acknowledge any form of hierarchy existing at
this juncture in the creation narrative (Belleville 2001, 140–47; Keener
2001, 62–63; Swartley 1986, 85; Trible 1978, 100–102). The notion of
the presence of hierarchy is disconcerting for them. Giles' comments
about the Trinity and hierarchy indicate the reason why. Drawing from
an egalitarian paradigm, he asserts that the relationality of the Trinity
reflects mutual submission, thus eliminating hierarchy within the Trinity.
Consequently, egalitarian relations among humans are the ideal. He
further argues that those who claim the Trinitarian relationships are hierarchical see the ideal being "ordered relations where some are forever
in the commanding role and others are in the subordinate role" (2002,
16). Identifying hierarchy in this portion of the narrative could appear
to strengthen the argument for stratified relationships and male dominance. However, the problem with such a conclusion is that hierarchy
as defined by dominance-subordination is the result of the events in
Genesis 3 and subsequent human history; it is not how Genesis 1 and 2
define hierarchy.

23   Belleville argues that the animals are created first in Genesis 1 and
this has no significance; therefore, the man's being created first in Genesis
2 has no significance either (2001, 144). Trible asserts that the woman is
created last to show that the woman is the culmination of the creation
(1978, 102). Trible's position would be strengthened if the man were not
the focus of the narrative section. She tries to address this weakness by
viewing the man as genderless until the creation of woman (see footnote
17, p. 29). Antonelli goes a step further and declares that woman's formation at the end of the creation process makes her the "crown of Creation"
(1997, 6). One limitation in denying primogeniture is that this text was
written in a cultural context that would have discerned primogeniture
in the narrative of Genesis 2. Paul evidently saw it. I maintain that we
should not seek to deny that primogeniture exists; rather, we should seek
to determine its meaning from the tenor of the story. The problem is
that we allow Genesis 3 and human history to define what hierarchy is.
However, the movement of God and the man in the narrative demonstrate
that hierarchy should not be defined as we understand it from human
history. Hierarchy as defined in human history is intimately related to

the exertion of power over others. This understanding of hierarchy is not justified by what we read in Genesis 1 and 2. Those who seek to image God in their relationships should seek to reflect the movement of God, which is other-focused, liberating, and empowering in intent, whenever hierarchy may appear and in whatever form it appears. When hierarchical relationships fall short of that goal, they are distorted and corrupted.

24   It is unlikely that the naming of the woman by the man supports a male-dominated hierarchy in social and conjugal relationships. Naming in Genesis appears to be a "memorializing" of the significant characteristic stemming from a specific incident or interaction (Belleville 2001, 143). Hagar names God in Genesis 16:13. Hagar is clearly not the superior one in that relationship. This memorializing is what we observe in the man's naming of the woman. The man sees that the woman is a female version of himself, and he draws the receptor's attention to this. Representative of the perspective of naming as an act of dominion, Wenham asserts, "Though they are equal in nature, that man names woman (cf. 3:20) indicates that she is expected to be subordinate to him, an important presupposition of the ensuing narrative (3:17)" (1987, 70). In contrast, Trible asserts that the man does not name the woman, because he does not use the "naming formula" (1973, 38; 1978, 98–99). George Ramsey asserts that there is little support for Trible's naming formula. Ramsey states, "I want to argue that the concern to correct male chauvinist inferences from the creation story is justified, but that it is an error to argue that Genesis 2:23 is not an instance of name-giving. The conventional interpretation of this verse needs to be challenged, but Trible has challenged the wrong point" (1988, 26).

25   Phyllis Bird recognizes this androcentric nature of the text (and of the Hebrew language) and struggles with it, yet she affirms that the Scripture remains "the richest resource for Christian theological reflection" we have (1994, 532–34).

26   This is in contrast to Calvin, who suggested that the woman was placed under a "liberal and gentle subjection" (1847, 172), and to Delitzsch, who felt that "the subordination of the woman to the man was intended from the beginning" (1888, 166). I would argue that Calvin and Delitzsch's thoughts were shaped by the rhetoric and patriarchy of history, not by the narrative itself.

27   See Belleville (2001, 140).

28 A patriarchal perspective of gender hierarchy does not describe this picture of the relationship between God and humanity and the relationship between the husband and wife. For a definition of patriarchal, gender-related hierarchy, see Goldingay (2003, 105).

29 Kenneth Matthews states that "what the man lacks, the woman accomplishes.... Woman makes it possible for the man to achieve the blessing that he could not do 'alone'" (1996, 214).

30 Procreation appears to be an implicit concern in the creation of the woman; however, it appears to have secondary significance in this segment of the narrative (contra Goldingay 2003, 104). The context seems to define "becoming one flesh" more by relationality than by procreation (see Birch et al. 1999, 52). Procreation arises as a central concern in the commission to fill the earth in Genesis 1 and in the discipline of the woman in Genesis 3.

31 Looking at John Wevers' notes on the Septuagint (1993) and Gordon Wenham's notes on the variant textual readings in his commentary for these first two chapters (1987), there do not appear to be any noteworthy discrepancies affecting meaning in the Greek and Hebrew texts. This is significant as we seek to determine what Paul may have understood as he approached these chapters of Genesis.

7

Explaining the Current Malaise: Genesis 2:25–3:24

THE RELATIONAL MUTUALITY and harmony described in Genesis 2:23,24 was about to be radically altered due to the tragic events of Genesis 3. After Genesis 2:22, Yahweh disappears from the scene after he presents the woman to the man. Yahweh reappears after the transgression. His absence is a narrative device highlighting the couple's freedom of action in Genesis 3.

The serpent, through his interaction with the woman, entices the couple to violate God's command. The consequences of their violation reverberate through every relational sphere. The couple's relationships with the serpent, the earth, their tasks, and each other are radically altered due to the judgments of God.[1] These judgments result in difficult living conditions which challenge the willingness and ability of the human race to celebrate the person and enjoy the union and the mutual regard that had characterized the couple's relationship. When humans succumb to the difficulties of life and allow their inclinations to shape their actions, their relationships become distorted.

The Curse of the Serpent

In 3:14, after the question and answer period, God begins to pronounce judgment upon the culprits. God addresses the serpent first. The context of chapter 3 suggests that the text lends itself to identifying the serpent through literal-naturalistic and/or figurative readings.[2]

As John Ronning points out, though the incident involves the initial couple, the incident is recorded for the implied receptor (1997, 126–27). The implied receptor would not fail to notice the inconsistencies caused by assumptions created within the text. The snake is compared to the animals of the field, and a part of God's good creation. Unlike all other animals, it speaks. From Genesis 1 and 2 the receptor would expect the animal to be somewhat "irrational and inferior to man in terms of spiritual and divine matters." Yet the snake's behavior in the temptation reveals that it is "evil, rational, and superior to man in knowledge of divine affairs" (ibid., 127). In addition, Ronning also points out that the existence of the cherubim (3:24) demonstrates the existence of other beings who are not mentioned in Genesis 1 or 2 (ibid., 131–32) and are not related to the earth. These inconsistencies and the presence of the cherubim broaden the potential of interpretation beyond the etiological or figurative.[3]

The identity of the serpent as a single personality is significant because God states that he will put hostility between the serpent and the woman, and between his seed and her seed.

How does God put hostility in their midst?[4] The wording of the final clause of verse 15 indicates that this hostility is a response to God's declaration:

And hostility I will set between you and between the woman,
and between your seed and between her seed,
he will strike you *on the* head and you will strike him *on the* heel.

The final clause is strikingly personal. Though the word "seed" functions as a collective noun in the second clause (15b), the text represents "seed" with a singular pronoun in the final clause (15c). This is opposite to how the text renders the collective noun *'adam* in 1:26. The text follows that collective noun with a plural verb form ("let them rule") to establish the collective sense of the word. In contrast, in this instance the text follows the collective noun with singular pronouns and singular verb forms.[5] This appears to be intentional to establish meaning. The personal nature of the clause indicates that the promise of the surety of death lies upon the serpent alone, implying that an offer of life exists for those of his seed who turn from evil.

The imperfect verb form is used, demonstrating the wondrous ambiguity of the Hebrew language. From this, one can infer a continuous struggle will ensue between the two seeds (see Wenham 1987, 80). However, the imperfect is also a way of speaking into the future. The immensely personal nature of the final clause and the contrast in places where the blows would be received are subtle indications of both the finality of the conflict and who will eventually be victorious (Fretheim 1994, 363; Wenham 1987, 80).[6]

Consequently, the declaration that the serpent will be killed may become the occasion for the serpent's hostility toward the woman, she being the source of his destroyer. The text gives no indication of how the serpent's hostility against the woman will manifest itself. The serpent's hostility will be contagious, spreading to his seed. Though there is no immediate indication of what the seed of the serpent means, the following chapters of Genesis indicate that the seed of the serpent refers to those who align themselves with wickedness (Ronning 1997, ii–iii). The woman's seed by contrast are those who align themselves with God in doing righteously. This declaration strikes down the notion that women are defective due to Eve's succumbing to the deception and upholds the integrity of female ontology.[7] The woman's seed is the seed of the righteous.

From Mutual Regard to Task Management

After dealing with the serpent, Yahweh Elohim addresses the woman. Genesis 3:16 is the judgment that anticipates and describes the nature of sexually oriented roles and relationships that subsequently develop.[8]

> To the woman he said, "Increasing I *will* increase your pain[9] and your childbearing,
> in pain you *will* bring forth children,
> and to your man (*ish*) *will be* your desire and he[10] *will* rule over you."

Immediately we can see that the woman's role as mother, the one who helps create the family, is negatively affected. The impact on the woman's role is paralleled by the impact on the man's role in tilling the ground: "In pain you will eat *from* her (the ground) all the days of your life" (3:17). Both of them will carry out their roles in *pain*. Life is going to be characterized by suffering, anguish, and death.

Adding to the woman's anguish would be the elusive nature of her aspiration for a loving relationship with her husband, an elusiveness which is indicated by the words "desire" and "rule."[11]

This idea is developed in the words God uses to speak to the woman. God addresses her as *isha* and refers to her man as *ish*. These words intentionally remind the receptor of the couple's previous relational harmony in 2:23,24 (Trible 1978, 128). As *isha*, the woman would still desire her *ish*, seeking the previous companionship and partnership in spite of the increased suffering in life.[12] However, the mutual regard of the previous section will now be elusive. The verb "rule" can imply domination as well as management (as in Eliezar of Damascus managing Abraham's house in Genesis 24:2; Joseph being placed as manager over his brothers in Genesis 37:8; and Joseph managing all of Egypt in Genesis 45:8). Through the use of the verb "rule," it appears that the relational oneness of Genesis 2 is going to be marred by stratification within the husband-wife relationship. The reason for this stratification can be seen as an outcome from the judgment of the man in Genesis 3:17–19, rather than being understood as an essential characteristic of future conjugal relationships, in the same way as the enmity between the serpent's seed and the woman's seed is not caused by God but is an outcome of the serpent's knowing that the seed of the woman will destroy him.

In Genesis 3:17–19 God does not speak to the man as *ish* but as *'adam*, reminding *'adam* of his relationship to *'adama* (the ground). God curses *'adama*, and the result is that it can no longer properly function in its role as a food producer for *'adam*. Consequently, humanity will have to struggle to survive. All of humanity will eventually lose the struggle because, having been made from the dust of the ground, they will return to it as dust.

It appears that this context of suffering and hardship will negatively impact the conjugal relationship. The challenge to survive will hamper the man's desire to be God-imaging, other-centered, and empowering. The primogeniture that enabled the man to move toward the woman will now be misused. The harsh conditions of life will incline the husband to be reluctant to view the woman-wife as a significant other. He will be inclined to reduce her to fulfilling a role, as someone to accomplish tasks in the household. The woman-wife will be viewed as one to be managed or controlled, rather than as a person to be cherished.[13]

Seeing this clause in 3:16 as descriptive of a relational aberration sheds light on the reason for the generalized application of Genesis 2:24. In that verse, the text jettisons the receptor out of the temporal particularity of the passage and embraces all of time, declaring that all men are to realign their allegiances and move in a God-imaging manner toward their wives. The text, addressing the present, marred relational context and writing about the past, recognizes that humankind has taken this path of relational degeneration as God had indicated they would. Consequently, the text utters a prophetic call in 2:24 to counter this degeneration. In addition, this relational degeneration and its subsequent impact on how people pejoratively came to perceive female ontology explain why the text intentionally ensures that the receptor would understand that women as well as men were made in God's image in 1:27.

Though the clause in 3:16 focuses on the husband ruling the wife, it does not mean that the receptor would view the husband as an isolated entity. This is the reason for the exhortation that all men are to leave their families and cleave to their wives in 2:24. The man-husband was part of a family-community. The struggle to survive apparently opened the door for a downward spiral toward oppression[14] as both men and women[15] in the family-community abused the positionally weak in the household.[16] Unfortunately, the path humankind had taken allowed the formation of stratified, hierarchical structures which devalued some and elevated others, making power a dominating factor in relationships.[17] It was up to each man to break with this pattern within his family-community and align himself with his wife, treating her as his *'ezer kenegdo*.

The naming of the woman in Genesis 3:20, though filled with hope because the blessing is not lost,[18] subtly reflects this shift in the man's orientation, from identifying his wife in terms of her close affinity to him to identifying her in her role as child bearer. In 4:1,2,25 the receptor observes this changed orientation toward women. The receptor sees the first woman functioning three times in the role of child bearer, and she subsequently disappears from view. The other three women in chapter 4, Cain's wife and Lamech's two wives, are nameless and voiceless child bearers.[19]

Conclusion

The decision to eat from the forbidden tree compels God to respond in a disciplinary way to humankind. His discipline radically affects their lives, their roles, and their relationships.

God curses the serpent and the earth, not the woman or the man (see Fretheim 1994, 363; Hess 2005, 90).[20] However, the curses drastically affect the couple's relationships and roles. Within the curse to the serpent is a strongly personal declaration that the serpent will be destroyed. One result of this declaration is the expression of the serpent's hostility toward the woman. However, no indication is given as to how the serpent's hostility against the woman will be manifested. It can only be assumed that the seed of the serpent will be the means by which the serpent will express its hostility, because this hostility is expanded to include the seed of the serpent against the seed of the woman. From the ensuing chapters of Genesis, the seed of the serpent are humans who align with the serpent. Thus fallen humanity will be the means by which the serpent will express his hostility toward the woman. In contrast, the ensuing chapters of Genesis reveal that the seed of the woman becomes those who align with God. By identifying the righteous with the seed of the woman, God negates any notion that the results of the first human couple's transgression are to negatively reflect on the nature of women.

The earth is also cursed so it can no longer produce abundant vegetation for them. Thus suffering and anguish become the salient conditions in which the humans will live their lives, ultimately ending in death.

Humanity's suffering is to radically affect their relationship with one another. Women will be inclined to seek for companionship and mutuality from their husbands. However, stratification is now going to become a dominant feature in the conjugal relationship. The primogeniture that the husband holds in Genesis 2 will apparently provide the occasion for this stratification. The position of the woman-wife, weakened in some way due to the suffering of childbearing along with the harsh conditions of life, will provide the occasion for her subjugation within the family system.

This stratification is an aberration of what was initially intended, and not a command of God that needs to be followed to maintain social order.

Though the rest of Genesis and the Pentateuch tend to display social and familial hierarchies characterized by large power distance, the overall tenor of the Pentateuch as well as the OT corpus does not support the notion that men are compelled to treat their women as laborers and needing management.[21]

A Summary of the Genesis Narrative

The narrative sections of Genesis 1–3, within the larger context of the book of Genesis and the Pentateuch, reveal that God initially intended the husband-wife relationship to be one that imaged the divine character. The conjugal relationship was meant to be a celebration of the other and be characterized by mutuality, partnership, and oneness.

However, that expectation remained unfulfilled due to the consequences of the couple's violation of God's command. Though the modern receptor is not privy to the exact social context of the implied receptor of the Pentateuch, the narrative in Genesis 1–3 does identify some of the problematic social values and conditions that negatively affected the common household. Stratification characterized the average husband-wife relationship, and the average woman held a significantly weakened position within her family unit. It is even possible that women were viewed as needing to be subjugated, managed, or controlled, and possibly even perceived as having inferior natures.

The text of the Pentateuch speaks prophetically into this deviant context in order to bring change. First, the text uses poetry and parallelism in

Genesis 1 to highlight the fact that both women and men were made in the image of God and enjoyed the commission of God to be God's royal representatives on the earth, and both were empowered to freely carry out this commission.

Second, the text closes the first narrative section with the rest on the seventh day. That was a day specifically hallowed by God to remind everyone to celebrate the significance of the person. That was a day that affirmed that there was no difference between women or men, or between those with more prestige and those with less. On the seventh day all rested.

Third, in Genesis 2, through the use of the theme of incompleteness, a compound prepositional phrase, a failed search among all the animals, and the building of the woman from a portion of the man, the text creates a narrative tension to emphasize the fact that there is no ontological difference between men and women. The pinnacle of this narrative development finds expression in the joy of the first man over the first woman. By having the man's first recorded words uttered in poetic form, the text affirms that the woman has the exact same nature as the man does. The only difference between men and women is in their sexuality, not in nature.

Fourth, the text demonstrates that an ontological difference and a corresponding hierarchy exist within and without the creation. Outside of creation God is the transcendent and sovereign one. Within the creation humankind enjoys an ontological and positional distinction. However, this difference and hierarchy is not meant to imply superiority and dominance. The creation narrative reveals that God empowered the different spheres of creation to have separate identities and appropriate levels of self-determination, with men and women enjoying the most significant level of self-determination possible.

Fifth, in Genesis 3 the text gives a reason for why the present social context does not resemble God's initial intention. The reason is that the first couple violated God's command. God's judgment on the couple resulted in a context of hostility, pain, suffering, and death that marred God's initial intent for the husband-wife relationship, and ultimately for the family and society. The stratification of relationships, the viewing of women as inferior, and the allegiance of the husband to his parents, family, and possibly tribe over against his wife were wrong.

God had declared that this deviation from his intended purposes would happen, but it was wrong. The seeming digression from the time-space particularity of the narrative to a universal application across all time and space in Genesis 2:24 was a prophetic call to change this distortion of God's initial intention. The text makes an all-encompassing application that all men are expected to realign their allegiance to their wives so they could potentially fulfill God's intention for the couple.

Sixth, in Genesis 3:15b the text reminds the receptors of the judgment of God that declared that the final victory over the serpent and all he represented would come through the seed of the woman. This statement affirmed that the nature of woman had not changed after the violation of God's command. Her seed is described in the rest of Genesis as the seed of the righteous. What had changed was humanity's willingness to image God in their relationships.

The reason for the woman's inferior position within society and within the family unit was the corruption of the primogeniture that the man had at creation. Initially this primogeniture enabled the man to move toward the woman and image God by being other-centered, serving, caring, and empowering. However, due to the curse of the earth and the struggle to survive, a stratification within human relationships developed, with women being fundamentally disadvantaged. Women were going to have to struggle within the households to gain positions of power.

Besides hardship and death, humankind faced an unidentified enemy, the serpent. His ongoing hostility would negatively affect the whole human race, and women in particular. This hostility was going to be ongoing; however, it would ultimately end with the seed of the woman being victorious. In making this statement, God upheld the integrity of woman's nature by identifying her seed as the seed that would ultimately overcome the serpent.

It is from this creation narrative that Paul developed his assumptions and values, and this is the interpretive paradigm from which to understand Paul's instructions in his letters.

---

1   The couple's relationship to God appears only somewhat affected (see Birch et al. 1999, 57). They are initially afraid of God and hide from him in fear. However, God has not changed. As in Genesis 1 and 2, God initiates the movement in the narrative and draws near to them. Even though he disciplines them, God remains their *'ezer*, clothing them appropriately.

2   The serpent and its curse have been interpreted naturalistically and figuratively (Ronning 1997, 2). The naturalistic interpretation views the serpent as a creature who could talk. The curse, therefore, is an etiological explanation of why snakes move about the way they do and why a seeming hostility between snakes and humans exists. Josephus naturalistically interpreted the story of the serpent (1961, 1.1.4.41–50). Philo blended the naturalistic and the figurative by viewing the serpent literally (1929, *Questions and Answers on Genesis* 1.31–36) but also as being an allegory for carnal desire (1961, *On the Creation* 56.157, 58.164) and a mouthpiece for the devil (1929, *Questions and Answers on Genesis* 1.36). The *Wisdom of Solomon* interpreted the serpent as the personification of the devil (2:24). Romans 16:20 indicates that Paul possibly interpreted the serpent as symbolically representative of Satan. The book of Revelation makes a connection between the serpent and Satan (12:9). In modern scholarship, von Rad rejects the idea that the serpent personified the devil (1961, 85). He understands it as representing evil (ibid., 90). Cassuto sees the serpent as the inner voice within the woman (1961, 142–43). Fretheim follows Philo as interpreting the serpent both literally and as figuratively; that is, as a snake and as representing anything that offers humankind alternatives to obedience to God (1994, 359–63). Goldingay follows Philo as well. Incorporating the totality of scriptural testimony, he seems to offer a more nuanced explanation than Fretheim. For Goldingay, the serpent is one of the ways Scripture explains why evil is present in the world (2003, 133–35; see also Wenham 1987, 80).

3   Seeing the serpent as representative of Satan "does not lie outside the narrative implications" of the text (Sailhamer 1992, 107). Matthews understands that the serpent is representative of Satan (1996, 232–35).

4   Does God cause the hostility or is it to be considered the moral agent's response to something else God does? My hermeneutical approach is derived from Trinitarian relationality and theistic freedom. Within this hermeneutic, it is impossible for God to cause moral agents to act contrary to moral law; that is, to cause hostility among others.

5   The Septuagint translates the pronouns in the singular as well (Wevers 1993, 44).

6   To the contrary, von Rad sees this as a curse upon both parties. The conflict between the two seeds will be an ongoing one, utterly destructive and hopeless for all (1961, 90).

7   Calvin recognized the positive nature of this phrase. Working from different categories, he wrote, "He mentions the woman on this account, because, as she had yielded to the subtlety of the devil, and being first deceived...so she had peculiar need of consolation" (1847, 170).

8   Fretheim (1994, 362) and Sailhamer (1992, 56) recognize that the judgments impact relationships and roles.

9   Carol Meyers asserts that "pain" refers to the wife's labor alongside her husband's (1983, 344–46; see also Hess 2005, 90–91). However, the parallel use of "pain" in verse 16 seems to underscore the anguish that now would characterize human life. In this vein, Cassuto asserts that "pain" regards both the woman's life in general and childbearing in particular (1961, 163, 165).

10   Robert Vasholz claims that the pronoun "he" in the final clause of verse 16 should be translated as "that" because he sees the pronoun modifying desire (1994, 51-52).

11   Even though Delitzsch believed that women were initially meant to be subordinate to men, he recognized that this comment reflected an aberration of the intended benevolence of the initial conjugal state (1888, 166). Augustine believed that "even before her sin woman had been made to be ruled by her husband and to be submissive and subject to him." He also recognized that in these words "there is a condition similar to that of slavery rather than a bond of love." However, he felt that "if this order is not maintained, nature will be corrupted still more, and sin will be increased" (Augustinus 1982, 11.50).

12   Wenham links "desire" to sexuality in this verse (1987, 81; see also Gunkel 1997, 21). Driver sees no connection (1909, 49). Wevers points out that the language of the Septuagint avoids interpreting "desire" as sexual (1993, 45). Childbearing is an integral part of the text, and humans are sexual beings. However, we are also more than sexual beings, having been made in God's image. Since the context of the man and the woman in the previous section is primarily relational, it is valid to view the woman's desire in this passage as primarily relational. This is in contrast to Calvin, who suggested that "desire" refers to the woman only desiring what her husband wishes (1847, 172).

The Hebrew word for "desire" is used only three times in the Old Testament: Genesis 3:16; 4:7; Song of Songs 7:11. Being that the Song of Songs was written by a different writer and at a different time, it is best to find the meaning of the word in its own narrative context. Susan Foh suggests that the meaning for "desire" in 3:16 corresponds to the meaning in Genesis 4:7. Thus it signifies the desire of the wife to dominate her husband (1974, 383; see Grudem 2006, 22–23). The problem with this suggestion is that it requires the receptor to break with the narrative flow and inject meaning backward, something that hasn't occurred yet in the Genesis narrative. There is no question that the use of the same words in Genesis 3:16 and 4:7 is intentional. However, the use of *ish* in 3:16 in referring to the woman's husband reminds the receptor of the prior relational harmony in 2:23,24, indicating that the desire is not to dominate but to enjoy a satisfying relationship. The next clause indicates that this desire will probably be elusive, only adding to the anguish of the woman. It is more likely that "desire" is used as a narrative device in 4:7 to keep the receptor's attention, not to parallel meaning (see Cassuto 1961, 212).

13   Regarding the issue of the man and woman's relationship to function and management, see Van Wolde (1994, 26–28).

14   Could it be that the serpent exacerbates these human predispositions and familial and social structures in order to express his hostility toward the woman?

15   Gerda Lerner asserts that women have always been active participants in the development of their societies (1986, 5).

16   Phyllis Trible states that the rule of the man over the woman is the result of sin, not a God-given right (1978, 128). Richard Hess asserts that this judgment describes life as "it will be lived," not as "it should be lived" (2005, 92).

17   This stratification of hierarchy was not limited to the husband-wife relationship. The inclination grew to encompass all human relationships. Albert Somit laments that societies seem predisposed to "hierarchical social organization and sharply delineated patterns of dominance and subordination" (1991, 26). He notices that most of the states in the UN are totalitarian regimes. Due to the prevalence of dominance relations in human societies, ethological studies have been conducted to try to demonstrate that there is a biological basis for such behavior (see also Peterson 1991). The root of this malaise is found in Genesis 3:14–19.

18   See Goldingay (2003, 143).

19   The woman's voice is not heard again until Genesis 16:2.

20   Graham Ogden also recognizes that verse 16 is not a curse on the woman (1985, 131).

21   See Schmitt's delineation of the healthy regard the Old Testament corpus portrays for the conjugal relationship (1991).

8

Recreating Oneness in 1 Corinthians 7:1–16

THE CREATION NARRATIVE contradicted the Greco-Roman world's assumptions and values about human sexuality. It created a new understanding of sexuality. This creational perspective shaped Paul's assumptions and values, which are evident in his writings. This is seen in Paul's treatment of the conjugal relationship in 1 Corinthians 7:1–16.

It appears from this passage that marriage was encountering some difficulty in Corinth. Drawing from the data within the letter, it seems as if some of the believers had merged Paul's teaching about the eschatological age of the Spirit[1] with a view of the world that was unhealthily dualistic. It looks as if some misunderstood what it meant to be "spiritual." They thought this meant that they had already experienced the resurrection and become like the angels (Fee 1987, 269; Talbert 2002, 54).[2] Their experience with the gift of tongues encouraged this misunderstanding of spirituality, because the language of angels was included in the *charisma* of tongues.[3] A dualistic approach to the material world influenced them to deny their natural desires and advocate sexual abstinence (Fee 2005b, 158–59).[4] Since they had become like the angels, some thought that this enabled them to transcend their sexuality.[5]

Paul was not dualistic in his outlook. He taught a unified view of reality, merging the spiritual with the physical. Paul's description of himself and the apostles in 1 Corinthians 4:9 demonstrates that during this eschatological age angels are watching the people of God as they live their lives on the earth:[6] "For I think that God has exhibited us apostles as last of all, like men sentenced to death; because we have become a spectacle to the world, to angels and to men."[7] However, for Paul, though angels and humans occupied the same sacred space, they remained in two distinct categories.

This misunderstanding of being spiritual along with an advocacy of abstinence threatened the integrity of the marriage relationship. Paul confronts this problem in 1 Corinthians 7:1–16. While Paul affirms the value of celibacy, he opposes any dualistically inspired asceticism. In addition, Paul upholds the goodness of human sexuality and marriage while turning upside down Greco-Roman patriarchal approaches to power within the conjugal relationship. Paul in addressing these issues creates a vision of interaction that recreates oneness in the conjugal relationship.

Asceticism or Celibacy?

Paul begins this passage by writing, "Now concerning the matters about which you wrote. It is well for a man not to touch a woman" (1 Cor 7:1). Some consider this to be a statement of Paul affirming celibacy; however, the scholarly consensus is that the discussion relates to whether or not a husband and wife should engage in sexual intercourse. This is because "to touch a woman" was an idiom referring to intercourse (Hays 1997, 113), and the Corinthians had raised this issue in their correspondence with Paul.[8] It appears that some Corinthians had come to believe that engaging in sexual intercourse indicated a deficiency in one's spirituality (Yarbrough 1985, 119).

Whatever the reasons for Paul's preference for celibacy in this passage, they do not nullify Paul's affirmation of human sexuality and his radical approach to mutuality and oneness in the conjugal relationship. Nonetheless, a few comments must be made about Paul's celibacy in order to clarify the significance of Paul's comments about marriage.

Paul's celibacy has been mistakenly understood as a form of asceticism.[9] Asceticism is a form of renunciation in order to enhance one's spiritual state.[10] For Paul, celibacy was not an ascetic practice of denial.[11] It was a gift from the Spirit which enabled a person to devote all his or her energies to serving God. Conzelmann points out that self-control which is the result of "celibacy-as-charisma" should also be understood as a charisma of the Spirit. Self-control in this context is not a virtue (1975, 120; see also Fee 1987, 284–85). Therefore there is a qualitative difference between ascetic abstinence and celibacy-as-charisma, a subtle but significant distinction that has been sometimes overlooked.[12]

What is clear through Paul's instruction in 1 Corinthians 7 is that he rejects asceticism while he affirms celibacy. For Paul, celibacy and marriage are both gifts from God.[13] For he writes, "I wish that all were as I myself am. But each has his own special gift from God, one of one kind and one of another" (1 Cor 7:7).

Sexuality and Oneness

While correcting the ascetic tendencies of Corinthian spouses, Paul introduces an alternative paradigm to the Greco-Roman conjugal relationship. Through prosaic parallelism Paul affirms the significance of both spouses within the marriage relationship and contradicts the Greco-Roman notion of male dominance and the related assumption about female ontological inferiority (Scroggs 1972, 294–95; Witherington 1988, 26–27).[14] (See table 2.) In addition, Paul creates a decision-making process between the spouses that elevates the position of the wife in the use of social power.[15]

Though there is no direct reference to the creation account, Paul gives practical definition to the celebration of human sexuality and the oneness that is exemplified by the primal couple in Genesis 2:23–25.

In verse 2 Paul asserts that a man should have "his own" wife, and the wife should have "her own" husband.[16] "To have" is an idiom for having sex (Garland 2003, 256; Hays 2004, 139). Paul achieves two objectives through his use of the reflexive pronoun *idios* (own). First, he identifies the conjugal relationship as monogamous. Second, he emphasizes mutuality in the relationship by placing the couple on equal footing.[17] Paul develops this concept of mutuality in verse 3 by referring to sexual intercourse as an obligation[18] within the relationship, and both spouses are required to fulfill it.[19] In verse 4 Paul raises the standard and goes beyond the Greco-Roman concept of obligation. He transfers the authority of one spouse's body over to the other spouse.[20] Drawing attention to Paul's rejection of the idea of male dominance, Witherington states, "Few Romans could have conceived of arguing that the husband's body *belonged* to the wife" (1995, 175; italics in the original).

TABLE 2: Parallelism in 1 Corinthians 7:1–16[21]

Verse	To the Man	To the Woman
2	Each man should have his own wife	each woman her own husband
3	The husband should give to his wife her conjugal rights	likewise the wife to her husband
4	The wife does not have authority over her own body, but the husband does	The husband does not have authority over his own body, but the wife does
5	Do not deprive one another except perhaps by agreement for a set time	

Verse	To the Man	To the Woman
10, 11	The husband should not divorce his wife	The wife should not separate from her husband
12, 13	If any believer has a wife who is an unbeliever, and she consents to live with him, he should not divorce her	If any woman has a husband who is an unbeliever, and he consents to live with her, she should not divorce him
14	The unbelieving wife is made holy through her husband	The unbelieving husband is made holy through his wife
15	If the unbelieving partner separates, let it be so; in such a case the brother or sister is not bound	
16	Husband, for all you know, you might save your wife	Wife, for all you know, you might save your husband

In verse 5 Paul elevates the status of the wife as he calls for the couple to mutually decide upon temporarily abstaining from sex. This is not a decision that the husband could make unilaterally.

Through this parallelism Paul refutes the notion that procreation is the primary purpose for sexual intercourse (Hays 2004, 142).[22] Paul, by encouraging sexual intercourse at the desire of either spouse, also implicitly contradicts any notion that sexual intercourse weakens the body[23] or impairs one's relationship with God.[24] Roy Ward writes, "Paul, in effect, redefined marriage as a context for the mutual satisfying of erotic desires" (1990, 286–87).[25] By putting sexual satisfaction strictly within the confines of monogamous marriage, Paul also protects the spouses from undermining the conjugal relationship by seeking sexual gratification in alternative ways, ways that are accessible within the broader Corinthian social context.

The cumulative effect of the parallelism of verses 1–5 is fourfold. First, Paul affirms human sexuality, being male and female.[26] Being in Christ does not entail transcending, ignoring, or negating one's sexuality. Second, Paul affirms the "goodness of marriage" (Instone-Brewer 2001, 243). Third, Paul clarifies that sexual intercourse within a monogamous marriage is a valid and pure expression of sexuality for the people of God as they live in the present age. Finally, Paul raises the status of the wife in the marriage relationship, placing her on the same level as the husband. She has the same rights as he does.[27] The two are to consider the other as they live out their marriage relationship.

In verses 12–16 Paul continues to negate dualism and affirm the integrity of female ontology. Paul contradicts the dualistically influenced notion that staying with a nonbeliever could have a defiling impact on the believer (Thiselton 2000, 528). He conversely declares that the believing spouse can positively impact the unbelieving spouse through their ongoing relationship (Fee 1987, 300–301). By paralleling husbands and wives in this sanctifying process, Paul contradicts the notion of female inferiority. Just as the husband has the power to sanctify his wife, the wife has the power to sanctify her husband.[28] In addition, if the unbelieving spouse does not want to remain in the marriage, both the female and the male spouse are empowered to make the decision to separate.

Conclusion

In conclusion, the marriage relationship was in jeopardy due to an unhealthy dualism and a misunderstanding of what it meant to be spiritual. Paul used the Corinthians' misunderstandings to create a new cognitive framework for understanding the marriage relationship.

Paul affirms the validity and the sanctity of marriage in two ways. First, he states that celibacy and marriage are mutually exclusive, spiritual gifts from God. Second, living as God's people does not require a person to deny one's humanity or sexuality. If one does not have the gift of celibacy, that person should marry. In this way Paul affirms the goodness and integrity of marriage. Marriage is not a sin. Paul also goes beyond Greco-Roman values by fully affirming the propriety and validity of sexual intercourse in marriage.

Paul contradicts the Greco-Roman notion of male superiority and female subordination in the marriage relationship through prosaic parallelism.[29] Paul gives wives the same rights within the marriage relationship as their husbands. They also have the equal responsibility to fulfill those rights. In addition, Paul raises the status of the wife by calling for mutuality in the decision-making process as the couple chooses to temporarily abstain from sex. Paul affirms the spirituality of women by stating that they could potentially sanctify their unbelieving husbands and children in the same manner as men. Finally, regardless of sex, spouses are empowered to withdraw from a marriage if the unbelieving spouse no longer wants to continue in the marriage.

Paul constructs an argument that protects the validity of sexuality and marriage while calling women and men to image the mutuality and oneness that the original couple demonstrated.

The Corinthian misunderstanding of spirituality and its threat to the marriage relationship did not find expression only in the conjugal relationship at home. This misunderstanding negatively impacted the way the community worshiped together. Paul addresses this problem in 1 Corinthians 11:2–16.

---

1   There is an "already" and a "not yet" dimension to Paul's understanding of this eschatological age (Hays 1996, 26–27). The Corinthians apparently did not understand the "not yet" dimension of this.

2   The angels are mentioned four times in 1 Corinthians: 4:9; 6:2–3; 11:10; 13:1.

3   See 1 Corinthians 13:1.

4   Regarding dualism and asceticism, Hays writes, "The correlation between piety and celibacy was a common feature of Hellenistic culture. The physical body belonging to the physical world was deprecated and regarded as inferior to the rational soul" (1996, 48). See also M. MacDonald (2004, 154). See Hurley for a description of what defilement might have meant to a Corinthian believer (1981, 131–32). In contrast, Will Deming asserts that there is no indication that the Corinthians avoided marriage due to dualistic influences. He maintains that the textual clues within 1 Corinthians 7 indicate that the Corinthians were influenced by the Cynic position against marriage in order that one have leisure time to devote for study and the development of virtue (2004, 109–10). However, as Judith Gundry-Volf points out, Paul states in verse 28 that the one who marries does not sin. The only reason Paul would have needed to make that statement is if some of the Corinthians believed that marriage was a sin (1996, 523). Lietzmann asserts that some Corinthians viewed "all sexual intercourse as improper—even within marriage" (1953, 135).

5   Robin Scroggs asserts that the Corinthians held to a gnostically influenced, spiritual asceticism where the distinctions between males and females were abolished (1972, 536; see also M. MacDonald 1987; Meeks 1973).

6   Fitzmeyer points out that two documents from Qumran demonstrate that some believed that the angels were "present at the gathering of the army for the eschatological war and at the meeting of the congregation or the assembly of God" (1957–58, 56). Paul reflects this belief but reshapes it.

7 As mentioned in chapter 1, in chapters 8–11 the biblical quotations are from the Revised Standard Version (RSV) except when otherwise noted.

8 See Fee (1987, 273), Garland (2003, 251), Hays (1997, 110–12), Horsley (1998, 95), D. Martin (1995, 205), and Talbert (2002, 53). Conzelmann sees 1b as a statement of Paul because of the use of the characteristically Pauline word *kalon* (good) (1975, 115). Garland, how-ever, points out that "good" is more likely part of a quote, "good for a man," which was drawn from the Corinthian correspondence (2003, 249). Baumert sees 1b as a statement by Paul, but asserts that Paul's state-ment is a response to his understanding of the working of the Spirit in a person's life (1996, 25–32). The Spirit draws a person to celibacy. The problem with Baumert's position is that it implies that a married per-son may be drawn to celibacy by the Spirit, which is the very issue Paul refutes. Paul's discourse indicates that the Spirit's boundary in gifting celibacy is that the person be single. Peerbolte sees this as a statement of Paul because "Paul appears to have his values determined by the coming *parousia*. It is no longer necessary for a man to marry a woman" (2000, 79). Wire sees it as a statement of Paul, and part of Paul's rhetorical strategy in 1 Corinthians 5–7 to persuade women to give up their sexual abstinence (1990, 73–79). Caragounis sees this as Paul telling the church that "it is better for people not to marry" (1996, 548). Lietzmann asserts that this is a statement of Paul's because Paul, influenced by Philonism and Hellenistic Judaism, believed that sexual intercourse was "of lower moral value and unclean" (1953, 135).

9 Maximos Davies, in his advocacy of celibacy, writes, "Celibacy in Eastern Christianity is seen primarily as a form of asceticism" (2002, 13). Jerome Murphy-O'Connor writes about Paul, "He himself lived a life of sexual asceticism" (1979, 59). Elizabeth Castelli assumes Paul was an ascetic (1999). Roetzel claims that Paul was an ascetic and his asceti-cism was rooted in "Jewish and Hellenistic traditions, a Christological focus on the cross and Jesus' self-denial, an apocalyptic mind-set, and an eschatological reserve emphasizing a continual struggle" (1998, 149). However, Jesus' self-denial had no correspondence with asceticism. If it did, the Gospel writer's contrast between Jesus and John in Luke 7:33,34 loses its meaning. In contrast, Fee is correct in stating that "Paul was simply not an ascetic" (1987, 276). Will Deming explains the dif-ference between celibacy and asceticism this way: "Indeed, Paul advises the Corinthians against the attempt to censure their (God-given) sexual drives, maintaining that if one is unsure of his or her ability to remain

continent, then marriage is the better choice. Celibacy for Paul was thus not the equivalent of sexual asceticism, a regime of self-induced privation and hardship" (2004, 216–17).

10   This definition is in line with Wimbush's definition of ascetic behavior, which is "a range of responses to social, political, and physical worlds often perceived as oppressive or unfriendly, or as stumbling blocks to the pursuit of heroic personal or communal goals, life styles and commitments" (1990, 2).

11   Conzelmann points out that "Paul differs from the Stoa in suggesting no spiritual training for the control of passion. The fact of the case—whether a man has the χάρισμα, 'gift,' of continence or not—is simply accepted" (1975, 116).

12   See E. Clark for how this difference was overlooked by the Patristic Fathers (1999).

13   This is in contrast to Deming, who suggests that sexual abstinence within marriage is the gift Paul addresses (2004, 124–25, 213–14). Paul is correcting the incongruous thinking that the Spirit would gift a person within marriage with celibacy.

14   David Instone-Brewer states, "Paul refers to both women and men whenever he discusses the marriage obligations. In fact he is so conscientious in making balanced statements, that he often repeats whole phrases in order to emphasize this" (2001, 234). In contrast, Antoinette Wire sees Paul's "egalitarian" stance as a means of subduing the Corinthian women who have devoted themselves to God (1990, 82–97).

15   Paul's response in verses 2–16 to the Corinthian assertion that "it is well for a man not to touch a woman" demonstrates that he did not prefer males above females. This is in contrast to Wire's assertion that Paul is actually demanding more from women than from men in this chapter by compelling them to give up abstinence in marriage (1990, 82–83).

16   Being that Paul is working to preserve the marriage relationship, one of the implications from the phrase "his own wife" is that it eliminates the possibility of having sexual intercourse with one's female slaves, which was somewhat frowned upon but permissible (see Martialis 1993, 1.84). However, Carolyn Osiek asserts it is an "overinterpretation" to state that the phrase "his own wife" does not rule out sex with one's slave

women (2003, 269–70). Yet John Clarke points out that an elite man was free to have sex with anyone, just as long as the person was not free-born (2003, 163; see also Martialis 1993 3.33; 3.73; 4.66; 12.58; 12.97). Clarke also states that non-elite men and women "were used to relatively unregulated sex with a variety of partners" (2003, 164). Such libertinism would have destroyed the creation intent of the marriage relationship. This libertine context of both men and women provides a background for Paul's inclusion of the phrase "her own husband."

17 See Hays (2004, 140) and Houghton (1976, 65). Loader points out that though there is a level of mutuality in these verses, "we should not read into it our modern notions of partnership. Avoiding sexual im-morality is the primary agenda, not marital love" (2005, 156). Loader is right that the immediate context is avoiding sexual immorality. Gundry-Volf seems to concur with Loader's view. She does make the distinction that Paul uses Adam and Eve as a model of lovers, not a model of parents. Thus Paul breaks with procreation as the purpose for marriage and sex (1994, 114). I disagree with Gundry-Volf and Loader, because Genesis 2 depicts much more than erotic love. It speaks of the transfer of allegiance and of the attainment of oneness in the conjugal relationship. Therefore I assert that Paul uses the crisis of Corinthian asceticism as an opportunity to raise the standard for the conjugal relationship, and he depicts a model of mutuality and love that the primal couple in Genesis 2 expresses.

18 Here Paul uses the noun *opheile*, a verb cognate being *opheilo*, which Paul uses in 1 Corinthians 11:7,10. It is a term that expresses the obligations one has to another with respect to any given relationship (Gundry-Volf 1996, 526; Winter 2001, 130–31).

19 See Blomberg (1995, 133) and Thiselton (2000, 503).

20 Paul uses a verb cognate of *exousia* in verse 4. The significance of this will be examined later in this chapter. Loader points out that Paul's formulation could be used to justify rape in the marriage, because "the rights are not one's own rights to be respected, but rights over the other which potentially subvert consent" (2005, 158). However, the defining characteristic of a disciple for Paul is love (1 Cor 13). Such a blatant violation of one's dignity contradicts the overall tenor of Paul's teaching. Even Loader has to conclude by saying, "We should probably assume that mutual love and respect are envisaged" (ibid.).

21 The verses in table 2 are from the NRSV.

22   Musonius Rufus in his discourse *On Sexual Indulgence* reflects the Greco-Roman notion that the purpose of sexual intercourse with one's wife is for procreation: "Men who are not wantons or immoral are bound to consider sexual intercourse justified only when it occurs in marriage and is indulged in for the purpose of begetting children, since that is lawful, but unjust and unlawful when it is mere pleasure seeking, even in marriage" (1947, 87). With regard to Philo on this point, see Loader (2004, 14). Though there is no explicit reference to the creation narrative in this section, the primal couple is identified as becoming one flesh and being naked and not ashamed. This potentially shaped Paul's understanding of the goodness of sexual intercourse in its own right within the conjugal relationship.

23   Soranus wrote, "Virginity, therefore, is healthful, since it prevents the excretion of seed…since men who remain chaste are stronger and bigger than the others and pass their lives in better health, correspondingly it follows that for women too virginity in general is healthful. For pregnancy and parturition exhaust the female body and make it waste greatly away, whereas virginity, safeguarding women from such injuries, may suitably be called healthful" (1991, 1.30; see also 1.32). See also Galen (1982, 93–94).

24   Loader suggests that Paul's permission to the couple to temporarily abstain from sexual intercourse indicates the tension that exists within Paul about sexual intercourse and purity (2005, 158). Judith Gundry-Volf states that the ascetics considered themselves superior to those who were weak and engaged in sexual intercourse (1996, 523). However, this is not the case. David Scholer writes, "Paul's argument is that sexual relations in marriage are not in conflict with true spirituality" (1993, 336). Paul allows a period of temporary abstinence in order that the couple may enter a liminal state and focus more intensely on God and prayer. Temporarily separating oneself from the daily rituals of life for a time of focused prayer is not an ascetic abstinence which purposes to obtain a higher level of purity.

25   This is in contrast to Dale Martin's assertion that Paul was concerned about eliminating sexual desire altogether, either by marriage or by celibacy (1995, 212–16).

26   This is in contrast to Daniel Boyarin, who suggests that Paul felt that a return to genderlessness would have been the ideal (2004, 34). I have demonstrated that the intent of Genesis 1:27 is to define *'adam* as

being an inclusive term of male and female, thus it is not to present a diachronic creation from androgyne to gendered being. Also, the phraseology of the poetry of Genesis 2:23 does not lend itself to seeing *'adam* as genderless. Thus I do not see the textual support for the notion of a primal androgyne. In addition, David Scholer asserts that Paul did not advocate for an "asexual humanity"; rather, Paul sought to eliminate the discriminatory elements associated with gender (1998, 7).

27 Paul went beyond Musonius (Rufus 1947) in his view on wives, as he wanted the couple to model the oneness that was reflected in the creation narrative. Paul's teaching is in marked contrast to the misogyny that we read of in Livy, where in the tussle over the Oppian Law, Marcus Portus Cato called upon husbands to keep a tight reign on their wives: "If each of us, citizens, had determined to assert his rights and dignity as a husband with respect to his own spouse, we should have less trouble with the sex as a whole; as it is, our liberty, destroyed at home by female violence, even here in the Forum is crushed and trodden underfoot, and because we have not kept them individually under control, we dread them collectively" (Livius 1953, 34.2.1–2).

28 Margaret MacDonald points out some of the issues involved in a woman remaining with an unbelieving husband and how strong she had to be in order to remain (1996, 193–95).

29 Also, in comparing Paul's teaching about marriage and divorce in 1 Corinthians 7 with Jewish, Greek, and Aramaic marriage papyri, David Instone-Brewer concludes, "The only facet which is not paralleled by the papyri is Paul's combination of equality and security of men and women in marriage" (2001, 242).

9

Affirming the Other in 1 Corinthians 11:2–16

CULTURAL INFLUENCES were threatening the integrity of the marriage relationship in Corinth. Dualism and a misunderstanding of what it meant to be spiritual inspired a trend toward asceticism.[1] On the personal level, this asceticism could lead to immorality and destroy the conjugal relationship. Paul addresses this problem in 1 Corinthians 7. However, these erroneous beliefs were also negatively impacting the Corinthian corporate worship experience. Paul tackles these impacts in 1 Corinthians 11:2–14:40.

In chapters 11–14 Paul seeks to properly enculturate the Corinthian church in corporate worship.[2] Chapter 14 shows that the Corinthians' corporate worship events were fairly chaotic. The Corinthians had elevated certain spiritual gifts over others (ch. 12) and were spontaneously expressing the gifts of tongues and prophecy (ch. 14). This uncontrolled spontaneity led to a considerable amount of disorder. In addition, wealthy Corinthians had also elevated themselves above the others in the assembly (ch. 11).

In an attempt to resolve these problems, Paul enculturates the Corinthians in how to worship as a community. In 1 Corinthians 11:2–16 Paul begins this process of enculturation by weaving together a conjugal relational paradigm drawn from creation and redemption, a renewed vision of human sexuality, and the cultural symbols of dress to make his points. Paul's purpose in this section is to counter the Corinthian misunderstanding of spirituality as well as Greco-Roman cultural inclinations toward self-assertion and elitism. Paul seeks to preserve corporate unity and the value and integrity of marriage by encouraging the Corinthian believers to affirm the value and the significance of the others in their midst.

A Relational Paradigm from Creation and Redemption

In verse 2 Paul begins the passage with a commendation.[3] As Paul begins the letter to the Corinthians praising them (1:4–9), here he also employs rhetoric that is meant to put the Corinthians at ease, transition to a new topic, and draw support for his upcoming commands from his previous teaching and church tradition.

Then Paul introduces the Corinthians to a hierarchical structure that appears to be drawn from the creation account and redemption. Paul writes, "The head of every man is Christ, the head of a woman is her husband, and the head of Christ is God" (11:3). The hierarchy appears to reflect the creation narrative (Gen 2:4–25), which ascribes to the man a level of primogeniture.[4]

Paul also places Jesus as the head of the man. By using Jesus' title, the Christ, he describes the impact redemption has had upon the creation model. Paul subsequently refers to the creation narrative in verses 7–9 in order to support the rationale for this hierarchy.

At first appearance, by placing men and women in this hierarchical structure through the use of the term "head," Paul seems to support the patriarchal structure that existed in his Greco-Roman world.[5] Dale Martin points out that the Greco-Roman conception of the body was hierarchically oriented, reflecting social and sexual superiority and inferiority (1995, 29–34). However, Paul does not affirm the Greco-Roman patriarchal model; rather, he radically subverts it along with its assumptions and values.[6]

The Assumption of Subordination

Paul subverts the Greco-Roman assumption of female subordination through dissonance and by injecting the term "Christ" into the hierarchy.[7]

First, in creating this hierarchy, Paul breaks with the conventional Hellenistic-Jewish triadic format.[8] The format for the triad was either ascending or descending. However, Paul starts in the middle, with "every man" in relation to "Christ."[9] In this way Paul creates a sense of dissonance within the receptor by not following the traditional ascending or descending order. This subtly indicates that Paul does not want to communicate the notion of subordination within the hierarchy (Garland 2003, 508).[10]

Second, in speaking of Jesus in relationship to "every man," Paul does not refer to Jesus as the Lord as he does in verse 11 and as he often does in

1 Corinthians.[11] Paul avoids this term because of its obvious connection with authority and submission.[12]

Third, in speaking of Jesus' relationship to God, Paul refers to Jesus as *the Christ*, not as the Son. In 1 Corinthians 15:28 Paul refers to Jesus in his relationship to God as the Son to emphasize subordination: "When all things are subjected to him, then the Son himself will also be subjected to the one who put all things in subjection under him, so that God may be all in all" (NRSV).[13] By referring to Jesus as the Christ, Paul frames this hierarchy around the work of Jesus, emphasizing Jesus' soteriological role as mediator and servant.[14] In effect, Paul creates a functional hierarchy.

This functional dimension of hierarchy parallels the nature of hierarchy as it is revealed in Genesis 1 and 2. The first section of the creation narrative affirms the necessity of functional hierarchies, as humanity is made in God's image and given a limited dominion over the earth. The completion of corporate tasks requires the creation of functional hierarchies. However, the first section of the creation narrative contradicts the large power distance assumption of existential or ontological superiority given to those higher within functional hierarchies.

In addition, the second section of the creation narrative reveals God as the servant-helper of Adam. Since the head of Christ functioned as a servant-helper to Adam, and Christ has functioned as a servant-helper to every man, then the impact of this hierarchy is that men are expected to function as servant-helpers to their wives.[15]

Also, Paul's use of "every man" parallels the universality of the declaration of Genesis 2:24, where each and every man is called to realign his allegiance from his parents to his wife.

Therefore the functional nature of hierarchy and the revealed character of God as helper in Genesis 2 shape Paul's description of hierarchy. By beginning his hierarchical structure with "every man" and by referring to Jesus as the Christ, Paul underscores the responsibility every man has with regard to his position in the hierarchy. Every man is supposed to image Christ, his head, who as the perfect man imaged God and functioned as the servant-helper to all.[16] In this way Paul further develops the theme of 1 Corinthians 10:23–11:1. Paul concludes that passage by encouraging the Corinthians to image him and Christ by living their lives out of consideration for the other. Paul by doing this subverts Greco-Roman assumptions and values embedded within the patriarchal model.

Kephale and Primogeniture

Kephale (head) is a hierarchical term, and Paul uses it in both literal and metaphorical senses in verses 3–10 (Fee 1987, 493–94). This has led to a discussion on how to interpret the word in verse 3. Some have argued that *kephale* should be understood to mean "source," as this would most adequately reflect Paul's egalitarian position on sexuality (Horsley 1998, 153; Mickelsen and Mickelsen 1986; Murphy-O'Connor 1980, 492; Talbert 2002, 86), or "origin" (Barrett 1968, 248), while others have argued that it means "authority over" (Grudem 2002; 1985, 51; see also Blomberg 1995, 208–9; Bordwine 1996, 18; Peerbolte 2000, 83).[17]

Gregory Dawes has shown that *kephale* functioned as a living metaphor at the time of Paul, eliminating the possibility for ascribing one fixed meaning. It has a range of meanings. Therefore the specific meaning of the metaphor has to be developed within its narrative context "by reference to the literal sense of the word" (1998, 127). Therefore the word should be translated as "head," and the context has to provide its meaning each time it occurs.

It appears that Paul chose *kephale* as it aligned with his understanding of the second creation narrative, which gives the male a level of primogeniture in the conjugal relationship. However, as we have seen, Paul deconstructs the receptor's understanding of the political dimension of that primogeniture, removes from it the notion of dominance or superiority, and reconstructs the receptor's understanding of the term to mean servant-helper.[18] While acknowledging the primogeniture the man has in the creation narrative, Paul reminds the Corinthians of the implication of this creational primogeniture by calling every man to image his head, the Christ, who became the servant of all in order to bring life to all. Following the pattern of the universal application of Genesis 2:24, Paul permits no exceptions. This is the responsibility of every man.

In this subtle way, Paul subverts the Greco-Roman patriarchal idea of male dominance and female subordination in the marriage relationship.

The Assumption of Ontology

Not only does Paul subvert Greco-Roman assumptions about female subordination, he also subverts Greco-Roman assumptions about female ontology.[19]

A first-century Mediterranean male assumed that women were ontologically inferior to men.[20] However, in verses 11–12 Paul contradicts this notion[21] and draws the receptor's attention to the fact that women and men are ontologically interconnected: "Nevertheless, in the Lord woman is not independent of man nor man of woman; for as woman was made from man, so man is now born of woman. And all things are from God" (ESV). Referring to the initial creation where woman was formed from man,[22] and to the subsequent process of procreation, Paul indicates that there is no ontological difference between women and men.[23] Paul recycles his paradigm of creation and redemption by paralleling "in the Lord" with "all things are from God" in order to emphasize this point (R. Collins 1999, 403).[24]

In addition, by basing men and women's interdependence "in the Lord" and by concluding with "all things are from God," Paul reminds the Corinthians of the inherent goodness of the creation and of humanity as female and male.

The Symbolism of Head Coverings

The Greek word *gyne* can mean either "woman" or "wife," and the Greek word *aner* can mean either "man" or "husband." The context is supposed to determine how the words should be translated. Therefore, does *gyne* in 1 Corinthians 11:3–16 refer to "wife" in particular or "woman" in general? Does *aner* refer to "husband" or "man"?[25]

In answer to this, Thiselton states that "the overwhelming majority of commentators convincingly argue that the issue concerns gender relations as a whole, not simply those within the more restricted family circle" (2000, 822). Witherington concurs:

> In some parts of the text it is clearly impossible to argue that *aner* means "husband" and *gyne* "wife," and elsewhere these translations are implausible, especially because Paul keeps saying things like "every man" or "any woman." The argument is not about family relations but about praying and prophesying in Christian worship. (1995, 235)

However, this assessment does not harmonize with the way *kephale* is used in verse 3 and the symbolic meaning of the head covering for women in verse 10.

First, the *kephale* relationship that Paul describes in 1 Corinthians 11:3 appears to be more appropriate within a husband-wife relationship than being descriptive of relationships between women and men in general.

The NRSV and the ESV translators have recognized this and translated *aner* as "husband" and *gyne* as "wife" in this verse. Second, Paul's reference to woman being made from man and woman being created for man in verses 8–9 is an allusion to the second part of the creation narrative. Raymond Collins recognizes that this "story evokes the image of a prototypical man and woman who cling to one another in marital union" (1999, 410).

Second, it appears that Paul's focus is on head coverings[26] because of their symbolic meaning. Mary Harlow points out that Roman clothing was a "material representation of the social world." Clothing represented "status, rank, age, gender, ethnicity, otherness, etc." (2005, 144). Likewise, Bruce Malina states, "The physical person (one's body) is normally a symboled replication of the social value of honor.... Honor and dishonor are displayed when the head is crowned, anointed, touched, covered, uncovered, made bare by shaving, cut off, struck or slapped" (2001, 38–39).[27]

Since head coverings were imbued with meaning, Paul was compelled to address the issue. As I will demonstrate below, the head covering indicated that a woman was married.

One final point: in this passage Paul addresses both men and women with regard to head coverings.[28] The primary focus of verse 13 is on the women who were praying and prophesying with uncovered heads; however, it appears that Paul was concerned about men covering their heads as well.[29]

A Symbol of Superiority

Why were the men covering their heads while they prayed and prophesied? Corinth was architecturally a thoroughly Roman colony (Winter 2001, 11), and the dominant social and cultural ethos was Roman (ibid., 25; Horrell 1996, 65). Richard Oster has shown that aristocratic Roman men covered their heads in their devotional and sacrificial worship of the gods (1988, 494–95).[30] In this light, David Gill asserts that the Corinthian men who were covering their heads were the social elite of the community.[31] These men were modeling Roman aristocratic men and were covering their heads with their fine togas in order to highlight their superior status within the group (1990, 250).[32] The men's actions reflected the stratification and factionalism that Paul addresses in 11:17–22 and alludes to elsewhere in the letter.

These men covered their heads in order to symbolically draw honor to themselves. In objecting to their behavior, Paul reconstructs their perception of honor and shame. Paul writes, "Any man who prays or prophesies with his head covered dishonors his head" (1 Cor 11:4). Paul uses "head" as a synecdoche (Thiselton 2000, 816) and as a metaphor for Christ. Rather than bringing honor to themselves, these men were actually shaming themselves as well as their head, Christ. Paul's appeal to the creation narrative puts perspective on their actions. These men did not recognize their own inherent honor as being the image and the glory of God. They were attempting to derive their honor from their status in society. In addition, they did not recognize the significance of the others in their community as being made in God's image and being reflections of God's glory.

A Symbol of Sexuality and Marriage

Why were the women uncovering their heads? As stated previously, it appears that some of the Corinthians had become sexually abstinent because they believed that sexual activity was sinful or a sign of weakness. Being spiritual, they had transcended their sexuality and become like the angels. As they engaged in ecstatic corporate worship, the women may have uncovered their heads to indicate their sexual continence even though they were married, or they were indicating that they had attained to a state of transcendence (see Fee 1987, 498; 2005b, 158–59).[33] Dennis MacDonald suggests that the women unveiled themselves because their worship services were liminal events where they transcended their own ontology and became like the primal androgyne (1987, 92–98).

We cannot be sure that the women were motivated by a pre-gnostic belief in a primal androgyne. However, if they were, it is understandable why Paul would react so strongly against an action that symbolized androgyny. The myth of the primal androgyne demeaned the value and significance of women, because the primal androgyne was male.[34] However, God had created humans as male and female; therefore, being female was good. Affirming the value of female sexuality is one of the reasons Paul speaks of the creation of the sexes by God and their interdependence in verses 11–12.[35]

While Paul needed to affirm the goodness of the female sex, he also had to address the other cultural implications of removing the head covering in the Greco-Roman world.

A woman's head covering indicated that a woman was married. "The very mention of the word 'veil' by Paul would automatically indicate to the Corinthians that the females under discussion in this passage were married" (Winter 2001, 127).[36] "Marriage" and "veiling" were interrelated terms in Latin.[37] The veiling of the bride was an integral aspect of the wedding. It indicated that the girl was leaving childhood and becoming a matron (Treggiari 1991, 180).

The married woman wore a woolen *stola* (long robe) over her tunic and a woolen *palla*, "which was used to veil her head when she went out in public" (Sebesta 2001, 48).[38] Croom states that "no respectable woman would leave her house without her head covered [by the *palla*] and her body concealed by it" (2000, 87). This is because the head covering was the culturally acknowledged symbol of propriety for a woman (Rousselle 1992, 315).[39]

The head covering also had a negative implication as it symbolized a woman's inferior status to her husband (BeDuhn 1999; D. MacDonald 1987, 89). In Rome some of the aristocratic women had become educated and economically independent. Their improved position enabled them to break traditional mores within Roman society that they considered restrictive (Winter 2003, 96). Therefore they went about with their heads uncovered.

Thus the head covering symbolized the propriety of the married woman or an inferior status, depending on the person. Some Corinthian women might have been influenced by these trends in Rome. Their desire for freedom from subjugation nicely dovetailed with their understanding of being like the angels in this eschatological age. These sociocultural conditions may have influenced them to remove their head coverings while praying and prophesying.[40]

The notion of freedom (*eleutheria*) and its synonyms, such as *exousia* (right/authority), recycle within this epistle (R. Collins 1999, 329).[41] In this letter Paul counters the Corinthian preoccupation with oneself with regard to freedom by declaring that freedom is not living for oneself but for the other (Fee 1987, 252).[42] Paul also overturns the Corinthians' concept of right. One example is when he addresses the sexually abstinent in 7:2–5. Paul denies the abstinent the right over their bodies and gives that right to their partners. Paul strengthens the force of his argument by stating that each person is obliged to fulfill the right of the other (Gundry-Volf 1996, 524–26). It was well understood within the Greco-Roman world that obligations existed within any given relationship, and for that relationship to meaningfully continue, one had to fulfill those obligations.[43]

Whether it was to communicate their transcendence of sexuality, or assert their independence, or a mixture of both, the text indicates that these women were violating an accepted social norm by uncovering their heads.[44] Paul's appeal in verse 13 that the Corinthians judge for themselves whether removing the head covering is right or wrong assumes that the values associated with head coverings are shared ones within the Corinthian community. His assertion that all the churches have one practice demonstrates that these were shared values throughout his world.

Why was the removal of the head covering wrong? As a symbol of propriety, a woman was bringing her own reputation into question by removing it. Also, since the head covering was a symbol of marriage, her husband and the community may have interpreted its removal as her slighting her marriage partner.[45] This explains Paul's allusion in verses 5–6 to the removal of the head covering being the same as if the woman cut off her hair.

In the Greco-Roman world, a woman would have her hair shorn if she had been found unfaithful to her husband and had committed adultery (Winter 2001, 128–29).[46] Thus Paul asserts that when the woman prays and prophesies without a covering she shames herself in the same way as if she had declared herself an adulteress.[47] Also, since the Greco-Roman world was a collective one,[48] a woman's action negatively impacted the reputation of her husband and family. By uncovering her head, the woman was not only shaming herself, she was shaming her husband.[49]

This possibility of the wife shaming her husband makes sense of Paul's digression from the creation narrative in verse 7. Paul refers to man being the image and glory of God, not the image and likeness of God as in Genesis 1:27. He then refers to woman being the glory of man.

This digression has been interpreted as a denigrating step down for women, as they are not identified as the image and glory of God as men are (Conzelmann 1975, 186, 189).[50] However, it would be inconsistent of Paul to denigrate the honor of women or wives;[51] rather, it appears that Paul purposefully digresses from the language of the creation narrative to highlight the cultural ramifications of the misuse of head coverings.[52] The cultural reality within the Greco-Roman world was that a woman's action had positive or negative implications for her husband. A woman could bring her husband glory (honor) or shame. The reality was that the women's action of uncovering their heads was bringing their husbands shame.[53]

The relational dimension of head covering helps to explain Paul's statement in verse 10: "That is why a woman ought to have a veil [*exousia*] on her head, because of the angels."[54] As he does in 7:3,4 in addressing the marriage relationship, Paul employs the themes of obligation and right/authority.

According to Roman law, a woman was expected to be one of the parties agreeing to the marriage. The law stated, "Marriage cannot take place
unless everyone involved consents, that is, those who are being united
and those in whose power they are" (Justinianus 1985, 23.2.2). In the
Greco-Roman world and especially within the redeemed community, a
woman was to exercise her own will and assent to her marriage. Wearing
a head covering in the corporate assembly while praying and prophesying apparently was a statement by the wife affirming the value, integrity,
and sanctity of her marriage relationship before the community.[55]

Thus Paul asserts that the woman is relationally obliged to have *exousia*
on her head. In other words, it is her obligation to demonstrate her power of action and affirm her marriage relationship by covering her head.
This is not a symbol of submission or subordination; it is her affirmation
of her husband and of the integrity and sanctity of their relationship as
husband and wife.[56]

By mentioning the angels, Paul reaffirms the value and sanctity of
marriage. Paul and the Corinthians believed that the angels were present
with the people of God during this eschatological age.[57] By linking the
woman's affirmation of her marriage with the presence of the angels,[58]
Paul ensures that no married woman would think of marriage as something that marginalized her or her spirituality.[59]

Conclusion

In 1 Corinthians 11:2–16 Paul addresses the expressions of self-assertion
and asceticism as they appear in corporate worship. Both of these issues
threaten the welfare of the community. Paul seeks to counter these by
creating a disposition that affirms the others in the congregation.

In order to accomplish this, Paul creates a paradigm for understanding relationships drawing from creation and redemption. Through this
paradigm Paul subverts the assumptions regarding sexuality within the
Greco-Roman patriarchal system.

First, Paul appears to agree with the Greco-Roman patriarchal system
by depicting the sexually oriented relationships within a hierarchical
framework. However, Paul creates a sense of dissonance within the receptor by beginning the form in the middle, breaking with the traditional
Hellenistic ascending/descending triadic form. In this way, Paul undermines the notion of male superiority and female subordination. Second,
Paul undermines the notion of male superiority and female subordination by referring to Jesus as the Christ. Paul avoids using a term that

denotes superiority or subordination. By the use of "Christ," Paul refers to Jesus' mediatorial role as the servant-helper of all humankind.

In this paradigm, Paul demonstrates a realistic approach to his world. Paul acknowledges the primogeniture that men have in the creation and in the Greco-Roman culture through his use of the term "head." However, by referring to Jesus as the Christ and as the head of men, Paul enjoins men to act like their head, who, as redeemer, has begun to bring creation back to its intended order. Paul's use of "every man" as he begins his hierarchical model reflects the universality of the appeal of Genesis 2:24, where every man is enjoined to transfer his allegiance from his parents to his wife and live in mutuality and oneness.

Paul also contradicts the assumption that women are ontologically inferior to men by showing the interdependence of the sexes in their creation by God and their ongoing existence. Woman initially came from man, but now all men are born from women. Thus there is no ontological difference between them.

Paul created this paradigm in order to address the issues that developed out of the misuse of head coverings. Head coverings had symbolic meaning, and men and women were asserting their own value by their misuse of that symbol. Their misuse of head coverings demonstrated that they did not understand the values of love and "being for the other" that the believing community was to embody.

Some men had been placing their togas over their head to show that they were higher in wealth and status than the rest of the men in the congregation. These men did not realize that their true significance lay in having been made in God's image. The men were also dishonoring Christ by thinking they were better than the others in their community. Therefore, by not covering their heads they were able to affirm the significance and value of the others in the community.

Likewise, some women were asserting their misunderstood elevated stature due to their being "spiritual" and "like the angels." They were uncovering their heads because they were influenced by a dualistic philosophy that perceived sex as sinful. The head covering demonstrated that they were married and sexually involved with their husbands. In addition, it is also likely that some of these women viewed the head covering as symbolizing a position of subjection and subordination from which Christ had liberated them. They were asserting their equality with men by removing their head covering.

However, this symbol meant much more than subjection in the Greco-Roman cultural milieu. Being a form of dress for married women, it signified femaleness, propriety, and marriage. By uncovering their heads, the women were negating the validity and significance of their sexuality, disrespecting themselves, and devaluing their marriage relationship.

Paul's teaching demonstrates sensitivity to the culture while contradicting its underlying assumptions. First, Paul understands that God has created femaleness and it is inherently good, not defective. Women do not need to blur their sexuality by rejecting fundamental cultural symbols and act like men to affirm their value and significance. Second, God has created sexuality. Sex is good within the monogamous marriage relationship. Therefore, being married is good and should be affirmed—at home, in the community, and in the corporate assembly. Third, being female is not a position of subjection. Paul makes this clear through his prosaic parallelism in chapter 7. He reiterates what he teaches in chapter 7 by crafting a relational paradigm that reflects the initial intention of God for conjugal relationships in the creation, which is meant to be restored through the redemption of Christ. Men are to view themselves as servants who image God, being for the other, not as those placed in charge of their wives. With this recreated paradigm of the conjugal relationship, Paul charges the married women to use the culturally relevant symbol of the head covering while they pray and prophesy in order to positively affirm the value and significance of their sexuality, their marriage, and their husbands.

It is likely that only elite women removed their head coverings. Were there issues that arose among non-elite women? This is apparently what Paul addresses in 1 Corinthians 14:33–35.

---

1   According to Gordon Fee, "It is hard to escape the implication that what is involved here are two opposing views as to what it means to be 'spiritual.' For the Corinthians it meant "tongues, wisdom, knowledge" (and pride), but without a commensurate concern for truly Christian behavior" (1987, 630).

2   Among those who accept Paul as author of this section (and all of the letter) are Garland (2003), D. Hall (2003), D. Martin (1995), Thiselton (2000), Winter (2001), and Witherington (1988). However, some have argued that 1 Corinthians 11:2–16 is a Deutero-Pauline interpolation because it is inconsistent with Paul's teaching of gender equality and because of its internal inconsistencies in logic (see Cope

1980; Trompf 1980; Walker 1975, 97). Jerome Murphy-O'Connor argues against seeing these passages as internally inconsistent and interpolations (1976; 1986), as do Joel Delobel (1986) and Ben Witherington (1988, 78–79).

3 This is in contrast to David Odell-Scott, who argues that 1 Corinthians 11:3–10,13–15 are assertions made by the Corinthians to which Paul responds in 11:11,12,16 (2005, 212–13).

4 Judith Gundry-Volf argues that Paul, as he struggled to help the Corinthians live within their cultural context, read the creation from contrasting paradigms—on one side, patriarchal, and on the other, egalitarian (1997, 152). However, I suggest that Paul's teaching harmonized and transformed the Corinthian cultural context with the teaching of the creation narrative. Raymond Collins, on the other hand, thinks that Paul naively interacted with the creation narrative because he saw it all as one narrative, rather than seeing it as a composite of J, E, P, and D (1999, 569). Even though the author(s) of the Pentateuch chose material from different sources, the outcome was one document. Paul may not have been as naive as Collins suggests.

5 Gerda Lerner asserts that it is wrong to isolate and blame patriarchy for women's oppression. She has shown that men have exercised authority over women in both patriarchal and matriarchal systems. Also, she claims that women have not only been victims in these systems but have also been active participants in their creation and perpetuation (1986, 29–30). The problem is much more complex. Identifying the oppressive dimensions within any social structure is vital, but important as well is identifying and changing the fundamental assumptions and values that sustain such oppression.

6 This is in contrast to BeDuhn, who states that Paul believed that woman, having originated from the man, had an "inferior ontological status" (1999, 308).

7 This is in contrast to Conzelmann (1975, 184), D. Martin (1995, 232), Økland (2004, 178), and E. and W. Stegemann (1999, 398), who contend Paul was advocating subordination of the woman to the man. It is also in contrast to Lone Fatum, who asserts that Paul sacrificed women's freedom for the sake of the community in Corinth (1991, 57; see also M. MacDonald 1990, 180–81).

8   For a brief discussion of the Hellenistic-Jewish triadic format, see R. Collins (1999, 405). Delobel recognizes that Paul's break with the traditional format is significant. He asserts that the break is due to the fact that the focus of the passage is to correct women's behavior (1986, 377, 379–80). Collins also recognizes the inconsistency in the order with the standard triadic form (1999, 205); however, he sees Paul's use of the term "Christ" as an expression of the Christian understanding of seeing creation through the redemptive act of Jesus (ibid., 399–400). Thomas Schreiner asserts that the hierarchy reflects voluntary submission (1991, 128). T. L. Scott also fails to recognize the dissonance in how Paul articulates the hierarchy (1998, 297), and concludes that "Paul clearly sees the subordination of women as essential to social order in the Corinthian assembly" (ibid., 303).

9   Paul's connecting every man with Christ does not have soteriological implications in this verse (Barrett 1968, 249). This is how Paul connects his discourse with Genesis 2:24.

10   This is in contrast to John Meier, who says the term "Christ" refers to his creative involvement, as per 1 Corinthians 8:6, thus Christ is the source of man's being. Therefore Meier asserts that this "chain of being" showing "the order of creation...necessarily involves subordination" (1978, 218). This is also in contrast to David Lowery, who holds that subordination is integral to Paul's meaning (1986, 157–58). He does not notice the disruption of the ascending or descending Hellenistic-Jewish form. This dissonance is also missed by Dale Martin, who concludes, "It is difficult to see how such interpreters, presumably wishing to save the text for contemporary egalitarian theology, can insist that Paul is here not teaching the subordination of women" (1995, 232). This is also in contrast to Loader, who states that Paul is working from "within the framework of Genesis 1–2 LXX, which does indicate a sense of hierarchy and appears to see some analogy between the man in the likeness of God and the woman in the likeness of man and so is probably to be assumed here and reflects the context" (2004, 100).

11   See 1 Corinthians 1:2,3,7,8,9,10; 2:8; 4:5; 5:4; 6:11,14; 8:6; 9:1; 10:21,22; 11:23; 12:3; 15:31,57; 16:23.

12   This is in contrast to Gillian Beattie, who asserts that the term "Christ" connotes authority due to its relationship with the term "Lord" in 1 Corinthians 8:6 (2005, 41).

13   Kevin Giles argues that the subordination of the Son was not reflective of the eternal relationship of Jesus with the Father. He grounds
his argument in the historical teachings of Athanasius and asserts that
Athanasius "rejects not only any suggestion whatsoever that the Son is
subordinate in being to the Father, but also any suggestion whatsoever
that the Son is eternally subordinate to the Father in function, role or
work" (2002, 38). Giles acknowledges that ontological inferiority was
one of the central aspects of the controversy between Athanasius and
Arianism, but he does not understand how this contextual assumption
impacted the shape of the church's argument. This lack of understanding
impairs the foundation of his argument. Augustine's defense of the divine nature of Jesus in *The Trinity* illustrates how underlying assumptions
about hierarchy determined the shape of his and Athanasius' argument.
Augustine declared that the economic subordination of the Son did not
indicate ontological inferiority in his divine nature: "So the Son of God
is God the Father's equal by nature, by condition his inferior. In the
form of a servant which he took he is the Father's inferior; in the form of
God in which he existed even before he took this other he is the Father's
equal.... And so it is not without reason that the scripture says both; that
the Son is equal to the Father and that the Father is greater than the Son"
(Augustinus 1990, 1:14).

It appears that large power distance assumptions about hierarchy
shaped the church's argument, because it was assumed that a lower position in a hierarchy not only meant subordination, but that it also meant
ontological inferiority and inequality (see J. Chrysostom 1956a, 150).
This assumption has remained influential in the church's discussion up
to the present day. Dennis MacDonald's question demonstrates this well:
"Does [head] here mean source as in a sequence of generation, or superior in ranking of ontological value, or both?" (1987, 73). If the eternal
Logos was also Son in eternity, being Son could not mean Jesus as God
is ontologically inferior or unequal. However, such familial terminology
would appear to support the idea that hierarchy exists in the Godhead.
This is something that Giles cannot accept. He distinguishes between the
economic and the immanent Trinity and asserts that the Cappadocians
were unable to uphold the equality of the Trinity because they were hierarchical in their view of the Trinity (2002, 43). However, the biblical
record reveals the immanent Trinity through the economic Trinity (see
Molnar 2002, 312), and Jesus is revealed as the submissive Son. Haydn
Nelson states, "Although it may be argued that in the economy God has

not revealed all he is…I would nevertheless still contend that he has not revealed *other* than he is" (2005, 165; italics in the original). Thus, from the biblical data, cognizant of the assumptions that were functioning during the Arian controversy, if one follows the Cappadocians and acknowledges a hierarchy in the Godhead, it is crucial to clarify that hierarchy does not denote inferior status or inferior ontology.

14   Jerome Murphy-O'Connor sees the use of the term "Christ" as connoting Jesus in his mediatorial role as well (1980, 493–94).

15   Scroggs asserts that hierarchy for Paul means service and empowerment. Men have a responsibility to ensure that their actions are Godlike (1972, 298).

16   Hays wrote, "The twin themes of conformity to Christ's death and the imitation of Christ are foundational elements of Paul's vision of the moral life" (1996, 31). Paul's teaching here reflects this. Also, Thiselton recognizes the "servantlike" responsibility of the man in the male-female relationship, but he develops his thought from the intertextual context of 1 Corinthians 8:1–14:40 (2000, 821).

17   David Lowery concludes that the word connotes subordination and origination (1986, 157). With regard to Grudem's research, Joseph Fitzmeyer's article on *kephale* supports Grudem's conclusion (1989). Though Grudem's analysis is thorough, his argument for the meaning of *kephale* as "authority over" is seriously weakened by Dawes' work. In his study of the function of metaphor and the metaphorical use of *kephale* in Ephesians, Dawes contends that in Ephesians 5:21–33 *kephale* cannot function as a metaphor for authority because it is modified by love (1998, 137–38). I will show that Paul uses *kephale* as a hierarchical term (head) in the 1 Corinthians 11:2–16 passage as it enables him to develop his argument. However, it is unlikely that *kephale* for Paul meant "authority over." Paul's view of hierarchy was transformed by what he discovered in Genesis 1–3.

18   As in 1 Corinthians 7, Paul digresses significantly from the values expressed by Musonius. Not even Musonius' egalitarian notions could rise above the assumption that men's higher position allotted them superiority in the conjugal relationship. In his discourse *On Sexual Indulgence*, Musonius wrote, "And yet surely one will not expect men to be less moral than women, nor less capable of disciplining their desires, thereby revealing the stronger in judgment inferior to the weaker, the rulers to the ruled.

In fact, it behooves men to be much better if they expect to be superior to women" (Rufus 1947, 89). On another note, Bruce Ware states that "Paul is arguing for the headship of man over woman" in this passage (2002, 85). However, Ware has missed Paul's point. Headship is not about being over anyone, it is about imaging God.

19   John Chrysostom noticed a link between ontology and Paul's use of *kephale*. Chrysostom asserted that one of the meanings implied in the use of *kephale* was that there is shared ontology between each of the pairs. He wrote, "For if 'the man be the head of the woman,' and the head be of the same substance with the body, and 'the head of Christ is God,' the Son is of the same substance with the Father" (1956a, 150). The problem with drawing data from Chrysostom is that he resembles his culture in his references to women more than he does Paul. In the same homily he wrote, "But when she made an ill use of her privilege and she who had been made a helper was found to be an ensnarer and ruined all, then she is justly told for the future, 'thy turning shall be to thy husband" (ibid., 151). In his homily *On Virginity*, commenting on Paul's teaching about marriage in 1 Corinthians 7, Chrysostom wrote, "To consider Paul's words more carefully, he increases the tyranny of marriage and makes the servitude appear more burdensome. For the Lord did not permit a husband to drive his wife from the house, whereas Paul takes away a man's authority over his own body and surrenders dominion over it to his wife, and he ranks a husband lower than a slave bought with silver. It is often possible for a slave to obtain absolute freedom if he can gain at some time enough money to pay his price to his master. But even if a husband had the most troublesome wife of all, he must bear with his servitude, and he can discover no deliverance or way out of this despotism" (1983, 38–39).

20   Soranus wrote, "Furthermore, the female is by nature different from the male, so much so that Aristotle and Zenon the Epicurean say that the female is imperfect, the male, however, perfect" (1990, 3.3).

21   This is in contrast to Dale Martin, who asserts that Paul believed a woman's body was ontologically inferior (1995, 233).

22   This man-woman ontological unity corresponds to the poetry of Genesis 2:23. Adam declares that woman is ontologically the same as he when he refers to her as *isha* and to himself as *ish*. The only difference between them is in gender, not in nature.

23   Delobel views verses 11–12 as having parallel meanings. The phrase "in the Lord" in verse 11 refers to Christ's role in creation as God's role is addressed in verse 12 (1986, 384). Barrett understands Paul in verse 11 to mean that this woman-man interdependency continues within the restoration of creation (1968, 255). Raymond Collins states that even though the pericope is a corrective of primarily women's behavior, Paul's "view of creation and of the new order is...egalitarian" and he is demonstrating that women and men "share a common nature" (1999, 403). This is in contrast to Hays, who sees patriarchal assumptions imbedded within the text and Paul advocating for an ontological preeminence for the man (1997, 184, 192), and Murphy-O'Connor, who does not see any allusion to ontology here. Rather, he sees Paul overturning the "chronological priority of the male in the creation" by acknowledging the "chronological priority of woman" in the birth of men. For Murphy-O'Connor this is how Paul argues for equality between the sexes, not complementarity (1996, 290).

24   Judith Gundry-Volf views the phrase "in the Lord" as referring to the equality women and men now have by virtue of being in Christ (1997, 163–64). Barrett concludes that the phrase intimates the Lord's intention in creation and in the restoration (1968, 255).

25   Keener asserts that Paul is referring to wives and husbands in the entire passage (1992, 32–36; 1995, 209–10).

26   The Greek says, "Every man praying or prophesying down from (the) head having." The obscurity of the phrase "down from the head" has opened the door for a controversy over whether Paul is concerned with hairstyles or head coverings. I concur with those who see Paul using hairstyles as an analogy to emphasize his points about head coverings (Barrett 1968; Garland 2003; Hurd 1963; M. MacDonald 2004; Talbert 2002; Winter 2003; Wire 1990; Witherington 1995). There are those who have argued that Paul is concerned with hairstyles (R. Collins 1999, 401; Fiorenza 1983, 227; Hays 1997, 185–87; Murphy-O'Connor 1980; 1988; Padgett 1984; Thompson 1988). However, Thiselton asserts that even though the argument for hairstyles is strong it is not conclusive (2000, 825).

If the myth of the primal androgyne had influenced the men and they were attempting to obscure their gender, then the ambiguity of the Greek clause could allow for the interpretation that the men were acting as women, having long hair. This would have effectively blurred the gender lines, and it could have also been interpreted by the Corinthian

society as a preference for pederasty and homosexuality, which a significant portion of the society abhorred (R. Collins 1999, 399). However,
this scenario is unlikely, because the image of the androgyne was not a
referent to gender neutrality. Dennis MacDonald shows that androgyny
implied "perfected masculinity" (1987, 98–102). Jorunn Økland points
out that Philo's perception of the primal androgyne provided a rationale
for male-dominated, hierarchical relationships between the sexes (2004,
181). Since the primal androgyne in the gnostic myth was the perfected
male, there was no reason for the men to demonstrate that they were not
male. However, if the Corinthians were motivated by the myth of the
primal male, there would have been a reason for women to show that
they had achieved that primal male status.

27 Croom demonstrates how clothing in the Greco-Roman world
signified position and status. For example, with regard to men, the color
of one's tunic indicated status. A white tunic with wide purple stripes
indicated the man was a senator; a thin strip indicated he was an eques-
trian. A leather belt indicated a man was a soldier (2000, 32). The *Digest
of Justinian* provides an example of how clothing indicated the status of
a woman: "If someone accosts a maiden, even those in slave's garb, his
offense will be regarded as venial, even more so if the women be in pros-
titute's dress and not that of a matron. Still if the woman be not in the
dress of a matron and someone accost her or abduct her attendant, he
will be liable to the action for insult" (Justinianus 1985, 47.10.15.15).
Glenys Davies points out how significant dress was to gender and to
status. He writes, "The essential point is that the toga in the imperial
period could not be worn by respectable women, and particularly not by
matrons." It was the form of dress abandoned by girls and taken up again
by prostitutes and adulteresses (2005, 128).

28 See also Thompson (1988, 104). This is in contrast to Fee, who
states that this is a hypothetical comparison since Paul is concerned with
the women uncovering their heads (1987, 505).

29 Though Raymond Collins believes the issue is primarily hairstyles,
he does concur that the primary "issue is the attire of women" (1999,
400; see also Witherington 1988, 86). This is in contrast to Thiselton,
who maintains that Paul is equally concerned about men covering
their heads as women (2000, 825). There are two reasons to question
Thiselton's position. First, Paul spends much more discourse on how
shameful it would be for a woman to be uncovered than a man to be

covered. Second, Paul concludes his argument with verse 13, not with verses 13–15 (Delobel 1986, 379–80; Garland 2003, 507). Paul's subsequent analogy to men and women's hair length in verses 14–15 is used to support his concluding statement (Barrett 1968, 256–57).

30 Raymond Collins points out that Jewish and Roman traditions had men praying with their heads covered and that the Greeks prayed with their heads uncovered (1999, 401).

31 Greco-Roman society was highly stratified with few people with wealth, position, and prestige. Symbols of wealth were particularly important within the city of Corinth for those seeking status. For a discussion on the significance of wealth for status seekers in Corinth, see Chow (1997, 114).

32 This is in contrast to Dana Thomason, who argues that the men were dramatizing "their transcendence of sexual distinctions by transvestite activities involving the way they wore their hair and by the use of their veils" (1987, 126). As I have shown, in the myth of the primal androgyne, the androgyne was male. There is, therefore, no reason to think that men were trying to transcend their own sexuality. In objecting to interpreting Paul as addressing hairstyles of men, Delobel stresses that Paul does not refer to cultural meanings to validate his points. Paul restricts the scope of his argument to saying that it is shameful for a man to cover his head because man is the glory of God (Delobel 1986, 374). However, though Delobel objects, the very use of the concepts of propriety and shame by Paul demonstrates that Paul is drawing from a shared set of cultural values besides the creation narrative. Regarding the social composition of the Corinthian believing community, Murphy-O'Connor says: "Among the believers at Corinth there were 'haves' and 'have nots,' and the former exhibited little or no concern for the latter.... Despite virtually unlimited opportunity, economic inequality was a fact of life, and believers did nothing to close the gap" (1996, 278). See also Horrell (1996, 95–101).

33 Another proposal is that the Corinthian women were modeling oriental cults (such as in the worship of Isis) and were uncovering their heads and letting their hair loose as they engaged in ecstatic worship (Fiorenza 1983, 227; see also Talbert 2002, 87). This suggestion seems implausible considering the nature of the Dionysian cult (Thiselton 2000, 830–31).

34   See endnote 27.

35   Thomason states that Paul draws on Genesis 2 to "demonstrate that in the beginning God created two distinct sexes, not one androgynous creature as the opponents claimed. By saying that the man was the 'source' or 'origin' of woman Paul could show that one sex was created prior to the other in time. If one sex preceded the other, it would mean that two distinct sexes were created. That, in turn, would rule out the need to restore an androgynous primordial ancestor." However, Thomason feels that Paul uses the term *kephale* to indicate the subordination of women to men (1987, 124).

36   What also may make this discussion a moot point is that almost every woman was married at that time (Keener 1992, 82).

37   Susan Treggiari points out: "Indeed, the verb used of the woman marrying, *nubo*, is related to *nubes*, a cloud, and means literally 'I veil myself.' From this come *nupta*, a married woman, *nova nuptia*, a bride, and *nuptiae*, the wedding" (1991, 163). Even though Paul uses Greek to speak to the Corinthians, and Greek was the *lingua franca*, Corinthians were heavily influenced by Roman culture.

38   This is in contrast to Houghton, who states that "some Greek and Roman women wore the covering, but felt no compulsion to do so" (1976, 413).

39   Rousselle argues that Paul is encouraging all Christian women to adopt wearing head coverings regardless of their status because of the positive connotation of the head covering. "Although the veil was a symbol of subjection, it was also a badge of honor, of sexual reserve, and hence of mastery of the self" (1992, 315). Sebesta says that the matron's dress "signified her modesty and chastity" (2001, 48). She adds, "In each stage of a Roman woman's life, costume served as a visual and tactile reminder of the virtue she should maintain and for which she should be respected" (ibid., 51). Douglas Cairns asserts, "That women in Greek societies veil, both as a regular public demeanor and as a response to particular events and circumstances, is demonstrated by a wealth of visual evidence and confirmed in literature. This veiling can manifest their αἰδώς (*aidos*) both as an occurrent affect (shame, bashfulness) and as an abiding quality or disposition (modesty)" (2002, 75). See also Houghton (1976, 106).

40 Though Hays sees this section referring to women in general, he asserts that the problem was that the head covering symbolized the woman's inferior status, therefore some women refused to wear it (1997, 184). Keener holds that the head coverings were needed in order to keep lust down in the assembly (1992, 29–30). This seems unlikely. When Paul was concerned about lust or immorality, he directly addressed the issue.

41 See 1 Corinthians 6:12; 8:9; 9:3–18; 10:23; 11:10. With regard to freedom, Stephen Barton writes that Paul gives himself as an example, how he "refrains from exercising his own *exousia* to receive financial support from the Corinthians so as not to place any hindrance in the way of their receiving the gospel.... For Paul the apostle, true freedom is found in being able to restrict one's freedom—which means becoming like a slave (*doulos*)—for the sake of 'saving' as many people as possible: 'For though I am free from all, I have made myself a slave to all, that I might by all means save some'" (1997, 13).

42 Compare 1 Corinthians 10:23 with 10:33.

43 For a brief discussion on the importance of social obligations in Greco-Roman society, see Winter (2001, 130–31). Also, the Corinthian society was an agrarian society. (This concept is discussed in more detail in chapter 4.) Relationships were the means by which people created their stability. Therefore obligations in relationships were much stronger than they are in contemporary middle-class North American cultures. With regard to the significance of the obligations embedded within one's relationships, George Foster writes, "The ideal of successful defense is... to be able to meet life's continuing challenges without help from others, to be able to avoid entangling alliances. Yet, paradoxically, the struggle to reach this goal can be made only by saddling oneself with a wide variety of obligations. Strength and independence in fact always depend on the number and quality of the ties one maintains. Hence the whole course of life consists of manipulating and exploiting the institutions and behavior forms one knows in order to achieve desirable obligations, to tap social resources so that life's dangers will be minimized and its opportunities maximized. On a formal and institutional level an individual is aided by his 'defense' by family...and friendship ties. These are legitimate forms of support in which obligations and expectations—whether or not honored in any specific instance—are clearly spelled out" (1967a, 214).

44   It is very likely that this was only a problem among elite women, as the head covering was only a problem among the elite men. A problem that arose among non-elite women is discussed in the next chapter in the section on the nature of the women's interaction in the assembly.

45   "As the veil symbolized the husband's authority over his wife, the omission of the veil by a married woman was a sign of her withdrawing herself from marriage" (Sebesta 2001, 48–49).

46   See also D. Chrysostom (1986, 64.3).

47   Shame and honor were fundamental values in the Greco-Roman world (deSilva 2000, 23–42; see Malina 2001, 27–57). With regard to shame and honor within the Greco-Roman social context, Cairns writes, "For the various manifestations of veiling are unified by the fact that social interaction in Greek culture is a matter of committing one's own honour in an arena in which it must find its own level relative to the honour of others. The operative Greek concept here is that of τιμή [*time*]. Τιμή constitutes the individual's selfhood or identity in so far as it is viewed socially; thus τιμή is the crucial concept in the interaction ritual of the Greeks, functioning as it does both as the claim to honour that one projects and the validation of honour that one seeks to receive in social interaction" (2002, 81). Paul understood this social dimension of honor and how important it was for the church to live out their lives in ways that drew honor to Christ. However, Paul radically reconceptualized the acquisition of honor within this social milieu. The men were charged to not cover their heads. This would have brought them honor in the large power distance Greco-Roman context, because it enabled them to set themselves apart from and above most others. However, according to Paul, the people of God derived their honor by seeing others as members of the body of which they also were a part. Those with more visible honor were to give more honor to those with less visible honor (1 Cor 12:12–26). For an overview of the reconstructed paradigm of honor in the NT, see deSilva (2000, 43–84).

48   For a discussion on the collectivist nature of Greco-Roman society, see Malina and Neyrey (1996, 154–57).

49   Thiselton points out that "people bring shame upon themselves... and perhaps also shaming the person or persons who were perceived as the generally more public associate of the woman (whether husband, guardian, father, or wider family)" (2000, 830).

50   Thomason argues that with this reference to the woman being the glory of man "Paul believed in the ontological inferiority of women," but "this ontological inferiority does not diminish the sociological equality" (1987, 137). However, the data indicate that Paul did not accept the assumption that women were ontologically inferior to men.

51   Thiselton asserts that the term "glory" has a positive connotation, not a negative one (2000, 834–35).

52   This is a significantly different position than the argument that Paul wants to preserve the creation order in worship and ensure only God's glory appears by having women cover their heads (see Witherington 1988, 89).

53   This is not to say that the women's action does not have implications upon God, or that the men's wrong action of covering does not bring dishonor to their wives. This is just the way Paul is developing his argument, as his focus is upon the wife's behavior at this point.

54   The RSV translates *exousia* as "veil," which signified the symbol of marriage. The NASB translates *exousia* as a "symbol of authority," and the NIV translates it as a "sign of authority." The TNIV translates verse 10 as, "It is for this reason that a woman ought to have *authority* over her own head, because of the angels" (italics added). These variances indicate that the verse has been a bit of a conundrum to translate. Schreiner asserts that *exousia* speaks of a woman's submission to male authority (1991, 135). However, *exousia* "cannot be a sign of the man's authority since there is no evidence for such a passive use" of the word in the literature (Gundry-Volf 1997, 159; see also BeDuhn 1999, 302–3). Therefore, *exousia* denotes one's right, authority, or power to act.

55   BeDuhn states that as a woman exercises control over her own head and covers it, she "demonstrates her faithfulness to her husband or her acknowledgment of her status" (1999, 303–4). However, BeDuhn holds that the woman is acknowledging her inferior status in the relationship by this.

56   This is in contrast to Beattie, who states, "The veil itself is not a sign of true authority…it is instead a sign of submission with which women choose to cover themselves. In one verse Paul both attributes authority to women and tells them how they must use it" (2005, 51).

57   As Collins and Fitzmeyer have pointed out, the Qumran literature speaks of angels being present among the worshiping community,
and anyone with an impurity or defect is to be kept out of the assembly (R. Collins 1999, 412; Fitzmeyer 1957–58, 55–56). Thiselton notes
that "from Paul to the Revelation of John Christian theology shares the
Jewish tradition that Christians worship the transcendent God of heaven
in company with the heavenly host" (2000, 840–41). However, Morna
Hooker takes a different tack on the angels and women reflecting the glory of man. She argues that this passage is about the need for all women
to cover their heads because the angels need to be shielded from being
misled as they view her glory. Only God's glory should be visible during
worship. By choosing to wear the veil the women glorify God (1964,
414–15). In this vein, see also Wire (1990, 121–22).

58   This is in contrast to those who view the angels as guardians of
the order of creation (see Witherington 1988, 88–89). With Paul's ear-
lier comment (6:3) about the people of God judging the angels, it does
not appear that his theology would view angels as the keepers of order.
Rather, Paul is concerned with the demonstration of godliness in all its
dimensions by the people of God.

59   To ensure that the men do not feel that they are somehow superior
to women by what Paul has just written, as his words in verses 8–9 could
be misunderstood to affirm that man enjoys a level of superiority since
woman was created for man, Paul immediately after verse 10 states that
both in creation and in redemption neither women nor men are separate
from one another. As I have mentioned, this denotes their ontological
sameness, thus invalidating the assumption that men are superior in nature to women.

10

Restoring Order in 1 Corinthians 14:33–35

IN 1 CORINTHIANS 11 Paul permits women to pray and prophesy in the assembly. In 1 Corinthians 14:33–35 Paul appears to contradict himself by charging the women to keep silent.[1]

> As in all the churches of the saints, the women should keep silent in the churches. For they are not permitted to speak, but should be in submission, as the Law also says. If there is anything they desire to learn, let them ask their husbands at home. For it is shameful for a woman to speak in church. (ESV)

Since this appears to be such a radical digression from what Paul teaches in chapter 11, Gordon Fee, among others, has argued that verses 34–35 are a later addition, an interpolation.[2] What seems to indicate that these verses are an interpolation is that they appear in some manuscripts (the Western ones in particular) after verse 40.

However, the argument for viewing the verses as an interpolation has been refuted on textual and contextual grounds.[3] First, these verses only appear after verse 40 in the Western manuscripts. The transposition of these verses in the Western manuscripts can be traced back to a single antecedent text in Northern Italy (Niccum 1997; Wire 1990, 149–52). This, and the fact that these verses appear in all the manuscripts, undermines the argument for the verses being an interpolation. Second, Ben Witherington has shown that certain words used in these verses are used elsewhere in the chapter, such as *laleo* (speak) in verses 2, 3, 4, 5, 6, 9, 11, 13, 18, 19, 21, 23, 27, 28, 29, and 39; *sigao* (keep silent) in verses 28 and 30; *hupotasso* (submit) in verse 32; and *ekklesia* (church) in verse 28 (1988, 91).[4] Therefore, these verses should be considered to be Paul's.[5]

The Context of 14:33–35

How do we explain this apparent radical departure from what Paul has already written? From 11:2 to this point in chapter 14, Paul has been en-culturating the Corinthians on how to appropriately engage in corporate worship. Paul concludes chapter 14 with an appeal that they do everything in a dignified and orderly manner (14:40). The Corinthians apparently had carried manners of worship that were suitable in the pagan cults, but were inappropriate for a Christ-centered assembly. Also, the Corinthian culture encouraged self-assertion and status-seeking. These had worked their way into their corporate worship and had marred their communal life. Men and women had been asserting themselves through the symbolic use of their dress (11:2–16). They divided themselves on the basis of their status when they came together to share the Lord's Table (11:17–34). They demonstrated elitism in the way they exalted certain *charismata* and persons above others (12:1–30). They had overemphasized speaking in tongues, feeling that this gift demonstrated how spiritual they were. And their misunderstanding of being spiritual influenced them into un-controllably expressing the gifts of speaking in tongues and prophecy. Witherington states that the Corinthians had been following a mantic model of spiritual inspiration. They could not contain themselves when they felt inspired, so when the inspiration hit they blurted out whatever came to mind (1988, 93).

In this context of division and disorder, Paul tries to turn the Corinthians' motivation for expressing the gifts away from themselves toward loving and caring for one another (12:31–13:13). Paul teaches them that the verbal gifts of tongues and prophecy are given by God in order to encourage and strengthen one another (14:1–19). In verses 20–23 Paul becomes quite strong in his attempt to release the Corinthians from their fixation on the gift of tongues. In verses 20–22 Paul tells them not to be like children and to think maturely about the gift. He adapts a quote from Isaiah 28:11 and writes that when Israel would not listen to God, God punished them by sending them the Assyrians, people who spoke in a foreign tongue. So then, tongues are a sign for the rebellious, not believers. In this manner Paul sarcastically marginalizes the gift that the Corinthians have exalted as a sign of being spiritual.[6] In verse 23 he admonishes them again by writing that if an unbeliever came in to their meeting and they all were speaking in tongues, the unbeliever would think that they were mad.

As Paul enculturates the believers on how to corporately worship in chapter 14, he is very inclusive. In verses 24–25 he proceeds to teach that prophecy is the more significant gift because all can benefit by it: "But if all prophesy…" He continues in this inclusive vein in verse 26: "When you come together, each one has a hymn." Paul's expectation is that everyone will be able to participate in corporate worship. He proceeds to instruct them on how their expressions of the gifts of the Spirit can be exercised in an orderly fashion. Participants do not need to immediately blurt out their messages when they feel divinely inspired. They can exercise control over themselves and take turns uttering their messages. In verse 31 Paul reiterates this theme of inclusiveness. He uses *pantes* (all) three times, asserting that all can prophesy so that all can learn and all be encouraged.

Paul concludes by referring to the character of God as the guideline for worship: "For God is not a God of confusion but of peace" (14:33a).

The Need for Enculturation

After this Paul shifts focus, and in verses 33b–35 he charges the women to keep silent and that they should save their questions for their men at home.

Does Paul suddenly contradict his inclusiveness of everyone in the community in prophesying, speaking out in a tongue, or interpreting a message spoken in tongues?[7] It is not likely. Since enculturation is the interpretive paradigm to understand the larger section of 11:2–14:40, so it is the proper paradigm to understand this charge to the women.

Thiselton points out that the numerical majority of the Corinthian community was the urban poor and slaves (2000, 26). Few of the male members of the community would have had any formal education,[8] and fewer of the women. Women were not formally educated outside the home; only the upper echelon could afford to hire tutors to teach their girls. Therefore, almost all women acquired their knowledge through nonformal means.[9]

Since most women had no formal education and were restricted in movement, most would have had little opportunity to attend any kind of meeting outside of family-oriented functions. Female artisans did participate in some *collegia* (guilds) (Arlandson 1997, 87–89); however, the data indicate that even among the artisan class, daughters were generally trained to take care of the home, not work in the crafts (Saller 2003, 195; Bradley 1991, 108).[10] This means that most women had little or no opportunity to be enculturated in how to conduct themselves in a corporate worship event.[11]

In addition, a good portion of these women would have been between the ages of fifteen and seventeen with young children, with fairly restricted and difficult lives. Getting together regularly at the assembly provided these young women with a venue to see one another without having the responsibilities of running a household and hosting guests. They would have been positively inclined to interact with one another.[12]

Kenneth Bailey points out that, due to the multiethnic composition of Corinth and the lack of formal education among the women, a number of the women may have had difficulty understanding the Greek language (1998, 218). This would have had one of two impacts. First, it may have increased some of the women's desire to understand what was happening in the meeting, and their interaction would have caused even more chaos as they sought clarification (Keener 1992, 81–85). Second, other women may have become bored and subsequently disengaged from the proceedings around them and interacted with one another. Both scenarios would have only added to the bedlam of the already-chaotic Corinthian assembly (Bailey 2011, 412–415).

In contrast, the males who had received formal education would have understood how to interact in a group setting. They would have intuitively understood Paul's injunctions on uttering their prophecies and then letting them be evaluated by other members of the assembly. Students were expected to openly evaluate what they heard and read with their teachers in school (Osiek and Balch 1997, 158). Male artisans would have belonged to their various guilds and attended those meetings. Third, there were also immigrant associations to which some of the men may have belonged (Meeks 2001, 131). Ernest Best points out that these "groups held regular meetings which members were expected to attend and their behaviour when they met for either business or social pleasure was controlled; disruptive conduct was not permitted; those who offended might be fined or in some cases expelled" (1998, 85). This exposure exposed men in how to conduct oneself in a meeting.

Jews who had attended synagogues would have been enculturated and would have intuitively known how to act in times of corporate worship. However, Gentiles who had not attended a synagogue may not have had the enculturation necessary to understand how to conduct themselves in a believing assembly. The issues that Paul addresses in 11:2–34 demonstrate that even the wealthy men of the Corinthian church did not know how to appropriately conduct themselves in a corporate worship setting.

In summary, Paul does not exclude anyone from participating in the meeting. All are free to pray and prophesy or bring a hymn, revelation, or teaching. He is seeking to minimize the distracting clamor of so many verbal events happening at once. The women had no training in how to properly participate in corporate worship, and it appears few did. The assembly was interacting in ways that created bedlam. Paul had dealt with the explosive nature of tongues and prophecy within the Corinthian church, and in these verses he addresses the interaction of the women.

The Nature of the Interaction

This context of the lack of enculturation helps to explain why Paul charges the women to be silent and to ask their men at home if they want to learn anything. As to the nature of the women's interaction, Paul's use of the conditional "if" in verse 35 indicates that learning-oriented[13] and non-learning-oriented interaction was taking place. To resolve this problem, Paul writes, "If there is anything they desire to know, let them ask their husbands at home. For it is shameful for a woman to speak in church."

Terence Paige builds upon the referent to shame in describing the nature of the women's interaction. Paige asserts that in the light of the cultural context in Corinth, Paul addresses the married women because he is concerned about the women's private conversations with nonrelated men. Such intergender interaction would have crossed the lines of propriety and would have ignited jealousy in their spouses. To rectify this problem, Paul exhorts the women to restrict their interaction to their husbands at home (2002).

Paige's reconstruction is unlikely. The average woman in the large power distance Greco-Roman society was probably not going to disregard a boundary of sexual propriety that had been instilled in her since birth, especially in a context of high uncertainty.

The Greco-Roman societies were agrarian societies.[14] George Foster has pointed out that one of the fundamental assumptions of an agrarian society is that people lack control over the circumstances of their lives. This results in a driving need to create stability; the means to create that stability is through one's relationships (1967b, 8–9). Lawrence Rosen describes how this looks in a contemporary context:

> It is a characteristic feature of North African social life that it is one's relationships with others that define the person and that these networks of attachment constitute, as it were, the molecular units from which society itself is built. Moreover, each of these webs of relationship…is inherently open-ended, subject to the capacity of

individuals to create networks…within which each person fashions that structure of mutual indebtedness by which he or she will be more or less secured in a world fraught with the potential for chaotic disintegration…. In a sense, then, what is at work is a "great game," a constant series of moves aimed at securing oneself in an uncertain world. (2002, xii)

Where uncertainty is the norm, the weak in status desperately need the support of the strong. In the insecure Greco-Roman world, the average wife would have been slow to undermine her husband's support.

In this light, a young wife would have been very cautious about inciting her husband's jealousy. John Chrysostom points out how intolerable a woman's life would have become if her husband became jealous of her. Her position would have been worse than that of the slaves in the house, for the servants would have taken advantage of her weakened position in her relationship with her husband (1983, 52.1–8).[15]

Witherington asserts that Paul could not be referring to the free interaction of the women, because every other time the verb "to speak" is used in this chapter it is used in the sense of "inspired speech" (1988, 99; see Barrett 1968, 332). Working from the context of verse 29 where the prophets are discerning one another's utterances, Witherington suggests that Paul is correcting those wives who are engaging in "uninspired speech,"[16] disrespectfully questioning the value and content of the spoken prophetic words during the times of weighing and discerning what was prophesied (1988, 103). Fiorenza describes it this way: "Wives had dared to question other women's husbands or point out some mistakes of their own during the congregational interpreting of the Scriptures and of prophecy. Such behavior was against all traditional custom and law" (1983, 232).

Thus some scholars assert that Paul sought to restrict the disrespectful questioning of the wives in the discernment process.[17] However, in the uncertain, large power distance Greco-Roman world, the average woman would not have been inclined to verbally challenge or disrespect her husband in the public sphere. Plutarch, in his *Advice to the Bride and Groom*, acknowledges that contentious communication did occur between spouses, but it generally happened in private—in the bedchamber (Plutarchus 1998, 39). Juvenal uses this common experience as fuel for his satire: "The bed with a bride in it is always full of disputes and mutual recriminations. Not much sleep there. That's when she's terrible to her husband, that's when she's worse than a tigress who's lost her cubs" (Juvenalis 2004, Satire 6:268–69).[18]

In light of the combined impact of large power distance and high uncertainty on spousal interaction in the public sphere, it is more likely that Paul was addressing the disruptive interaction of the primarily poor and slave women who had never been enculturated in how to conduct themselves in a group setting outside of family-oriented functions. Some may have been spontaneously asking one another questions about the proceedings, trying to understand what was happening, while others may have just disengaged from the meeting and freely interacted with one another.[19] Paul's point is that the sacred event of corporate worship is not the place for disruptions or to carry out private conversations.[20]

This reconstruction distinguishes between the proper participation of the women, their praying and prophesying, and the kinds of interaction that would have been detrimental for the order of the assembly and the spiritual growth of the women. Women were free to do the former, restricted from the latter.

Submission and the Law

In 1 Corinthians 14:34 Paul follows his charge of the women being silent with the charge: "but should be in submission, as even the Law also says" (ESV).

This charge to be submissive has been understood to mean that the women needed to submit to their husbands due to Genesis 3:16's declaration of the woman's subordination to her husband (Bruce 1971, 136).[21] While acknowledging that subordination as the teaching of the creation account, D. A. Carson states:

> By this clause, Paul is probably not referring to Gen. 3:16, as many suggest, but to the creation order in Genesis 2:20b–24…. Paul understands from this creation order that the woman is to be subject to the man—or at least the wife is to be subject to the husband. (1991, 152)

Carson assumes Paul is referring to Genesis 2 as he refers to the Law;[22] however, Paul does not ask the women to submit to their husbands.[23] In fact, Paul does not provide an object to the verb (Jervis 1995, 66). Husbands are not mentioned till the independent clause of the next cognitive unit.[24]

With regard to the verb "to be submissive," Thiselton states that the verb is used in verse 32 to refer to self-control and controlled speech (2000, 1153).[25] Therefore in this verse Paul asks women to be self-controlled and "keep to their ordered place" (ibid., 1155).[26]

Paul's reference to the Law is probably a reference to the Pentateuch as a whole.[27] The Pentateuch begins with God responding in an orderly way to the *tohu* (formlessness) and *bohu* (emptiness) of Genesis 1:2. Also, Yahweh organizes the nation of Israel by giving the regulations that governed the cult as well as the daily life of the community.[28]

Paul's appeal to silence and submission is to create an orderly assembly that will enable the Corinthians to edify and build up one another as they come together to worship.[29] Paul has asked the speakers of tongues to be quiet, and he has asked the prophets to be silent while another prophesies. Here he speaks to the women, who were likely from the lower economic strata, who had been interacting too freely for everyone's good.

An Appeal to Shame

Paul concludes this brief charge to the women with an appeal to shame in 14:35: "For it is shameful for a woman to speak in church" (ESV).

Paul's appeal to shame is a strong one.[30] However, the broader context might explain why. First, the women's interaction had to have caused a significant ruckus for Paul to have addressed the problem in the first place. Second, Paul has been quite sharp in his dealings with other problems that were occurring among the Corinthians (see 3:15–21; 4:18–20; 11:22).[31] In this same manner, Paul is quite strong with the rest of the congregation in 14:36–38:[32]

> Or was it from you that the word of God came? Or are you the only ones it has reached? If anyone thinks that he is a prophet, or spiritual, he should acknowledge that the things I am writing to you are a command of the Lord. If anyone does not recognize this, he is not recognized. (ESV)

Therefore, Paul's appeal to shame does not necessarily indicate that the behavior was disrespectful or violating moral codes. It does indicate that the behavior was excessive, violated what was considered proper and orderly behavior, and needed correction. Paul's sharp rebuke may indicate that some Corinthian leaders had tried to correct these women and they had been slow to respond to local correction. Wanting the church to be spared from being laughed at by those who come to visit, Paul appeals to the value of shame, alerting the women to the fact that their noncompliance to his directive will negatively impact the reputation of the believing community in the broader social context of Corinth.

Conclusion

1 Corinthians 14:33–35 comes at the end of a lengthy section (11:2–14:40) in which Paul has been enculturating the Corinthian believers in proper and orderly engagement in corporate worship. In the pursuit of spiritual gifts, some of the Corinthians have forgotten how important the others are in their community. The spirituality of some of the socially elite has degenerated into self-preoccupation and self-promotion. In 11:2 Paul begins to correct these problems, demonstrating that true spirituality is other-focused.

In chapter 14 Paul emphasizes that everyone is expected to participate in the corporate worship events. However, the meeting is to be conducted in an orderly and fitting way so that everyone can benefit from the proceedings. Paul requires that the participants control their spiritual speech events so that others can participate by introducing songs, praying, interpreting messages that come in the form of tongues, and prophesying. Paul notes that the Spirit does not override people's personalities and compel them to utter tongues or prophecies; each person is expected to exercise control over their behavior.

Subsequently, in 14:33–35 Paul requires that those women who are talking among themselves control their unrestricted interaction in the meeting. Their interaction is disrupting the meeting. If these women feel a need to ask questions to understand what is going on during the meeting, they are directed to ask their men at home. Also, they are not free to disengage from the meeting and interact among themselves. The worship event is to be understood as a corporate one, open to the orderly participation of everyone, even if that participation is to listen.

Paul charges the women to submit, but he does not include an object with the verb. Therefore, since Paul is concerned about order, it makes sense that Paul expects the women to submit to the principle of order.

It may have been that some of the Corinthian leadership had previously asked the women to submit to this rule of order, but the women were not abiding by their instruction. This may be why Paul is as strong with them as he is with others in the letter. Paul also appeals to shame to let the women know that their disruptive behavior could negatively impact the reputation of the believing community in Corinth. Thus this passage was a meaningful, culturally connected way to gain their attention and encourage them to cease their disruptive behavior.

---

1   I assign verse 36 to Paul's concluding remarks, following Horsley (1998, 189) and the translators of the ESV.

2   Fee strongly argues that this is an interpolation on the basis of transcriptual probability (primarily) and internal incohesiveness (secondarily). Most texts place these verses after 33a; however, the Western texts place them after verse 40. This discrepancy suggests to Fee that it is an emendation. With regard to the internal evidence, Fee asserts that the material is internally inconsistent with what Paul teaches in chapter 11, allowing women to pray and prophesy. Also, the verses disrupt the flow of Paul's thought in chapter 14. For these reasons, Fee asserts that these verses should not be considered a part of the original text (1987, 702; 1994, 272–81; see also Hays 2004, 146; Murphy-O'Connor 1996, 290). Conzelmann states, "This self-contained section upsets the context: it interrupts the theme of prophecy and spoils the flow of thought. In content, it is in contradiction to 11:2ff, where the active participation of women in the church is presupposed.... This section is accordingly to be regarded as an interpolation" (1975, 246).

3   Thiselton is quite strong on how the vocabulary of 34–35 parallels vocabulary from the preceding section, demonstrating internal consistency (2000, 1152; see also Witherington 1988, 91).

4   See also Thiselton (2000, 1152).

5   Talbert takes the view that verses 34–35 are a Corinthian assertion (as 7:1b was a Corinthian assertion) and verse 36 is Paul's response (2002, 114). Keener refutes this position and concludes, "What ultimately leaves this explanation most unconvincing is that Paul's citations of the Corinthian positions elsewhere are at least partly affirmed, though seriously qualified" (1992, 76). See Witherington's refutation of a similar position to Talbert's taken by D. W. Odell-Scott (1988, 98). See also Jervis' refutation that this is an interpolation (1995, 52–59).

6   With regard to tongues and this disciplinary action by the hands of the Assyrians, see Bruce (1971, 132–33).

7   This is in contrast to Walter Maier, who asserts that Paul is restricting women from speaking in tongues and prophesying (1991, 86). See also Holmyard (1997).

8   Witherington states that, at most, between 10 and 20 percent of the population could read in Paul's time, with Jews having a higher literacy rate than the other peoples (1998, 92).

9   The fact that women did acquire and use their nonformal learning is evidenced by the fact that women did work in family businesses, and even operated businesses on their own (Saller 2003, 193–94).

10   However, data from Egyptian censuses indicate that children of both sexes are registered as weavers (Bradley 1991, 120).

11   Kenneth Bailey is one of the few scholars who seem to see the significance of this lack of enculturation among the women. This is because he has experienced it firsthand (1998). Having experienced it as well, I can see the value behind Bailey's position. It appears to me that Western scholars are not aware of how important enculturation is in knowing how to act in whatever context one finds oneself. Evelyn Hatch writes of the "scripts" that we have embedded within our minds that inform us of how to carry out everyday interactions (1992, 85). For example, simply purchasing items at a store requires a significant process of enculturation. In the US, a highly contextual language is used (e.g., "cash or plastic," "credit or debit," "swipe your card," etc.), and special behaviors are required. Having lived overseas for many years, I have become acutely aware of how cultural insiders take for granted issues related to enculturation. John Chrysostom described the impact of the lack of enculturation as it appeared in his church in Antioch: "'And if they will learn anything, let them ask their husbands at home.' Then indeed the women, from such teaching, kept silence; but now there is apt to be great noise among them, much clamor and talking, and nowhere so much as in this place. They may all be seen here talking more than in the market, or at the bath. For, as if they came hither for recreation, they are all engaged in conversing upon unprofitable subjects. Thus, all is confusion" (1956, 435). Chrysostom does not demonstrate much understanding or compassion for the women's situation and so he denigrates their behavior.

12   When reconstructing the context in this way, I am not resurrecting the misogynistic stereotype of women as "chatterboxes." There were valid social reasons for the women to talk to each other, to which I draw

the receptor's attention. When people are deprived of meaningful social interaction outside their own houses or compounds, it is just normal to want to interact when they get the chance.

13 L. Ann Jervis states that this was learning-oriented communication (1995, 60).

14 In the 1960s and 1970s agrarian societies were referred to as "peasant societies." Hiebert and Meneses refer to them in this fashion (1995, 185–232). In reference to the Greco-Roman world, Malina labels the first century, Greco-Roman agrarian societies as "ruralized societies" (2001, 81–82).

15 Chrysostom writes, "Then do the servants and the handmaids treat her more insolently than her husband. This class...when it sees its masters quarrelling with each other, it uses that discord as a fine pretext for its own abusive conduct. For then it is possible for servants to invent and fabricate as much as they want completely unafraid, and in this way do they increase the atmosphere with their slander. For the soul once afflicted with this miserable disease easily believes everything.... From then on the wife is compelled to fear and tremble no less before those living with her" (1983, 52.4–5).

16 Excluding free interaction from the implication of "uninspired speech" appears rather arbitrary.

17 Ellis agrees that this was a situation where husbands were involved in prophesying and the wives were involved in testing the husbands' prophecies. This caused shame as the wives were breaking the rules of respect and propriety (1981, 218). See also Bruce (1971, 136) and Thiselton (2000, 1158). D. A. Carson also concurs but adds that Paul did not want women engaged at all in the process of discerning and weighing the prophesies (1991, 151–53). L. Ann Jervis states that the "context argues against understanding the speaking as glossolalia, or teaching.... This fact has led several interpreters to conclude that the behavior Paul is censuring is that of the discerning of prophecy. Yet Paul uses the word ἐπερωτάω [eperotao] here, rather than διακρίνω [diakrino], the word he uses when discussing the weighing of prophecy." Jervis concludes by saying that it "is best to understand Paul censuring a type of speaking which he regards as unspiritual and uninspired" (1995, 60–61).

18 This is not to say that no woman would ever disrespect her husband in public. The issue is one of degree and context. In *Satire 6*, Juvenal

mocks the wife who shows off her knowledge before her guests at the dinner table, much to her guests' chagrin, and criticizes her husband's grammatical mistakes. Poking fun at a husband's grammatical peculiarities is as close as Juvenal gets to having an educated, aristocratic wife verbally disrespect her husband in public (Juvenalis 2004, Satire 6:456). Plutarch acknowledges that a wife might air her "recriminations and disagreements in the presence of others." He labels such behavior as a disgrace, which indicates what most people must have thought about it. By referring to recriminations and disagreements, Plutarch indicates that the context for such words is one of unresolved conflict in the marriage relationship (Plutarchus 1998, 2.Advice to the Bride and Groom.13). This is not the context of 1 Corinthians 14.

19 Harold Holmyard asserts that 1 Corinthians 11:2–16 refers to women praying and prophesying in nonchurch settings and this context refers to women speaking in church settings. Therefore, women are supposed to not speak at all in any church setting (1997). However, this is not possible as the section on corporate worship begins with 11:2. It is also not possible because of Paul's repeated inclusiveness in 14:26–31.

20 Stephen Barton recognizes this distinction between sacred and profane spaces in this discourse. He suggests that verses 33b–35 are a "non-Pauline paraenesis…which has been added by Paul in a marginal note at 14.33a because of its appropriateness to his express concern with the regulation of verbal noise in church and with the role of wives" (1986, 229). It is true that Paul is concerned about verbal noise. However, the suggestion that he is concerned about the role of wives adds a pejorative dimension to the context. In that pejorative light, Barton suggests that authority, "expressed in terms of gender and sex-roles, is one of the issues at stake—and this is always a factor in boundary definition and the construction of a social world" (ibid, 231). The problem with Barton's conclusion is that he does not understand the context properly. There seems to be a consistent lack of understanding in the scholastic reflections about the impact the lack of enculturation has on behavior. This appears to have caused assumptions to rise that there is a power struggle taking place between the women and the men as they evaluate prophecies. In this vein, Barton proceeds to show that male domination was the typical format in the public gatherings that took place in private space, and this influenced Paul. The problem with making such parallels is that, as Barton so clearly recognizes in another article, Paul in 1 Corinthians is seeking to create a new, alternative society that functions by different

rules (1997, 10–12). Domination of any kind is antithetical to the character that Paul exemplifies.

21 Earle Ellis takes this position: "The reference to the law is in all likelihood an allusion to Gen. 3:16, which stipulates the wife's subordination to her husband" (1981, 217).

22 Raymond Collins concurs that Paul is referring to women being submissive to their husbands (1999, 521).

23 This is in contrast to Witherington, who says that "Paul is telling the women to be subordinate to their own ἀνήρ [aner]" (1988, 101). Fiorenza notes that "the text does not say that wives should subordinate themselves either to the community leadership or to their husbands. It asks simply that they keep quiet and remain subdued in the assembly of the community" (1983, 232).

24 Beattie points out that this charge to be submissive is part of a chiastic structure "in which the central prohibition on women's speech is flanked by two sources of authority, and proper submission is equated with silence." Beattie presents the chiastic structure in this way:

A. As in all the churches of the saints,
B. let the women be silent in the churches;
C. for it is not permitted to them to speak,
B'. but let them be in submission,
A'. as the law also says (2005, 55).

This structure demonstrates that the husbands are not part of this cognitive unit but part of the next one.

25 To clarify his position, Thiselton argues that Paul addresses the disruptions the women cause during the discerning and sifting period as the prophets judge the content of the prophecies (2000, 1156).

26 Carson objects to this notion of the women's subjection to the principle of order. He states, "Equally unlikely is the view of Kähler, to the effect that the subordination Paul had in mind is not of women to men, but of women to the order of worship he is establishing. But we must ponder why women are singled out. Do not men also have to submit to the ecclesiastical structures Paul is setting forth? Moreover, the verb for "submit" or "subordinate" normally involves subordination of a person or persons to a person or persons, not to an order, procedure, or institution" (1991, 146). Though the word may normally involve subordination

to a person, it does not exclude the possibility that it could be to the rule of order. Carson assumes it involves subordination to husbands because of tradition, not because there is a contextual reason for it. Paul draws the women's attention to the Law, not to their husbands. This is because the problem is their disorderly speech in the meeting, not a lack of submission to their husbands.

27   F. F. Bruce says that it is a "reasonable assumption that the law is the Pentateuch" (1971, 136).

28   Thiselton writes, "The patterns of order demonstrated in divine actions of creation through differentiation and order and in the Levitical and Deuteronomic codes are integral to the Pentateuch" (2000, 1153).

29   L. Ann Jervis writes, "Given the chief concern of 1 Corinthians 14—that the expression of oral spiritual gifts be done so as to build up the church (14.12) and witness to the character of God (14.25)—it is as likely that the mysterious law to which Paul alludes underlined this concern than that it was a law about wifely submission. In fact, the larger context of the passage makes it more than reasonable to suppose that the women are to be in submission in a general way: to the cause of the good functioning of the Christian assembly. As speakers in tongues are to control the expression of their gift for the good of all (vv. 27-28) and the prophets are to submit the spirits of prophecy for the sake of peace and order in the assembly (v. 32), for the same reason the women are to be in submission in regard to their speaking" (1995, 66–67).

30   Beattie says that if Paul really is "dealing with disruptive chatter here, then the remedy he proposes seems an alarmingly strong one for a relatively mild disease" (2005, 57). She questions why only the women are dealt with here if chatter is the issue.

31   Paul's response to the Corinthians in this letter is so sharp that Murphy-O'Connor describes it as "unchristian" (1996, 282).

32   Describing Paul's sharp tone in 14:36–38, Horsley labels Paul as being blunt and threatening (1998,189). See also Wire (1990, 154).

11

Transforming Relationships in Ephesians 5:22–33

EPHESIANS 5:22–33 is part of a section that extends to 6:9 and is labeled as the *Haustafel* (household) passage. 5:22–33 is a passage that incites strong emotions in some readers. One woman told me that she simply ignored this passage because Paul was a misogynist. At first glance it appears that Paul adopted a patriarchal pattern for the conjugal relationship and sacralized it, making it the standard for all cultures across all time.[1]

What this woman in particular and other readers like her fail to realize is that Ephesians 5:22–33 reflects the content and style of 1 Corinthians 11:2–16.[2] Paul uses the same creation-redemption relational paradigm that he uses in 1 Corinthians 11:3 to construct a new model for the conjugal relationship. Though Paul still shapes the model in a hierarchical manner, which appears to be adapted to his Greco-Roman cultural context,[3] Paul radically modifies the Greco-Roman pattern by comparing the conjugal relationship to the relationship between Christ and the church.[4] Through this parallel, Paul undermines the assumptions and values behind the Greco-Roman patriarchy and the *sine manu* marriage arrangement and injects new assumptions and values into the conjugal relationship.[5]

The Context of 5:22–33

The NIV and the NRSV begin this household passage with verse 21.[6] The idea of mutual submission is encouraged in verse 21. However, there were no punctuation markers in Greek, so it is not clear if verses 22–33 are connected to verse 21.

The reason the NIV and the NRSV begin the household passage with verse 21 is that verse 21 provides the verbal sense for verse 22. There is no verb in verse 22. Verses 21 and 22 literally are: "submitting to one another in the fear of Christ, the wives to their own husbands as to the Lord." However, the word "submitting" in verse 21 happens to be the fifth participle in a series of participles that begins in verse 19 (speaking, singing, making, and giving). Therefore, verse 21 appears to be part of Paul's admonition to the community in verses 19 and 20. It appears that Ephesians 5:21 is actually part of a sub-section that begins with 5:19 and serves as a transitional verse for the sub-section that begins with verse 22.[7]

5:19–21 and 5:22–33 appear to be two sub-sections of a larger passage that begins in verse 15: "Look carefully then how you walk, not as unwise but as wise." Paul's admonition to be continually filled with the Spirit in 5:18b is the climax of his instructions that begin in 5:15. 5:19–21 and 5:22–6:9 are the outworking of this admonition to be continually filled with the Spirit. Being filled with the Spirit changes the manner in which the believing community interacts (verses 18-21), and being filled with the Spirit changes the way people live out their lives in their households. The participle "submitting" provides a seamless transition from the instructions to the community to the instructions to the households.

Seeing that the household codes of 5:22–6:9 are a sub-section of a larger passage that begins with verse 5:15 enables us to understand Paul's intent. Paul is not sacralizing the Greco-Roman nuclear household as the pattern for all households in all cultures across all of time. Paul is simply instructing the members of the Greco-Roman household, as he has just instructed the members of the community, how their relationships will appear if they are continually filled with the Spirit (5:18).

Creating a New Foundation for Marriage

Paul begins this section by encouraging the wives (or brides)[8] to be submissive to their own husbands as they are to the Lord.

It appears that with this exhortation Paul is trying to recreate the marriage paradigm in order to free it from the negative impacts of the *sine manu* marriage arrangement. In the *sine manu* marriage the wife remained under her father's authority (Hoehner 2002, 728–29). Therefore, a woman's allegiance likely remained with her family and was not transferred to her husband. A wife could be encouraged (or compelled) to divorce her husband to marry another man (Cantarella 2002, 273).[9] This is one of the factors that made marriages in the first century fairly unstable (Bradley 1991, 173; Yarbrough 1985, 63).

To rectify this instability Paul creates a new foundation for marriage. First, he does this through his use of *idiois* (own) in verse 22. This reflects Paul's usage in 1 Corinthians 7:2, where he encourages each man to have his own wife and each woman to have her own husband. In that context Paul is stressing the importance of monogamy. This usage of *idiois* (own) in 5:22 indicates that Paul is seeking to uphold the standard of monogamy.[10] Second, Paul compares the woman's submission to her husband to the woman's submission to the Lord. This comparison indicates that her submission is voluntary (Best 1998, 532; Hoehner 2002, 731).[11] This appeal to voluntary submission reflects Paul's understanding that compelling or forcing submission is antithetical to the nature of God and to the nature of the Church. Therefore, it is also antithetical within the marriage relationship.

Since the woman was not motivated by cultural standards to transfer her allegiance to her husband, Paul instructs her to voluntarily align with her husband. She is to view him as her one and only husband. Paul's comparison means by implication that the husband is committed to this standard of monogamy as well.

One factor that could have caused the wife to be reluctant to submit to her husband was the dominant (or more negatively, domineering) role husbands had in the marriage relationship. In a relationship where there is dominance, a latent struggle to minimize this dominance naturally ensues (Hofstede 2001, 98). It is human nature that if some do not have some level of ascribed power in the relationship, they are likely to resort to alternative means to get some power. Jack and Judith Balswick observe: "Women who lack power are more likely to become depressed, to give in, or to use other means of gaining influence, such as pretending to be weak and dependent or manipulating a spouse" (1995, 300). It appears that Paul's injunction to the woman to submit to her own husband was intended to remove this struggle over power from the woman's side of the relationship. If the wife were truly filled with the Spirit, then she would desist from engaging in the all-too-common human struggle over power.

Paul moves beyond an appeal for monogamy and voluntary submission and begins to lay a theological foundation for marriage.[12] Paul does this in verse 23 by using the relationship between Christ and the church as an analogy for the marriage relationship: "For the husband is the head of the wife as Christ is the head of the church, his body, and is himself its Savior" (ESV).

By conceptualizing marriage through the lens of the relationship between Christ and the church, Paul contradicts the first-century notion that marriage was simply a contractual arrangement (Lincoln 1990, 363). Marriage is intended to be monogamous and permanent because it is a visible reflection of the mystical and abiding union between Christ and the church. Since the Greek word for church (*ekklesia*) is feminine, it is perfectly suited for this usage. This abiding union is intimated by referring to the church as "his body."

With these new assumptions about marriage, and by viewing her husband as her head (*kephale*), the wife is given a solid basis to transfer her allegiance from her family to her husband. Thus, Paul in verse 24 writes: "As the church is subject to Christ, so let wives also be subject in everything to their husbands" (ESV).

Paul does not delineate how the wife's submission should appear. The phrase "in everything" appears uncompromising to the modern reader. There are three qualifications for understanding this phrase. First, Paul assumes the spouses are Christians (see Best 1998, 532). Paul does not even consider the possibility that the "wives' submission to their husbands might conflict with their submission and obedience to Christ" (Lincoln 1990, 373).[13] Therefore, Paul is presenting an idealized pattern for the marriage relationship. Second, markedly absent from the passage is the contemporary notion of romantic love. The woman is not even asked to love her husband. She is asked to submit to him and respect him (v. 33). This indicates that the Western models we employ for conceptualizing the marriage relationship are inapplicable for the Ephesian context.[14] Third, though Paul conceptualizes this hierarchy within the vertical paradigm of the Greco-Roman marriage relationship, he undermines the assumptions of the paradigm by comparing the husband to Christ as the self-sacrificing Savior. In this regard, Miletic writes:

> Although the author thinks within an androcentric frame of reference, he nonetheless radically challenges its orientation by changing the meaning of subordination and headship language. Thus while he maintains an androcentric conceptual structure, he rejects its potential for domination....The patriarchal structure remains intact (i.e., the wife is subordinate to the husband), but the dynamics within that structure are radically refocused on the wife's well-being. (1988, 116)

In the light of Christ's redemptive work, Paul creates a solid foundation for marriage, enabling the wife to transfer her loyalty to her husband. Thus, Paul describes in verses 22–24 how being filled with the Spirit would shape the wife's relationship with her husband in the first century, Greco-Roman world.

Creating a New Image of Hierarchy

Paul continues to reshape the marriage relationship as he instructs believing husbands in 5:25-32. In comparing the husband to Christ, Paul works within his cultural framework, maintaining the Greco-Roman hierarchical model of the marriage relationship. However, Paul radically changes the way this "hierarchy" is meant to function.

By comparing the husband to Christ, Paul does not provide a sacred basis by which the husband could view himself as elevated above the wife. Though Paul appears to maintain the Greco-Roman patriarchal paradigm for the conjugal relationship, resembling large power distance in the political dimension of relationships in Greco-Roman society, there is no reference to Christ being Lord in his instructions to the husbands and no mention is made of Christ ruling over the church. In these subtle ways Paul reshapes how the hierarchy in the marriage would be actualized. By being filled with the Spirit, the husband is to live a life of devoted self-sacrifice toward his wife. This parallels Paul's meaning in his usage of "Christ" in 1 Corinthians 11:3.[15]

Paul's emphasis in his instructions is to create a portrait of the husband who images Christ in Christ's self-sacrificial love to the church. Paul's command to love, which is given three times (vv. 25,28,33), reconstructs the way husbands are to use their position of power within the marriage relationship. This theme of self-sacrificial devotion reflects the theme in the creation narrative of God "being for the other" and the theme of the husband imaging God and "being for the other."

Though empowerment is not explicitly mentioned in 5:22-33, empowerment is mentioned in Ephesians 4:7-13, where Christ gives gifts to the church so that the church may be equipped to serve and come to maturity. Since the analogy to Christ and his church is clear, the seed is sown with the notion of the husband empowering the woman. Also, the notion of empowering the wife would not have been a novel idea. In the *Oeconomicus*, Ischomachus, in his discussion with Socrates, speaks of how he, as a good husband, trained and empowered his wife to carry out her duties within the house (Xenophon 1997, 7.10–43). This discussion in *Oeconomicus* is particularly relevant as it portrays some of the characteristics of a marriage at that time. The husband was older than the wife, and she lacked the experience needed in running a Greco-Roman household. The husband was expected to train and empower his wife so that she would be able to adequately carry out her duties in running the household.

However, the notion of empowerment through the comparison of the conjugal relationship with Christ and the church moves beyond the comparison with Ischomachus. In Ephesians 2:6 the church is seated with Christ in the heavenly places as a present spiritual reality. The church shares in Christ's rule and reign (1:20–22). This creates a new vision of what empowerment should mean to the husband as he seeks to empower his wife.

With regard to empowerment as a model for the conjugal relationship, Jack and Judith Balswick write:

> The empowerment model…purports that each spouse can use personal resources to move the other from a position of weakness to one of strength. Empowering is not merely one spouse yielding to the wishes of the other. It does not involve giving up one's power to empower others. Rather, *empowering is the active and intentional process of each spouse developing and affirming power in the other.* (1995, 311; italics in the original)

Paul's appeal does not reflect the mutuality in the Balswicks' description of empowerment of the other. Rather, Paul lays the responsibility of empowerment entirely on the husband. This is appropriate given the vertical nature of the Greco-Roman marriage relationship.

Finally, this is an idealized representation of marriage. Paul's purpose is not to provide the final word on marriage but to provide a theological foundation for why Christian marriage is monogamous and permanent (vv. 31,32), as well as to transform assumptions about the use of power within the conjugal relationship.

Contradicting the Assumption of the Impaired Nature

In this passage Paul contradicts the Greco-Roman assumption about the inferiority of female ontology. In verses 28–29 Paul compares the woman to the man's *soma* (body) and *sarx* (flesh). This use of "flesh" enables Paul to assert that the woman should be viewed as the husband's own flesh. By his dual use of the terms "flesh" and "body," Paul asserts that there is no ontological difference between the sexes. He reinforces this by equating the wife with the husband's very being in verse 28: "He who loves his wife loves himself."

Paul culminates and cements his recreated paradigm of the conjugal relationship and his assumption about female ontology by comparing these to the mystical and permanent union of Christ with his church. Christ became "one flesh" with his church. Paul leaves this unexplained, content to leave it in the realm of mystery. This lack of explanation appears to be a rhetorical strategy to increase the couple's awe of and respect for the marriage relationship.

Conclusion

Paul worked in the Greco-Roman context. He spoke into that context understanding how relationships would be transformed in the Greco-Roman household if the members of the household were in Christ and filled with his Spirit. In Ephesians 5:22–33 Paul describes how this transformation would be expressed in the husband-wife relationship. Paul goes beyond this and creates a theological paradigm for Christian marriage, emphasizing monogamy and permanence. The portrait of the conjugal relationship in the passage reflects the large power distance in the political dimension of relationships in Greco-Roman society. Paul apparently does not try to alter the form of that model; rather, he radically alters the assumptions behind that model.

First, Paul contradicts the assumption that the female is inherently ontologically inferior to the male. This is done by comparing the wife to the husband—to his self, to his flesh, and to his body.

Second, the passage undermines the assumption that the husband is to dominate his wife. Paul compares the role of the husband in the conjugal relationship to the role of Christ in his relationship with the church. Christ expresses his love for the church in utter devotion and self-sacrifice. There is not one hint of Christ's domination over the church, or that the church exists to serve Christ. Paul presents Christ as one who lives self-sacrificially so that the church can become perfect. In this way Paul goes beyond reducing the power distance between the husband and wife. Through the comparison to Christ and the threefold command to love, Paul creates a notion of empowerment which eliminates the ideas of domination and control. Empowerment seeks to release power and build capacity in the other, not restrict.

Paul does this while acknowledging the realities of Greco-Roman society, that the wife/bride was usually younger and much less experienced in life than the husband. The injunctions to the wife to submit to and to respect her husband demonstrate the vertical relationship that existed between the husband and wife. However, Paul's injunctions to the wife indicate a cognizance of the potential for the wife to misuse the husband's motivation for her benefit. By submitting and respecting her husband, the wife would refuse to compete or seek to usurp power in the relationship.

Finally, the passage demonstrates that Genesis 1–2 shapes Paul's paradigm for the marriage relationship. Genesis 1–2 reveals God as being for the other. This being the case, and since man is made in the image of God, the man is expected to image the Christ-God as he relates to his wife.

In addition, Paul uses the direct reference to the two becoming one flesh to highlight the intensity of the mystical union that Christ experiences with the church. This reference to Genesis 2 brings to a climax Paul's theological paradigm for Christian marriage. Marriage is to be the visible reflection of the love that Christ has for the church and the mystical, permanent union that Christ has with the church. As a person made in the image of God, the husband is to image this love and union in his relationship with his wife.

---

1   Though the early church universally accepted Paul as the author of Ephesians, New Testament scholars in the last two centuries have rigorously debated if the letter was written by someone else. The discussion has revolved around differences in language, style, and theology between Ephesians and the uncontested epistles of Paul, as well as Ephesians' close, seemingly dependent, literary relationship with Colossians (see Best 1998, 20–35; M. MacDonald 2000, 15–16; O'Brien 1999, 4–33). Harold Hoehner itemizes the position of a number of scholars on this issue from the time of Erasmus, showing the diversity of opinion (2002, 9–18). Hoehner's chart indicates that the debate is in process with no immediate hope of unanimity.

Though scholars rigorously debate its authorship, there is a solid consensus that the letter is Pauline in character. This is because the letter intimately reflects Paul's thought and is dated toward the end of Paul's life or shortly after, somewhere between AD 60 and 90. The dating is due to Ignatius' and Polycarp's references to the letter (Best 1998, 15–19; Kümmel 1975, 366) as well as possible references to it in 1 and 2 Clement (O'Brien 1999, 4; contra Best 1998, 15–16). The strength of the Pauline nature of the letter is reflected in the conclusions of Muddiman, Best, and Lincoln. Muddiman looks at the arguments for and against viewing Paul as the author and asserts that the author of Ephesians built upon a letter written by Paul (2001, 20). Best concludes that the author of Ephesians stood in the Pauline tradition while adapting and developing it (1998, 27). Finally, Lincoln asserts that the author had been a member of a Pauline "school" (1990, lxxii). Since it is part of the canon, whether by Paul or by a disciple, the letter is part of the canonical Paul's corpus.

2 For a discussion of how the author of Ephesians draws from Genesis 1–2 and 1 Corinthians 11, see Miletic (1988, 69–74).

3 Frances Young illuminates why the vertical structure was so important: "Since each household was regarded as a little state, the proper ordering of households ensured the proper ordering of society" (1994, 82). This is in contrast to Sharon Gritz, who argues that the passage places both spouses on equal footing (1991, 90).

4 The word *ekklesia* (church) is feminine and is aptly suited for this comparative purpose.

5 The conjugal hierarchy made the passage relevant for its time. Though the pericope is androcentric in character, there is no need to apologize for it. This reflects the fact that the Scripture was formulated in time and space. Just as the forms of the OT were part of the revelational process and should be respected, so too should the androcentric nature of the revelation of the NT. The primary issue for the contemporary exegete is hermeneutical, how we interpret this androcentric form within our present context (see Marshall 2005, 187).

6 The UBS divides the text by attaching verse 21 with 5:22–6:9. Contemporary scholars follow suit, building an argument for an egalitarian conjugal relationship through mutual submission. However, this is unnecessary. Paul was writing to a specific group of people at a specific time in history. Thus, the Greco-Roman hierarchical pattern for the marriage is not necessarily universal. Even if one disagrees with this premise, I shall demonstrate that the theological basis for developing a conjugal relationship which facilitates the contemporary desire for an egalitarian relationship over a hierarchical one exists within the relational paradigm of Ephesians 5:22–33.

7 Ernest Best argues for attaching verse 21 to the previous section, beginning at verse 15. He presents three reasons for this. First, the participle in verse 21 is part of the sequence of participles in verses 19–20 (speaking, singing, making, giving, and submitting). Second, verses 19–21 address communal relationships while 5:22–6:9 addresses household

relationships. Third, verse 21 highlights mutual submission in horizontal relationships while 5:22–6:9 speaks of submission in vertical relationships. Best recognizes that verse 21 serves to link verses 18–20 with the household codes of 5:22–6:9 (1998, 515–17). Though Andrew Lincoln connects verse 21 to the household codes, he sees the larger section beginning in 5:15 and his analysis suggests why 5:15-6:9 is one interconnected passage. The section that begins with verse 15 exhorts its receptors to be wise in the way that they live. In verse 18 the receptors are told to be continually filled with the Spirit. The result of being filled with the Spirit impacts the manner in which the community interacts (vv. 18–20). Being filled with the Spirit also impacts the way people live out their lives in the household (1990, 338,363). I concur with Lincoln and Best's analyses and suggest that the larger section is 5:15–6:9, while agreeing with Best that the two subsections are 5:15–21 and 5:22–6:9. Verse 21 serves as a transitional verse from the section on relationships within the community to the section on relationships within the household.

8   Best notes that it is not clear if Paul is addressing wives or brides in this passage because of the referent in verse 27 where Christ presents the church to himself (1998).

9   This problem also existed among the Kapsiki of Cameroon (Van Beek 1987, 123).

10   The double use of the reflexive pronoun *idios* in verse 28 also indicates that Paul is concerned with establishing monogamy as the rule for Christian marriage (Hoehner 2002, 747–48).

11   This is in contrast to Muddiman who writes, "The attempt to find more significance in this verse with reference to some particular quality in the church's obedience to Christ that ought to inform the submissiveness of wives is therefore mistaken. Lincoln, for example (372), suggests that the point is that it should be freely and willingly given. But in the days of arranged marriages, and when brides had scarcely reached puberty, that implication would probably be lost on the receptors" (2001, 263). Muddiman is correct that the brides would have been young and that the marriages would have been arranged. However, having an arranged marriage does not imply that the bride had no choice in the matter. Having lived in a culture where arranged marriages are the norm, I have seen how young brides often conform to the societal expectations and marry willingly. It is the natural outcome of having been enculturated in that cultural context. In addition, as the conjugal relationship developed over

time and outside pressures, especially from the wife's family, negatively impacted the relationship, Paul's instruction would have increased in significance.

12   This is in contrast to Best, who says, "The idea that marriage need not be monogamous and permanent is not contested" (1998, 561). Though Best is right that this is not addressed overtly, the point of the passage is to lay a foundation for viewing marriage as permanent and monogamous.

13   This qualification is given in Colossians 3:18: "Wives, be subject to your husbands, as is fitting in the Lord." Also, Paul does not indicate to the husband what he is to do if the wife does not submit to him (Best 1998, 532). Judging from the number of words utilized for each spouse in the passage, Paul is more concerned with the husband abusing his position in the relationship than with how the wife will act.

14   In this light, Eva Cantarella's objection to Susan Treggiari's assertion that within the Roman marriage the couple had a "strong and affectionate" personal relationship seems well-founded (2002, 272). Cantarella points out that people's marriages were significantly influenced by allegiances the spouses had outside of their conjugal relationship.

15   On how *kephale* cannot mean "authority over," see Dawes (1998, 138). In addition, Paul digresses from Plutarch's example in his *Advice to the Bride and Groom*. In that work, Plutarch directs the bulk of his instruction to the wife. In contrast, in this passage Paul uses forty-one words to instruct the wife, while he uses 116 words to the husband (Hoehner 2002, 746).

12

Restoring Harmony in 1 Timothy 2:9–15

BY REFERRING TO EVE'S DECEPTION and transgression in 1 Timothy 2:13,14, is Paul affirming the Greco-Roman assumption that the woman's nature is inferior to the male's?[1] If so, this would be a radical departure from what Paul had taught thus far, and it would be a marked digression from the teaching of the creation narrative.

Yet this is the way the passage has been interpreted. Doriani points out that some have argued that the passage affirms that women cannot teach in the church because they are more easily deceived (1995, 262; see also Lock 1924, 29). Contemporary scholars of the complementarian school have shied away from stating that women have a weaker ontology than men and instead assert that the passage states that Eve was deceived and transgressed because she did not maintain her subordinate place under her husband's leadership (see Knight 1992, 131; Moo 1991, 190; Piper and Grudem 1991, 73).

If we assume that Paul thought and acted consistently, and if we assume that the passages that we have read do not sacralize one particular cultural approach to viewing and managing sexuality but rather demonstrate how Paul applied the truths of the creation narrative and the impact of Christ's redemption upon these truths to the Corinthian and Ephesian cultural contexts, this is what we should expect to see in 1 Timothy. In this light, it appears that Paul employs the analogy of Eve not to identify the inherent inferiority of a woman's ontology or a subordinate status but to correct the misuse of social influence and power by certain wealthy women in the Ephesian congregation.[2]

Paul's Focus: Wealthy Women

In 2:9–15 Paul evidently is concerned about wealthy patronesses who exercise significant influence in the church (see Towner 2006, 196;

Witherington 2006, 217–18, 232). This is because in 2:9,10 Paul contrasts elaborate and expensive attire with godly virtue. Such ostentatious displays of elaborate hairstyles and jewelry were only possible for the wealthy. In the Greco-Roman world, the purpose of such displays was to create and enhance an elitist divide between the few rich and the rest of the society.[3] One of the characteristics of large power distance is that those higher in the hierarchy "try to look as impressive as possible" (Hofstede 2001, 43). Paul's admonition that the believing women should adorn themselves with virtue and good deeds was a corrective to this self-advancing, elitist behavior (2:10).

The expression of the women's self-aggrandizement was not limited to their elaborate attire. They seem to have been contentiously engaged in the assembly. This is indicated by the use of the words *aidos* (decency) and *sophrosune* (self-control/propriety) (2:9). Paul's bracketing the passage with *sophrosune* (2:9,15) demonstrates that acting properly is at the heart of his correction (see Towner 2006, 205–10).[4] This is because included in the range of meaning for *sophrosune* was the idea of being reserved in public. *Aidos* also carried the connotation of being reserved in public and treating others with respect (Bultmann 1983, 1:171). It appears that Paul is using these words as synonyms.

What were these wealthy women arguing about in the assembly? It is not clear if some of the women were teaching;[5] however, Paul's charge that women should learn quietly and not teach (2:11,12) indicates they were verbally engaged in the assembly. Paul's charge that they should not exercise authority over men (2:12) indicates that these wealthy women were likely engaged in a power struggle, which also suggests that their verbal engagement was contentious in manner.[6]

In the Greco-Roman patron-client world, wealth was social capital. It appears that the wealth of these women had enabled them to exercise a disproportionate amount of influence and control in the assembly.[7] It is likely that heretical teachers had come under their patronage and the women were aggressively promoting these heretical teachers and their teachings in the assembly.

What were the heretical teachings about? The teachings were likely similar to what had occurred in Corinth, marginalizing the goodness of marriage and sexuality (Towner 2006, 234; see also Mounce 2000, 146; Scholer 1990, 7–8). Added to this, it is likely that the Cynics' notion that one should have leisure time to pursue the study of philosophy in order to become virtuous had influenced the lives of these patronesses and had become a part of these teachings (see Deming 2004, xxi, 81–84).

Elsewhere in the letter, Paul argues that the women and teachers' leisure and study are producing exactly the opposite of what they have been pursuing: useless knowledge and the antithesis to godly virtue (see 1:3–7; 4:7; 5:6,13).

Paul's Method of Correction: Creative Rhetoric

Into this contentious context, Paul attempts a corrective measure. It appears that Paul analogously appeals to the creation order and the first transgression in order to warn these women. He writes, "For Adam was formed first, then Eve; and Adam was not deceived, but the woman was deceived and became a transgressor. Yet she will be saved through childbearing—if they continue in faith and love and holiness, with self-control" (2:13–15 ESV).

Paul's intention in this correction becomes clear as we follow his use of nouns and pronouns: Adam, Eve, Adam, the woman, she, they. It is impossible to follow Paul's thought without paying attention to this progression. The progression in nomenclature from *Eve* to *they* demonstrates that Paul's rhetorical strategy in referring to the first woman's deception is to create a parallel between Eve (the first woman) and these women. Paul begins with the singular *she* but then employs the plural *they* as he ends the passage. In the *she* clause Paul artistically alludes to Eve's role in salvation by producing the seed who would crush the serpent's head and bring humanity its final deliverance. The use of *she* enables him to transition from the analogous Eve to all the women (*they*) involved in promulgating the heretical teachings (Fee 1988, 74). The purpose of this analogy is to show that the teachings these women are supporting are wrong and that they are deceived. Paul is cautioning these women about misusing their wealth and influence in the church and that they should discontinue their efforts to domineer over the authorized male teachers in the assembly (see ibid., 73). In addition, through this progression in nomenclature Paul is cautioning them that, as Eve became a transgressor due to being deceived, they will also transgress if they do not accept his apostolic correction (Scholer 1990, 10).

In developing his teaching with the comparison to the deception and transgression of Eve, is Paul indicating that Eve and all women are more prone to being deceived than Adam and men? This cannot be for three reasons. First, Paul does not state that women are more prone to deception than men. It was Eve who was deceived, not all women.[8] Second, Paul could not mean women are somehow more prone to being deceived because of what we have learned from the exegesis of Genesis 1–3 and from Paul's teaching in 1 Corinthians and Ephesians. All these passages demonstrate that women are not ontologically inferior to men. Third, Paul uses the example of Eve's deception in 2 Corinthians 11:3 to assert that anyone, female or male, could be deceived.

Does Paul mean to indicate that Eve was deceived and transgressed because she did not maintain her subordinate place under her husband's leadership? This does not appear to be the case, because Paul leaves his reference to the creation order undeveloped (Fee 1988, 73–74; contra Schreiner 2005, 105–6). Paul's lack of development of the creation order stands in marked contrast to 1 Corinthians 11:2–16 and Ephesians 5:22–33. In these passages Paul purposely uses the creation-based primogeniture of Adam to shape the way the husband is to image Christ as a servant in the conjugal relationship. It is possible that Paul does not develop the creation order theme in this passage because he is not dealing with a husband-wife issue, the parameter in which Genesis 2 constructs the notion of male primogeniture. It appears that Paul's reference to Adam simply facilitates him in developing his warning about the deception of Eve and her subsequent transgression.

Paul's Cultural Solution: Constructive Work

Paul's appeal about bearing children only makes sense when viewed in the light of the Greco-Roman sociocultural context. There were few avenues for constructive work in the society outside of the responsibilities that were integrated with marriage and family. The wealthy women may have been patronizing the false teachers because their teachings favored asceticism and demeaned marriage, enabling the wealthy women to move away from the dangers associated with bearing children as well as the responsibilities associated with family life. Their wealth combined with these teachings enabled them to misuse their freedom and pursue their own leisure and self-aggrandizement.

In verse 15 Paul counters these cultural and heretical trends against the fabric of marriage, and possibly against the bearing of children. Stating that a woman will be saved through childbirth acknowledges the inherent goodness of marriage and of childbearing. It grounds the goodness of marriage in the promise to Eve that her seed would eventually destroy the seed of the serpent. It also redirects the women away from idleness toward working constructively. Through this analogy Paul encourages these women to give up their elitism and the teachings that attack the foundations of marriage and return to propriety, at home and in the believing community.[9]

Paul is not arguing that childbearing can provide eternal salvation. Paul assumes that these women are already Christians (Fee 1988, 75–76). This assumption is implied by the word "continue" in Paul's final clause: "if they continue in faith and love and holiness, with self-control" (2:15 ESV). The salvation childbearing provides is from being deceived and falling into sin. Being married and fulfilling the responsibilities of familial and communal living will protect the women from the behaviors and teachings that will prove to be ultimately self-destructive.

Conclusion

In conclusion, 1 Timothy 2:9–15 does not indicate that women are ontologically inferior to men. Paul's appeal in verses 13–14 to the order of creation, and to the fact that Eve was deceived and transgressed, is apparently an attempt to correct a problem caused by some powerful, elite women within the congregation at Ephesus. Paul's teaching can be summarized in this way: As Eve was deceived, these wealthy women are too. As Eve transgressed, they might also if they do not heed Paul's correction.

Paul's appeal that Eve was saved by childbearing enables Paul to affirm marriage and childbearing, because Eve, as the first mother, set a chain of childbearing in motion that eventually produced the Messiah. This reference to Eve's childbearing is a rhetorical device which enables Paul to indirectly appeal to the wealthy women in Ephesus to discontinue their support for heretical teachings against marriage, as well as their misguided pursuit of leisure and knowledge which had resulted in improper, self-indulgent, self-advancing lifestyles. In this reference to childbearing Paul encourages these wealthy women to adopt constructive roles within the community. In the Greco-Roman context, the parameters for these constructive roles were generally limited to the responsibilities of the wife/mother. By adopting these roles, the wealthy women would save themselves from the negative consequences of the false teachings and the self-absorbed lifestyles that they had adopted.

Therefore this passage shows Paul making a specific and contextual application of the truths of the creation narrative to the difficult situation in the Ephesian church. Paul restricts the women from teaching and exercising authority over men because of the contentious and heretical nature of their interaction.

1   1 Timothy (as well as the other Pastoral Letters) is the center of scholastic controversy. Debate abounds over authorship, the *Sitz im Leben* (the life setting) and the implications the letter has on women in ministry: whether the letter restricts women in ministry throughout time (see Moo 1991; Schreiner 1995), or restricts women only during a specific crisis in time (see Scholer 2003; Towner 2006), or reflects a return to patriarchal social structures after Paul (see Beattie 2005; Quinn and Wacker 2000, 240). There is no way that I can do justice in reviewing the issues in this debate and keep this discussion within a reasonable length. However, it is sufficiently acknowledged among scholars that the letter is "Pauline"— even if not written by the hand of Paul—written in the last half of the first century (Dunn 2000, 781; Quinn and Wacker 2000, 19; contra R. Collins 2002, 9). Philip Towner reviews the arguments of the majority who argue for pseudonymity and concludes that even though their arguments have substance, they do not have the strength to conclude against Pauline authorship (2006, 15–84; see also Fee 1988, 1; Mounce 2000, xlvi–xlviii). Being that the scholastic dialogue is in process, I will affirm that the letter reflects Pauline thought and refer to the author as Paul. This accords with my assumption that the letters, being part of the canon, are valid expressions of the canonical Paul.

2   I will not address the implication of this passage with regard to women's roles in the church, as such a discussion is a communal task of the church and falls outside the boundaries of the purpose of this book.

3   Ostentatious dress in the Greco-Roman world maintained social distance between those with and those without power and status (Hales 2003, 29–32; see also Tacitus 1943, *Annals* 3:55). Pliny stated that women loved to display their wealth through their pearl necklaces (Plinius, *Natural History* 13.29.91–95). The clamor over the removal of the Oppian Law in 195 BC indicates how important displaying wealth was in the Greco-Roman world. One of the reasons given in the appeal for the removal of the law was that the women of the allies of the Romans could display their new wealth but the Roman women could not (Livius, *Livy* 34.7.5–6). Valerius Maximus lamented the repeal of the Oppian Law because of the pompous display of wealth that had developed among the aristocrats (2000, 9.1.3). Though some conservatives like Maximus did not like the wealthy displays of women, the majority apparently did as the law was repealed.

4   It is well accepted that the attire of the women and their behavior in the assembly violated shared standards of propriety. This is indicated by the use of the word *aidos* ("modesty" as per ESV), and by Paul bracketing the pericope with the word *sophrosune* (self-control/propriety). The question has been over what this impropriety meant. Some notable scholars have interpreted the women's ostentatious dress as being sexually alluring (see Fee 1988, 71; Scholer 1990, 9; Towner 2006, 205). It was embedded in the Greco-Roman worldview that a woman's lack of self-control would result in immorality. However, the word *aidos* included the notion of being reserved in public (Bultmann 1983, 1:171). Jerome translates *aidos* with *verecundia*, which can be translated as "modesty" (1984); however, the semantic range of *verecundia* includes "diffidence." Valerius Maximus uses *verecundia* in a diatribe against women's lack of reserve in the public sphere: "Nor should I be silent about those women whose natural condition and the modesty of the matron's robe (*verecundia stolae*) could not make them keep silent in the Forum and the courts of law" (2000, 8.3.preface). Since Paul links *aidos* with *sophrosune* it appears that the rhetoric of 2:9 indicates that Paul, in his addressing the women's attire, is primarily concerned about their elitist display of wealth and their abuse of social power due to their being contentious in the assembly. Thus, it does not appear that Paul was concerned about the women dressing in a sexually alluring manner.

5   Towner suggests that women may have been teaching (2006, 198, 232–33). The text does not overtly state that women were teaching (Grudem 2006, 162–65). However, it seems likely, because Paul's admonition that they should not teach implies that some were teaching. Whether they were teaching or not, the text indicates that women were in some way promoting the false teachings (Mounce 2000, 120).

6   Mounce argues that the word "authority" is used in the positive sense of exercising authority (2000, 128). However, the immediate context of 2:8–15 (the fact that instruction was needed implies that something was amiss) and the broader context of the occasion of the letter (correcting heresy) are negative. Therefore, it is only natural to conclude with Fee that the exercise of authority that Paul addresses in this passage has a negative sense to it (1988, 73). That the women's interaction was contentious accords with verse 8, which is the opening verse of this pericope, instructing the men to pray corporately without quarreling.

7   "Patronage was a means of putting oneself in a position of superiority and power over others" (Witherington 1995, 341). Witherington
points out that Paul's refusal to come under the patronage of some in
Corinth caused him problems with the Corinthian assembly (ibid.). In
contrast, the false teachers in Ephesus would have profited by becoming
clients of wealthy women in the church (Towner 2006, 198).

8   This is in contrast to Towner, who argues that verse 13 was a reminder to the women that they were complicit in the Fall (2006, 232).
However, Towner is reading this notion into the text, not deriving it from
the text.

9   This contextual reconstruction is reinforced by Paul's instructions
in 1 Timothy 5:4,8,10,14,16.

Part III

The Pashtuns and Paul:
Sexuality, Culture, and Transformational
Involvement

I have become all things to all people,
that by all means I might save some.
I do it all for the sake of the gospel,
that I may share with them in its blessings.

1 Cor. 9:22,23 ESV

13

Commonality and Coherence

IN THIS SECTION I SUMMARIZE and synthesize the material that we have looked at thus far. Chapter 13 synthesizes the data of the Pashtun setting, the Greco-Roman world, and the Pauline instructions. The parallels between the Pauline instructions and the Pashtun context guide Christ-centered development workers in adapting to how sexuality is viewed and managed elsewhere in the Islamic world. Chapter 14 builds on the particularity of Paul's example in his world and suggests a model for transformational engagement for the contemporary Christian worker that accepts the ways in which cultures express themselves while at the same time seeking to challenge and transform any assumptions and values that undermine the dignity of the person and transform the ways power is used in relationships.[1]

The Twenty-First-Century Pashtun Urban Context

Pashtuns are Pashtun and Muslim, which means that they engage discursively with their religion.[2] Islam influences the shape of their world, and Pashtun culture shapes the way Islam is held and expressed.

This interactive relationship between culture and religion is evidenced by the manner in which Pashtuns approach sexuality and its management. Islamic sacred writ has given parameters for gender-oriented interaction, both in the society and at home. However, Pashtuns have taken those parameters and interpreted them in ways they deem appropriate for their context. The diversity of the manners in which these parameters are expressed demonstrates their independence in interpreting the Islamic injunctions. The consistency of expression demonstrates that Islam is an integral part of Pashtun society.

Purdah: Assumptions and Values

The system of managing intergender interaction that the Pashtuns have developed in the light of Islamic writings, large power distance orientation, and traditions is called *purdah*. A collage of integrated assumptions, values, and cognitive paradigms provides the framework for the system.

A fundamental value interconnected with purdah is *hayā* (modesty). *Hayā* is a broad term that encompasses abiding by the culture's mores as well as exercising moderation in social behavior; in addition, *hayā* specifically applies to appropriate gender-oriented interaction.[3]

The manner in which Pashtuns conceptualize people and approach trust impacts the way purdah is shaped. People are conceptualized by intrinsic, bounded categories (as insiders or outsiders). This is significant because outsiders are not automatically given trust. Pashtuns operate from a pessimistically inclined, relational trust paradigm. This paradigm fluctuates from the absence of trust to mistrust, with a marked inclination toward mistrust.

This trust paradigm is shaped by four or possibly five assumptions. First, the male outsider is perceived as a potential sexual predator. This explains the compelling need for sexually oriented boundaries within the society. Males are expected to live up to certain moral standards, but it is anticipated that they will not. Therefore boundaries are vital to protect the integrity of the family and the continuity of the society. Second, both men and women are regarded as weak in resisting temptation. Third, being restricted in movement in the public realm, women have limited practical experience in relating to men. Therefore they are considered to be naive with regard to the malicious intentions of men and can be easily deceived by miscreant males. Fourth, women are ontologically inferior to men. One of the impacts of this inferiority is that women are not as intelligent as men. This makes them even more prone to being deceived. Finally, women have been traditionally understood as having a sex drive that is ten times greater than that of men.[4] This fifth assumption is in transition, losing some of its support among the educated; however, it still exercises significant influence upon the society.[5]

The assumptions that women are ontologically inferior, that men and women are weak in resisting temptation, and that males are not to be trusted are reinforced by Islamic sacred literature. The assumption that women's sex drive is greater than men's is rooted in folk understanding.[6]

The categorization of people into outsiders or insiders is not static. There is potential for movement across sets. An outsider can earn trust through an ongoing relationship with an insider. On the other hand, an insider may quickly grant an outsider trust if the outsider has significant influence, power, and prestige, which can potentially benefit the insider. However, trust among positional equals tends to be earned gradually as the relationship between the insider and outsider develops.

Thus the importance of modesty and the pessimistically inclined, relational trust paradigm and its related assumptions support the need for purdah within the society. The practice of purdah creates a sense of stability and moral order within the community.

Purdah: The Forms

Alongside these values, assumptions, and paradigms, Pashtuns have a series of cultural forms that express purdah. The first form is their division of space. Pashtuns have two distinct domains of movement for men and women—the public and the domestic.[7] Males have the right to move freely about in the public domain. Women have the right to move about in the domestic domain. Males and females encounter restrictions when they seek to move into the other's domain.

Females are granted limited access to the public sphere in times of necessity. Since women have a limited right to access the public sphere, Pashtuns have created special female space (i.e., on buses, in queues, in offices, etc.) in order to protect them. In addition, the society has created the additional boundaries of cloth and companion in order to protect the females as they enter the public domain. These boundaries are expressed in varied ways within the urban setting, depending upon how the family interacts internally among themselves and externally with their community. Education and globalization also influence the manner in which these boundaries are expressed in the urban areas.

Males encounter restrictions if they seek to enter the domestic domain. They encounter the restrictive boundaries of walls, betak, and sound. Since Pashtun women may marry cousins, which is the traditionally preferred union, postpubescent, marriageable male relatives encounter these boundaries as well.

The practice of these boundaries creates a sense of moral stability within the society. However, for traditionalists, the urban fluidity in the expression of these boundaries creates a level of cognitive dissonance. Some traditionalists have difficulty in adjusting to the diversity of expression found in the urban context.[8]

Purdah and the Conjugal Relationship

Purdah and the Pashtuns' fundamental assumptions, values, and cognitive paradigms about sexuality also impact the way in which the conjugal relationship finds expression.

Influenced by Islam, Pashtuns understand marriage to be a contractual arrangement.[9] However, even though polygyny is permissible within Islam, Peshawaris do not readily accept it.[10] A wife's brothers may threaten the brother-in-law if he considers taking a second wife.

The husband and the wife hope that they will develop *an understanding*, where they are able to accept, appreciate, and live in harmony with each other. The wife has an expectation that there will be a communicative relationship with the husband through which trust can be developed and maintained. However, this does not appear to be a primary concern for the husband. The husband's primary concern is that the wife will adjust to her new life in his house with his family. Due to the pessimistically inclined, relational trust paradigm toward women and the assumptions about their deficiencies, it is common for men to try to ensure that their wife will not do anything to shame their family.

Due to the virilocal living situation, the assumptions about women's nature, and the Pashtun trust paradigm, women need to be managed. This need dovetails with the hierarchical paradigm of male dominance and female subordination in the conjugal relationship. The Pashtuns' understanding of Islamic sacred writ sacralizes this stratification of the conjugal relationship.

Therefore a woman is expected to submit to the authority of her husband and accept the restrictions that her husband and the husband's family place upon her. The woman's submission is to be of such a nature that she is to never do something without her husband's permission. As a woman bears children and gets older, she can earn trust and gradually acquire greater freedom of movement.

The Pashtun virilocal lifestyle impacts how the management of the wife finds expression. Urban Pashtuns live in extended family units, which means that the husband's mother (and if present in the household, his sisters) wields a significant degree of power over his wife's day-to-day activities. A husband is expected to maintain his allegiance to his mother (and if present, his sisters) and keep his wife submissive to her.

Purdah: Education and Employment

Education and a growing economy are impacting the manner in which purdah is expressed in the urban setting. Some fathers are allowing their daughters to get educated and find employment in female-friendly environments. Husbands want their wives educated up to the metric level[11] or a bachelor's degree,[12] but they are reluctant to let their wives work. There is still a significant level of community pressure against married women working. However, the perceived benefit of having additional income in the household is gradually granting women more flexibility to work than they have previously had. As a result, women are working. Some jobs are deemed more acceptable than others, such as being a doctor or a nurse in a private clinic or as a teacher. It is preferred that women work in female-only contexts.

The First-Century Greco-Roman Urban Context

The first-century Greco-Roman urban societies were large power distance, stratified ones. Those higher in the social order saw themselves as either ontologically or existentially better than those lower in the social order. Men were ontologically better than women. People born free were existentially better than slaves or those who had gained their freedom. Therefore freeborn women enjoyed a higher status than freed or slave men.[13] Those with wealth were better than the poor. Those who earned their money through farming were better than merchants. The merchants (or slaves) who were able to amass a considerable amount of wealth rose positionally above many others, though this did not mean that they had social power. Properly used, their wealth could gain them influence with the few in local governments who had power. Ultimately, pedigree, land, and money meant everything in the Greco-Roman world.

Similar to the Pashtun context, the Greco-Roman urban context divided space into the *polis* (public/civil realm) and the *oikos* (household).[14] Men had free access to the public realm. Women were granted access to the public realm, but they were expected to be restrained in speech and demeanor.

Marriage in the Greco-Roman world was primarily a contractual agreement between families. It was not necessarily expected to be a permanent relationship, though the ideal woman was one who had been married to only one man. A woman with significant independent means could potentially divorce her husband. In addition, due to the *sine manu* marriage, a woman's allegiance could remain with her family after her marriage. A wife could be encouraged to terminate her marriage and marry someone else to benefit her side of the family.

The conjugal relationship was stratified, with men being dominant and women being subordinate. Most girls were married in their mid-teens, while the men were older. Girls were less educated and had little experience in running a household. Thus the husband was expected to train his wife how to run a household. The age and the bride's limited life experience encouraged the stratification of the conjugal relationship.

The assumption that women had an inferior nature to men also contributed to this stratification. Women were seen as less intelligent than men, more emotional, and irrational. Therefore a husband was expected to manage his wife. If a woman did not have a husband, she was to have a guardian to manage her.

The average wife was expected to live in harmony (*concordia*) with her husband, produce children, and maintain the household, which in Rome included slaves. Even poor families in Rome had one or two slaves in the house. In addition, aristocratic or wealthy women were expected to philanthropically use their personal wealth for the benefit of the larger community.

Due to the prevalence of subsistence-level living, the average woman's life was filled with domestic responsibilities, and she enjoyed very little liberty in movement. In contrast, a few wealthy women exercised a considerable amount of personal freedom in the public sphere. Some of these women tested the boundaries of propriety in deed and speech.

This freedom of movement and expression caused considerable consternation among the traditionalists. The women's behavior was interpreted as undermining the very foundations of society. One of the assumptions of the time was that the society depended upon everyone knowing their place in the social order and staying in that place.[15] In addition, it was assumed that women suffered from an inferior nature and needed to be properly managed by their husbands. The women's lack of compliance to social norms in the domestic and public spheres was an indication that the society was coming apart at the seams.

The Pauline Response

Paul spoke into this highly stratified, large power distance context. In harmony with the creation narrative, Paul accepted the existence of hierarchies. In particular, he worked within the Greco-Roman expression of hierarchy in the conjugal relationship. For example, Paul referred to husbands as the head (*kephale*) of their wives (1 Cor 11:3; Eph 5:23). He also enjoined wives to submit to their husbands (Eph 5:22; Col 3:18). However, Paul did not allow this conjugal, hierarchical cultural form to remain under the assumptions and values of the Greco-Roman world. He subverted the assumptions and values that governed this hierarchy by inserting an alternative set of assumptions and values. Paul's assumptions and values about sexuality were drawn from the content of the creation narrative.

Paul's Locus Classicus *on Gender: The Creation Narrative*

Genesis 1–3 appears to be the interpretive *locus classicus* for Paul on sexuality, because he refers directly or indirectly to Genesis 1–3 when speaking of gender-related issues in 1 Corinthians 11:2–16; Galatians 3:28; Ephesians 5:22–33; and 1 Timothy 2:9–15. This is supported in two other ways. First, though the Christ-Spirit event (the life of Jesus, his crucifixion, death, and resurrection, and the giving of the gift of the Spirit) radically transformed Paul's understanding of the Old Testament, his thoughts were completely rooted in these sacred texts. Paul did not quote from the OT texts to support novel and discontinuous ideas; he quoted them because he understood himself and the other people of God to be living out the narrative themes of those texts within his present day. Second, Paul understood the redemption of Christ to be the beginning of the renewal of creation. In this light, there is ample reason to view the creation narrative as the pivotal interpretive text for Paul with regard to gender.

In addition, Paul was sensitive to the prophetic function of the creation narrative with regard to sexuality, hierarchy, and power, because the narrative was written to encourage its recipients to reflect this God in whose image they were created.

God as Creator

The context in which the creation narrative was written was a large power distance context, one in which those with power and prestige felt they were ontologically or existentially better than those below them. Stratification prevailed in the societies and in the ways that sexuality was understood. Women were viewed as inferior and subordinate.

The creation narrative addresses these effects of power distance. However, the narrative does not approach these effects in a linear, systematic, propositional manner. Power distance is addressed narratively through the example of God's relationality with his creation.

The narrative offers no explanation for God. He simply appears in the story as the primary actor and is understood by what he does.[16] The implication of God's creative activity is that God is ontologically distinct from and superior to all that he makes. However, in direct contradiction to the large power distance context at the time of the writing of the narrative, God acts in ways that bring him near to and caring for his creation. God not only speaks and creates, which signifies an action which only God could do, but God also "makes," which signifies God's personal involvement in the act of fashioning (McComiskey 1980, 701). The narrative portrays God making humankind, and authorizing and releasing them to be his divine representatives on the earth. God's activity subverts the exclusive notion that political leaders are somehow existentially better than others. Also, it contradicts the notion that political leaders enjoy exclusive status as representatives of the gods. The narrative asserts that all humans are God's representatives and all share equally in the right to exercise dominion on the earth.

The second portion of the creation narrative continues to develop the theme of God's otherness and loving relation to the creation.[17] God is portrayed as actively forming the man[18] and planting a garden for him. God also pays close attention to the needs of the man, noticing the incompleteness of the man's condition—his aloneness. As a result he works to rectify this incompleteness. God shapes all the animals and presents them to the man for the man to name. In doing this God assumes the role of a servant-helper for the man. The theme of the inadequacy of man's condition recycles, because the animals are an inadequate solution to man's need for a suitable helper. God responds to this inadequacy by extracting a portion of the man's side, shaping the woman, and presenting her to the man.

The narrative does not provide any motive for all this divine activity. However, it portrays God as creating and making for the benefit of humankind in Genesis 1, and God is portrayed as acting for the benefit of the man in Genesis 2. Thus, even though God is the all-powerful regent over all the heavens and the earth, God reveals himself as the empowering servant-helper and as "being for the other" in all his creative activity.

In God's Image
Understanding God was vital for Paul because Paul recognized that humankind had been created in God's image. Variations of the theme of God's people being God's image bearers occur in his letters (Rom 8:29; 1 Cor 11:7; 2 Cor 3:18; Eph 4:22–24). In addition, Paul understood redemption in Christ and living by the Spirit as inaugurating a transformational process in the people of God so they might effectively image God in their actions.

Though the creation narrative does not explicitly define what being in God's "image" means, Genesis 1:27 makes it explicitly clear that women and men are created in God's image. The content of the narrative implies that relationality, humankind's ability to carry out God's commission as royal representatives, and freedom are all integral aspects of what it means to be in God's image.

Image: The Commission and the Seventh Day

God's commission of humanity to exercise a limited dominion over the earth involves completing tasks. To accomplish those tasks, humans will have to create hierarchies. These hierarchies are to be functional—a means to an end, not a demonstration of existential or ontological superiority. The example of God and the seventh day are meant to shape humanity's understanding of hierarchy.

Even though God is ontologically other than the creation and superior to all he has made, God draws near to the creation, actively shaping it. In addition, God authorizes creation's different spheres to have separate identities and appropriate levels of self-determination. In terms of hierarchy, God radically reduces the power distance in his regal relationship to the creation and to the human couple by his actions.

The inference, therefore, is that people are to image God in the way they relate to one another and in how they create hierarchies in order to carry out their commission. Since God is one who empowers and who acts for the benefit of the other, it is expected that they would image God and be empowering and act for the other as well.

To reinforce this understanding of decreasing the power distance within hierarchical relationships, the first section of the creation narrative concludes with the seventh day of rest, an allusion to the Sabbath. The Sabbath was a weekly reminder to humankind that any hierarchical relationships formed for the utilitarian purpose of exercising their limited dominion on the earth were functional. They were not demonstrations of existential or ontological differences. The Sabbath equalized all hierarchies, because on the seventh day all were to rest: women, men, those with more status, and those with less. The Sabbath allowed the people of God to celebrate the significance of each person by setting aside all corporate tasks and nullifying any associating hierarchies.

Image: Man and Woman as Helper

Genesis 2:4–25 further defines the meaning of imaging God. The narrative reveals God as the helper of the man. It is the narrative's assumption that the male is to image God as helper since he enjoys a position of primogeniture in the story.[19] Since the woman has a tertiary and passive role in this portion of the narrative, the narrative intentionally includes woman as being in God's image by twice identifying her as helper. This is the narrative's way of ensuring that both sexes are understood to be image bearers of God, which mirrors the narrative's purpose in Genesis 1:26,27, showing that women and men were equally made in God's image.

The narrative's focus is on the man in Genesis 2:4–25, giving the man a level of primogeniture in the conjugal relationship. Since superiority and dominance are inappropriate terms to describe God's ontological and positional difference from the creation, these terms are inappropriate to describe this primogeniture of the male. Primogeniture implies that the male is responsible to image God as helper of the woman, as being a person for her.

This understanding of the Genesis 2:4–25 account is strengthened by the narrative device of jettisoning the specificity of the temporal dimension of the narrative and making a universal appeal to all men across time and space to transfer their allegiance from their parents to their wife. This transfer of allegiance to one woman allows two distinct persons to enter into a relationship that merges them into oneness.

The transgression of God's command upsets the utopian harmony of Genesis 2:23–25. Genesis 3:16 indicates that due to the consequences of the transgression the male will no longer be inclined to image God. The task-orientated nature of God's commission along with the difficulties and pain that come with carrying out the divine commission will provide the occasion for the misuse of position and power at many levels of human relationships. The male's creational position of primogeniture will become a platform for preeminence, allowing the man's misuse of power in the conjugal relationship. Humanity's disinclination to image God and the hardships of life will occasion the stratification of human relationships. Conjugal relationships will be especially affected.

Paul and Monogamy

The creation narrative presents the conjugal relationship as a monogamous one. However, the Greco-Roman urban marriage was fairly unstable. Divorce was common. In Ephesians 5:22–33 Paul lays a theological foundation for viewing marriage as a permanent, monogamous relationship between a wife and a husband by comparing the husband-wife relationship to the relationship Christ has with the church. There is only one church (Eph 4:4), and Christ's commitment is unending.

Using the words of Genesis 2:25, the creation text that describes conjugal union, Paul solidifies his analogy by describing the union Christ
has with his church. This argument reflects Paul's appeal for monogamy
in 1 Corinthians 7:2, where he asserts that each man should have his
own wife and each woman should have her own husband. Paul mirrors
this appeal for monogamy in Ephesians 5:22, where he asserts that the
woman should submit to her own husband.

This analogy of the conjugal relationship to Christ and his church also
negates any gnostic-influenced notion that marriage and conjugal sexual
relations are somehow profane or unclean. By conceptually connecting
marriage with the Christ-church relationship, Paul creates the potential
for elevating marriage from the realm of the profane into the realm of
the sacred. The people of God are holy due to their union with Christ.
Therefore marriage can also be seen as holy, because it is a reflection of
this divine-human community of faith. This allusion to the sacredness
of marriage by conceptual connection with the holy appears first in 1
Corinthians 11:3, where Paul describes marriage as part of a cosmic hierarchy with God and Jesus.

Paul and Conjugal Hierarchy
The creation narrative demonstrates that though the man held a level of
primogeniture, this primogeniture was an opportunity for the man to image God, who was his helper. Due to the Fall, this level of primogeniture
became an occasion for dominance.

In the Greco-Roman world males were expected to exercise dominance in the conjugal relationship. The average wife was younger and
more inexperienced than her husband. Though this was not true in every
case, it was true to a significant degree. Whether this on-the-ground reality affected Paul's outlook, or whether he was working solely from his
understanding of the creation narrative, we do not know. Yet, while Paul
acknowledged the primogeniture that the male had in the creation, he
contradicted the assumption that this was to be equated with dominance.

In 1 Corinthians 11:3 Paul adapts the form of male primogeniture in
the marriage relationship by referring to the husband as the head of his
wife. Nevertheless, Paul's rejection of the notion of male dominance is
clear but subtle. He conceptualizes the conjugal relationship within a
cosmic hierarchy, including God and Jesus. Paul portrays this hierarchy
within the traditional Hellenistic triadic format; however, Paul breaks
with the traditional format. The traditional format would have been expressed in an ascending or descending order, like this:

> God is the head of Christ,
> Christ is the head of the husband,
> the husband is the head of the wife.

However, Paul begins the triadic form in the middle, stating, "The head of every man is Christ" (1 Cor 11:3). Paul not only breaks with the traditional pattern and begins the form in the middle, he also refers to Jesus as the Christ, emphasizing Christ's mediatory role as self-sacrificial Savior. Paul does not refer to Jesus by his authoritative title, Lord, or by his subordinate title, Son. This reference to Christ rather than Lord or Son reflects the intent of the creation narrative, instructing that man is to image God as a servant-helper and as "being for the other." The break with the traditional ascending or descending order and referring to "every man" is a narrative device that unequivocally stresses the man's responsibility to be a servant to his wife. In this way Paul undermines the assumed paradigm of male dominance in the conjugal relationship.

Paul employs and further develops his tactic of subversion in Ephesians 5:22–33, where he calls the man to image Christ, the servant-helper. Just as he does in 1 Corinthians 11:3, Paul compares the husband to Christ, using the same term for "head," *kephale*. His purpose is evidently to invalidate the conjugal relational paradigm of dominance and subordination by comparing the conjugal hierarchy with the Christ-church relationship.

In the Greco-Roman world, dominance implied exercising power over others, and subordination implied that the one lower in the hierarchy had less importance. Neither term accurately reflects the nature of the relationship Christ has with his church. Paul shows that the church is immensely important to Christ, not less important. In addition, Paul describes Christ as sacrificing himself for the benefit of the church. The Christ relational paradigm exemplifies him as "helper" and his "being for the other."

In conclusion, by referring to Jesus as head and Christ in 1 Corinthians 11:3 and Ephesians 5:23, by explicitly referring to Jesus' self-sacrificial example in Ephesians 5, and by referring to the creation narrative in Ephesians 5:31 and in 1 Corinthians 11:7–9,12, Paul demonstrates that the creation narrative is instrumental in forming his understanding of God, Christ, and the conjugal relationship.

In his teaching, Paul sought to transform the Greco-Roman hierarchical paradigm of the conjugal relationship. Though Paul maintained the traditional form of hierarchy within the conjugal relationship, he clearly subverted the underlying Greco-Roman assumptions about dominance and subordination in the conjugal relationship. Paul presented Christ as the true example of what it means to be a husband: a person who lives to benefit the other.

Paul and Ontology

The creation narrative demonstrates that women's and men's natures are the same; the only ontological difference between them is their sexuality. However, male dominance in the Greco-Roman world was based on the assumption that a man's nature was superior to a woman's. Paul countered this in three ways.

First, Paul clarifies in 1 Corinthians 11:12 that men and women are ontologically interconnected. The first woman came from man, but now all men are born of women. Second, in Ephesians 5:28,29 Paul compares the woman to the man's flesh and body. He stresses this comparison by use of the reflexive pronoun. Finally, Paul equates the wife to the husband's own being: "He who loves his wife loves himself" (Eph 5:28).[20] Thus there is no valid rationale for viewing women as ontologically inferior to men.

Due to this, though Paul alludes to Eve's deception in 1 Timothy 2:14, he does not make that reference to indicate that women are ontologically deficient and more prone to being deceived than men. It is part of his rhetorical strategy in developing a parallel between the Ephesian wealthy patronesses and Eve to show them that they are wrong to accept the heretical teachings that are being promulgated in Ephesus and that they should respond to his apostolic correction.

Paul and Power

The creation account in Genesis 2 concludes with the man completely aligned with his wife and the two becoming one flesh. This denotes that any primogeniture that the man had was subsumed into oneness, negating any notion of a struggle for power in the relationship. As Paul contradicts the notions of dominance and ontological superiority in Ephesians 5:22–33, he also contradicts the traditional patterns about the struggle over power in this relationship.

At first glance it may not appear this way. In the Ephesians 5 passage, Paul follows the traditional, hierarchical marriage form in a rather uncompromising manner by instructing the wife to submit to her husband in everything. However, Paul's strategy is to transform the traditional, large power distance structure and the inherent struggle over power in the marriage relationship. This emerges from his conceptualizing the conjugal relationship within the paradigm of redemption. This is similar to the manner in which Paul conceptualizes the conjugal relationship in 1 Corinthians 11:3.

By comparing the husband-wife relationship to the Christ-church relationship in Ephesians 5, Paul asserts that marriage is to be a permanent and monogamous relationship since it is the visible reflection of the mystical and abiding union between Christ and the church.[21] For this reason the wife no longer needs to be primarily aligned with her family for her stability. Her husband is to completely devote himself to her as Christ is devoted to the church. The wife, therefore, is to detach her allegiance from her family and fully commit herself to her husband as the church is fully committed to Christ. Also, it is a recognized pattern in relationships that the weaker in the relationship can be tempted to resort to manipulation and deception in order to achieve the upper hand.[22] Paul's exhortation that the wife submit in everything recognizes the potential for a struggle over power from the wife's side and seeks to eliminate this from the conjugal relationship.[23]

By conceptualizing the marriage relationship within the framework of Christ's relationship to the church, Paul gives no room for the notion that the husband has a right to dominate his wife. Christ is not presented as using power to control the church so it becomes perfect; rather, Christ is portrayed as self-sacrificially doing everything possible in order to perfect the church. Jesus' self-sacrificial role is seen in Ephesians 4:7–16, where the relationship Christ has with his church is described as one of empowerment so that the church may grow to maturity.

The passage of Ephesians 5:22–33 is complemented by 1 Corinthians 7:1–11. The Corinthian passage also challenges the notion of male dominance and female subordination in three specific ways. First, the decision-making process regarding sexual activity is squarely placed in the hands of both husband and wife. Second, though the power over the woman's body is transferred to the husband, the power over the husband's body is transferred to the wife. Third, women are given the same authority as the men to separate from their spouse if the unbelieving spouse is not willing to stay married. Later on in chapter 7, this empowering of women is reinforced as widows are given the power to choose another husband for themselves (v. 39).

Paul also addresses the use of power in the 1 Corinthians 11:2–16 passage. In verse 10 the woman is exhorted to exercise her power and cover her head, affirming the integrity of her marriage relationship with her husband. Therefore the wife's covering of her head is an authentic demonstration of personal power among the community of faith. It also is an implicit affirmation that the woman has the authority to exercise self-determination in whom she marries.

In these ways Paul contradicts the Greco-Roman notions about the use of power in the conjugal relationship.

1 Timothy 2:9–15 deals with the problem of the misuse of power by wealthy women in the Ephesian assembly. It appears that they had been overly asserting themselves and trying to exercise dominance over men. Paul does not develop a theology of male dominance by drawing from the creation narrative and the Messianic redemptive event. This absence of theological development and the purposeful, rhetorical development of the reference to Eve in an analogous manner to the wealthy women of Ephesus indicates that Paul's intent was limited to correcting the women's abuse of wealth, status, and power.

Paul and Symbols
Paul employs the culturally sensitive model of maintaining forms while subverting and transforming assumptions and values as he tackles the symbol of the marriage relationship, the head covering, in 1 Corinthians 11:2–16. In this passage Paul exhorts the wife to cover her head.

There are three possible reasons why some women were uncovering their heads. First, due to the heightened asceticism within the Corinthian community, some women may not have wanted to indicate that they were involved in ongoing sexual relationships with their husbands. Second, in their overrealized eschatology, those who thought that they were spiritual may have wanted to indicate that their spirituality enabled them to transcend their sexuality. By seeking to indicate a transcendence of their sexuality, the women were inadvertently demeaning the female sex. Third, some women may have perceived the head covering as an indication that the woman held an inferior status to her husband. Their uncovered head indicated that they were liberated from oppressive, traditional norms.

Paul sought to correct the problems of asceticism and self-assertion while clarifying that being female was good. With regard to asceticism, in 1 Corinthians 7 Paul argues that sexuality within a monogamous marriage is good and valid in its own right. Sexual intercourse is not to be seen as an act that is performed for the purpose of procreation alone. As the creation narrative indicates, sex is good. It is a gift from God to the human couple. The first couple became one flesh and they were naked and not ashamed. In addition, sexuality, particularly femaleness, is good and something to be affirmed. To uncover one's head to demonstrate some higher form of spiritual attainment was a deception. Therefore Paul calls for maintaining the symbol of the head covering.

With regard to self-assertion, Paul insists that the women assert the integrity and validity of their marriage by covering their heads. Marriage was something that they had chosen, and they should choose to affirm it.

In demanding that the head covering remain as a symbol of marriage, Paul did not allow the demeaning assumptions behind the symbol to remain untouched. He contradicted the assumption that a woman's nature was inferior to a man's by showing that woman initially came from a man and that all men subsequently came from women. Therefore, for anyone to assert that male nature was somehow inherently better was absurd. Also, he countered the assumption that males held a position of dominance in the relationship. As has been mentioned, though Paul affirmed a conjugal hierarchy in the wife-husband relationship, the primogeniture the man had in creation resulted in a responsibility to serve, not a prerogative to be served. As the creation narrative and Ephesians 5:22–33 indicate, the cultural form of conjugal hierarchy is ultimately meant to be subsumed into oneness.

Paul and Shame

In 1 Corinthians 11:2–16; 14:33–35 Paul constructs part of his argument on the appeal to shame. Shame only has significance when the values that are violated are shared ones within a community. Paul recognized that the church was itself a community, and it also was a community within the larger social milieu. What individuals did affected their relationships within the believing community and also impacted their relationships with their broader urban community. Though it has been argued that this appeal to shame was to restrict women from full emancipation in fear of what the community might think (see M. MacDonald 1996, 145–46), this does not agree with the tenor of Paul's teaching. Paul sought to get the believing communities to behave as those redeemed and not conform to the self-destructive and community-destructive ways of the world around them—e.g., avoid stratification, arguments, jealousy (1 Cor 3:3), lawsuits (1 Cor 6:1–6), and immorality (1 Cor 6:9–20) (cf. Rom 12:1–3; Eph 4:17–24).[24] Paul's appeal to shame was based on the fact that the values he was asking the community to uphold were entirely appropriate for a believing community. That these values also were shared values within the society at large reinforced their significance.

Thus in 1 Corinthians 11:2–16 Paul argues that women should cover their heads while they pray and affirm their marriage. Marriage was good, even potentially sacred. There was no reason for women to shame their husbands by trying to show that they were not married. Also, in 1 Corinthians 14 Paul argues that order in the believing assembly is inherently good because it is a reflection of the God who likes order. The outside community shared the value of order within their meetings of the guilds and associations. Therefore it was a customary value that women should not disrupt an assembly by disconnecting from the proceedings of the meetings and engaging in their own private conversations.

Commonality

As we compare the first-century Greco-Roman urban context with the twenty-first-century Pashtun urban context, we can identify commonalities in spite of the differences. The commonalities are evident in the assumptions, the paradigms for marriage and the conjugal relationship, the categorization of life spaces into the public and domestic spheres, and the forms that express propriety and modesty.

In both contexts it is assumed that women are inferior in nature to men. Along with that assumption, the communities operate on a paradigm of male domination and female subordination in the conjugal relationship. Wives are expected to be submissive, produce children, and work primarily within the household. Husbands are expected to manage their wives.

TABLE 3 Similarities Between Urban Greco-Roman and
Pashtun Assumptions, Values, and Forms

	Urban Greco-Roman		Urban Pashtun
1.	Space was divided into public and private spheres.	1.	Space is divided into public and private spheres.
2.	The conjugal relationship was hierarchical: men were dominant and women were subordinate.	2.	The conjugal relationship is hierarchical: men are dominant and women are subordinate.
3.	Men were ontologically superior to women.	3.	Men are ontologically superior to women.
	a. Women were less intelligent.		a. Women are less intelligent.

Urban Greco-Roman		Urban Pashtun	
	b. Women were more emotional.		b. Women are more emotional.
	c. Women were more irrational.		c. Women are more irrational.
4.	Husbands were to manage their wives.	4.	Husbands are to manage their wives.
5.	Women were to have limited access to the public sphere and to show restraint when in public.	5.	Women are to have limited access to the public sphere and to show restraint when in public.
6.	Women were to wear head coverings in the public sphere.	6.	Women are to employ the boundary of cloth in the public sphere.
7.	Marriage was a consensual contract, not a permanent, monogamous relationship. Divorce was permissible.	7.	Marriage is a consensual contract. Polygyny and divorce are permissible though discouraged.
8.	One primary expectation of the wife was that she would bear children, primarily sons.	8.	One primary expectation of the wife is that she will bear sons.
9.	The family was nuclear with slaves. Wives were to manage their households.	9.	Families predominantly live virilocally, and the husband's mother manages the house. The wife manages the house after the in-laws have passed away.

In both contexts space is divided into public and domestic spheres. In both contexts the expectation is that women are to be restricted in movement and in speech in the public arenas. Though the women are restricted within the public sphere, women enjoy a significant level of movement within their private, domestic spheres.

In both contexts the women are expected to employ the boundary of cloth in the public arenas. Though the expression of the boundary of cloth in the first century was different in style than the expressions of the Pashtun women, the boundary of cloth in both contexts symbolizes modesty and propriety. In the Roman sphere, this boundary also indicated that the woman was married. This is not the case in the Pashtun sphere. All postpubescent females are required to employ some form of boundary of cloth in public.

Coherence

These commonalities in assumptions, values, paradigms, and forms provide a platform for identifying how the Pauline instructions about sexuality and its management cohere and inform life and approaches in transformational engagement in the urban Pashtun context. We now turn to these coherences. Though there may be similarities between the Greco-Roman urban world and the contemporary Pashtun urban world, there is not a one-to-one correlation between the two worlds. However, establishing a one-to-one correlation between the two contexts is unnecessary. From the Pauline instructions a model emerges that provides a framework for identifying coherences and for engagement in context.

The Pauline Model as an Interpretive Paradigm

Paul's dependence on the creation narrative to determine his fundamental values about sexuality and his retention of cultural forms provides an interpretive framework for identifying how the Pauline instructions to his communities cohere with the urban Pashtun communities.[25] Paul's example is transcultural, for it allows people in any culture to absorb biblical values and allows these values to organically shape them rather than being shaped by theological responses to other cultural contexts.

Distancing Paul from Western Theologies

One issue that arises from Paul's model stems from his adoption of cultural forms. Did Paul's advocacy of maintaining the Greco-Roman hierarchical form in the conjugal relationship establish this hierarchical form as the model for conjugal relationships for all cultures across time?

Answering this question in the Western context is problematic, because the assumptions and values in Western societies have shaped the manner in which theologians have approached the biblical texts. In interpreting these gender-oriented texts, contemporary theologians have formulated two contrasting paradigms: the complementarian and egalitarian.

Complementarians answer the question of the universal applicability of forms in the affirmative, emphasizing hierarchy and prescribing conjugal roles (Knight 1991; Piper 1991, 35–52).[26] The problem with universalizing the particularities of the first-century Greco-Roman urban marriage relationship, and from those particularities prescribing conjugal positions and roles across cultures and time, is that this universalization and prescription contradicts the tenor of the creation narrative.[27] The creation narrative does not define roles for either the husband or the wife. It does, however, define the nature of the husband's and wife's motivation within the relationship. They are both to image God by being for the other and by seeking to help and empower the other. The narrative is clear: the male's primogeniture is meant to be lost in oneness and mutuality.

The complementarian attempt to prescribe the shape of the conjugal roles ultimately narrows the independence of the couple in mutually determining their expression of what it means to be wife and husband. This freedom in mutual determination is an inherent right based upon the creation narrative.

The apparent intent of the Pauline instructions, which are based upon the creation narrative, is to provide a theological framework for conceptualizing, valuing, and affirming a monogamous marriage relationship. The Pauline texts follow the prophetic nature of the creation narrative by seeking to end the misuse of male preeminence in the conjugal relationship. The instructions provide the basis by which a couple can develop meaningful mutuality within their relationship while eliminating a struggle over power from either side.

In contradiction to the complementarians, the Pauline instructions do not provide itemized role or job descriptions for either the husband or the wife. The instructions give a couple within any given social context a theological framework by which they can create a stable monogamous relationship that releases them to seek the benefit of the other as well as the freedom to allow their individual personalities, desires, and gifting to shape how they live life together within their community and culture.

Complementarians therefore err by enshrining their perception of the Greco-Roman patriarchal paradigm as the biblical/authoritative pattern for the conjugal relationship. Their descriptions place undue emphasis on hierarchical structure and subordination and miss the prophetic dimension of the creation narrative, seeking to rehabilitate all those who are culpable for the mistreatment of wives. The Ephesians 5:22–33 discourse reflects a sensitivity to male culpability as the discourse is primarily directed toward instructing men. Thus the complementarian treatment of the texts contradicts the prophetic tenor of the creation narrative, the character of God as expressed in the narrative, and the fundamental freedom of mutual determination granted to the couple in expressing their oneness.

On the other hand, egalitarians answer the question of the universal application of forms in the negative. Egalitarians demonstrate sensitivity to the prophetic intent of the Scripture and the gender-related, inherent freedom of expression. However, their interpretation of the sacred texts reflects a strong influence of their specific cultural context. While seeking to stop the abuse of male preeminence as it has been historically manifested in the marriage relationship and society, egalitarians argue for a woman's equality and independence by denying or ignoring the presence of hierarchy in the biblical texts. The difficulty egalitarians have with hierarchy is due in part to values developed within their Western industrial and postindustrial contexts, and these values have shaped their interpretation of the texts (for a description of industrial and postindustrial societies, see Shaw and Van Engen 2003, 131–35).[28]

An example of the influence of Western cultural egalitarian values upon the reading of these texts is the TNIV's dynamic equivalent translation of 1 Corinthians 11:10, which is, "A woman ought to have authority over her own head." The implication in the translation is that the woman is an independent agent and should exercise her independence. This translation highlights the individuality of the woman rather than highlighting the relational connectedness of the woman along with the moral responsibilities embedded within these relationships. Such an implication is disconnected from Paul's recurring theme in 1 Corinthians of abiding by one's obligations within one's relationships. In 1 Corinthians 11:10 Paul is not arguing on behalf of women's independence that women can do what they want with their heads. He is arguing that women have a relational obligation to affirm their marriages. The TNIV translation reflects the tendency of Western cultures to elevate the individual over the group.

Therefore Western egalitarian theologies, like their complementarian counterparts, are culturally contingent and are not inherently transcultural.[29] The Pauline model, on the other hand, is prophetic, compelling the people of God to adopt biblical values on sexuality drawn from the creation narrative, and it is flexible for various contexts because it does not challenge cultural forms. This enables the Pauline model to be transcultural.

Paul and the Pashtun Boundaries

The Pauline model allows a people to retain their cultural forms. The implication of this is that Pashtuns can continue to practice purdah in all its various dimensions, such as the division of space into public and private spheres and the various boundaries associated with those spheres.

The expression of public boundaries within Pashtun society may be varied; however, there is a communal expectation that some expression of the boundaries be manifested. This is because the Pashtun society has constructed these boundaries to create a sense of security and social order in intergender relationships in accord with the pessimistically in-clined trust paradigm toward women and outsiders. Failure to adopt the forms is interpreted by the community as lasciviousness. The Pauline model allows for the retention of these forms in order to avoid this pe-jorative labeling.

The Pauline instruction about head covering coheres with the Pashtun context. Pashtuns employ the boundary of cloth for women as they enter the public sphere. Even within the domestic sphere, some form of cloth boundary is almost always worn, whether a *dupatta* (sheer, narrow cloth) or a small *chaddar* (sheet-like covering).

The head covering was not a neutral symbol in the Greco-Roman world. Some viewed it as a symbol of inferiority. However, Paul insisted that a wife wear her head covering when she prayed. This was because the head covering had other symbolic value within the Greco-Roman context. First, the head covering symbolized that a woman was married. By cover-ing her head while she prayed each woman affirmed that her marriage was a legitimate and holy state in the presence of the *ekklesia* (church), the angels, and God. Second, the head covering was widely acknowledged to be the symbol of propriety for a married woman, both by the *ekklesia* and by the wider community. Since the form of the head covering was so intricately interwoven with the meaning of propriety and its removal was an egregious sign, Paul argued to have the form remain in use.

Likewise, it could be asserted that the boundary of cloth for the wom-an in Peshawar is a symbol of inferiority. However, it is clearly a symbol of propriety. A woman asserts her respectability to all in the public sphere as she adopts the symbol. Therefore, wearing the head covering coheres well with the Pauline instruction. Since there are a variety of styles for head coverings in the Peshawari context, it would appear that the specific socioeconomic context of each woman should inform what style she should adopt.

The additional boundaries of sound and companion exist both to pro-tect women as they move about in the public arena and to demonstrate that the women are connected, proper, and modest. Paul's model would affirm the continued use of such forms since they communicate propri-ety and enhance the community of faith's reputation within the larger society. In addition, since the boundaries of sound and companion offer women protection as they move about in the public arena, and as these are the forms of protection that the society provides, it is only wise for men and women to adopt these boundaries in order to protect them-selves from any untoward behavior by aggressive males.

In addition, the boundaries of walls and *betak* are protective and defensive in nature. These are the result of the Pashtuns dividing their world into two separate spatial spheres. Paul lived in an environment where a similar division occurred. Though we have no passage in which Paul directly addresses this spatial separation, we can generalize from his advocacy of the utilization of forms that he would have had no problem with it.

While Paul's example demonstrates that he would have challenged the demeaning values that underlie any of these forms, he would have advocated that the forms be utilized. It is perfectly valid for a family to preserve its honor within the community and protect themselves from predatory males.

Paul and the Pashtun Conjugal Relationship

The Pashtun conjugal relationship begins with a large power distance, hierarchical model, with the potential of the power distance diminishing over time. The conjugal relationship in the Greco-Roman context operated on a similar model.

With regard to hierarchy, Paul accepted the Greco-Roman model within the conjugal relationship as a valid, organizational model because the husband was often older and more experienced than his younger wife. However, Paul modified this hierarchical model by conceptualizing the husband-wife relationship within a cosmic framework which included God, Christ, the husband, and the wife. Paul referred to the man as the head of his wife, giving the husband a "higher" position in the relationship. However, Paul conceptualized this conjugal hierarchy through creation and the redemption of Christ. Thus he rejected the operating values within the model, those of large power distance.

Paul negated the Greco-Roman assumptions, and similarly would have negated the Pashtun assumptions, that provided the rationale for the stratification of the conjugal relationship. The man is not ontologically or existentially better than the woman. The female is not less intelligent than the male, nor is the female inherently more prone to being deceived.[30] The Pashtun premise that a woman is more susceptible to being deceived by a cunning, predatorial male because her experience with men is limited may have a degree of validity. However, this would be due to limited experience, not to deficiency in nature.

Paul expected the husband to model himself after Christ. This meant that the husband's position was to be used to benefit the wife. The husband had a clear responsibility to care for his wife as he cared for himself, earnestly pursuing his wife's development and seeking to empower her in the process. This turned the "higher" position within the hierarchy to that of a servant-helper.

Pashtun virilocal living creates unique pressures for the husband as he seeks to align himself with his wife and be her servant-helper. How can he convince his mother of his loyalty to her (and possibly to his sisters) and enable her to maintain order in the household, satisfy the demand to treat equally everyone in the household, while at the same time demonstrate his unfeigned devotion to his wife? Paul does not offer any advice, as he did not encounter the problems of virilocal living. Advocating against virilocality is virtually impossible in the urban Pashtun context due to the Pashtuns' limited economic means, the cultural-relational requirements related to hospitality, and the unreliability of the infrastructures within the society. Few have the means to not live virilocally.

One Pashtun provided a solution that reflects the intention of the creation narrative while being creative for the virilocal context. He said that the husband's duty was to privately make his wife understand it was essential for him to demonstrate his loyalty to his mother while he was in his mother's presence. However, the husband, while alone with his wife, needed to make his wife confident that she had the first position in his heart.

Paul's instructions also sought to eliminate the struggle over power between the spouses. On the husband's side, the husband is not permitted to view his position as one of dominance and his wife's position as one of subservience. On the wife's side, being in a "lower" position in the hierarchy, she is not to manipulate and deceive to achieve her own ends. The wife is enjoined to submit to her husband and respect him. Enjoining the wife to submit to the husband "in everything" is not intended to enslave the wife to a domineering husband; it apparently is a rhetorical device utilized to remove the latent struggle over power that exists in large power distance relationships.

Thus coherence can be identified between Paul's instructions to the Greco-Roman urban communities and the context of the Pashtun conjugal relationship. Though Paul accepted a hierarchical model for the conjugal relationship, he did not accept the assumptions and the values that made that model operational. Though virilocal living is very different from the Greco-Roman family context, and the manner in which a husband can demonstrate his love to his wife has to find creative expression, Paul's instruction requires that a husband align himself to and support his wife. In addition, the wife is expected to affirm and respect her husband.

Conclusion

In conclusion, Paul's model does not object to the forms of purdah. Purdah is how Pashtun society defines and ensures propriety in male and female interaction. In this way purdah provides stability for the society. The boundaries of purdah also ensure that a woman is protected. However, Paul's model does not accept the fundamental values that underlie the system. The model would subvert those assumptions and values, seeking to elevate the dignity of the person and transform the way power is used in relationships.

What Paul's model demonstrates is sensitivity to context. Such sensitivity is essential. For when change is introduced into a cultural system, there are unanticipated impacts. Highlighting this, Charles Kraft writes:

> Even apparently superficial changes produce a ripple effect throughout a culture, affecting both surface and deep level structures. Extreme damage has been done by cross-cultural agents of change who, whether through ignorance or neglect, have not considered the interrelatedness of the many parts and aspects of a cultural configuration. (1996, 439)

The Pauline model lays a foundation for organic and gradual change to happen by challenging nonbiblical assumptions and values and seeking to transform them. Transformed values create a potential for positive change in the social structures. However, it cannot be assumed that change will occur. Paul Hiebert discusses the relationship between assumptions as values (he would classify them as cultural systems) and social structures (social systems). He states that "the two act as semi-autonomous systems that reinforce each other. Changes in one often, but not always, produce comparable changes in the other" (1996, 143). As Hiebert points out, a change in values does not guarantee changes in social structures. The danger when that happens is that an "unreformed social order, in time, can subvert the most fundamental cultural changes" (ibid.).

With this in mind, how then should a Christian development worker address the issue of change within Pashtun social structures? It is to this issue we now turn.

1 As I have previously mentioned, the theoretical basis for this approach is given by Shaw and Van Engen: "Exegete Scripture within its own historical grammatical and cultural context, provide a transitional hermeneutic to the circumstances, and draw out the theological principle that relates the two" (2003, 51).

2 Ronald Lukens-Bull provides a helpful overview of how this discursive relationship between Islam and local cultures has been described and how it complicates formulating a coherent definition of Islam (2007).

3 Though modesty is a fundamental value that includes both sexes, a double standard exists within the culture. Males enjoy a certain amount of flexibility in overtly violating these codes without dishonoring themselves.

4 With regard to the woman's sex drive, Charles Lindholm states, "It is believed that the rigid seclusion of women is enjoined in the Koran and that the licentious nature of women (who are seen as being ten times as passionate sexually as men) would compel them to cuckold their husbands were the women not kept under close guard" (1982, 218–19).

5 When a Pashtun friend of mine realized his wife did not demonstrate this heightened level of desire, he asked her to go to the doctor and get herself fixed.

6 An Afghan scholar, Zia Nodrat, now deceased, informed me that this assumption developed from ancient Greek science. The Greeks had discovered that a woman's orgasm was greater than a man's. Therefore it became conventional wisdom that a woman's sex drive was greater than a man's.

7 There is one caveat. This division of space becomes operable when individuals near puberty. This division does not exist for small children.

8 Three examples demonstrate the difficulty Pashtun and also Pakistani traditionalists have with the diversity of expression in the Khyber-Pakhtunkhwa province and throughout Pakistan. The first example was in an ESL class in Peshawar with men in their early twenties. I asked the students what they considered proper purdah to be. Some students considered some of the local expressions as well as those in Lahore and Karachi not to be valid expressions of "true" purdah. As we talked about the variety in expression, one student spoke up and said that we should discontinue the discussion because it was too contentious. The second example is the assassination of Zill-e-Huma Usman, the late minister of social welfare of the Punjab province, on February 20, 2007. She was murdered at a public event by Muhammad Sarwar, who considered her attire and position in the government un-Islamic (*The News International* 2007). After the murder of Zill-e-Huma, some Pashtun traditionalists threatened a principal of a girl's school in Mardan (a city close to Peshawar) that the school would be bombed if the students and teachers did not start wearing veils and *burqas* (Rahman 2007).

9 The conjugal relationship is not envisioned to be a reflection of the divine character as it is in Christianity.

10 Of all the Peshawaris that I had contact with during my field research, only one was planning on taking a second wife. However, this man was secretly marrying the second wife, because it would cause too many problems if the first wife found out about it. The plan was that the man would regularly visit his second wife, but never reside with her. The woman who was to become the second wife had actually gone after the man and encouraged him to marry her. She was willing to accept the limitations of this arrangement because the advantages of having a husband far outweighed the fact that he could not live with her. She needed a husband and children in order to avoid the shame of being single and to avoid being sexually harassed.

11 The US equivalent is the tenth grade.

12 The US equivalent is an AA degree.

13 It is possible that Luke lists Priscilla first before Aquila in Acts because she was freeborn and he was a freedman (see Moody 1995, 95–96).

14 For an acknowledgement of these gender-oriented realms in the Greco-Roman world, see Elliott (2000, 505), M. MacDonald (1996, 30–41), and Stegemann and Stegemann (1999, 364–73).

15 Knowing one's place and keeping in it is what keeps order in large power distance contexts (Hofstede 2001, 98).

16 This is the thesis of Colin Gunton's book *Act and Being* (2003).

17 I derive these terms, rather than use "transcendence" or "immanence," from Colin Gunton (1997).

18   It has been argued that this first "man" was androgynous, and that sexuality did not begin till the forming of the woman. This is untenable for two reasons. First, I have shown that the Hebrew text does not support this notion. Second, the Hellenists who believed in this notion of androgyny perceived the primal androgyne to be male, not a blend of maleness and femaleness. Therefore, the notion of the primal androgyne fundamentally demeaned femaleness.

19   As I have shown in the research, some contemporary scholars object to seeing primogeniture in the second section of the creation narrative. They argue that Genesis 1 shows that men and women are equal, and the Genesis 2:2–25 pericope has to be interpreted in the light of the equality shown in Genesis 1. Their objections raise a significant issue that is further developed by feminist theologians. Feminist theologians assert that this primogeniture that the male receives in the creation narrative sacralizes male dominance over women. History adds fuel to their argument, because the text has been used in this manner. These theologians assert that male dominance is given additional sacred sanction by the Pauline Epistles. In response, one of the functions of Genesis was to provide an understanding of why the world of the Hebrews was the way it was. The world was predominantly male dominated and treated women in a demeaning fashion. The narrative explains why this is the case. It is not the text's fault that the world has not significantly changed. Even though the contemporary feminist movement has been very active in Western countries for over thirty years, Western countries are still characteristically male dominated. Many, if not most, of the world's contexts, whether patriarchal or matriarchal, are male dominated. There have been exceptions, such as the Iroquois nations (L. Klein 2004, 77–79). Male dominance, though not a completely universal paradigm for all cultures, is the dominant human paradigm. The purpose of the creation narrative is to rectify this endemic problem. The creation narrative not only addresses the excesses caused by male dominance, but also the abuses of position and power. It is our responsibility to allow the sacred text to instruct us how to properly conceptualize male primogeniture, hierarchy, and power.

20   As we have seen, 1 Timothy 2:13–15 does not declare that a woman is intellectually inferior to a man (i.e., more easily deceived than a man). The fundamental issue was that Paul was addressing a problem in the Ephesian context, where certain elite women were involved in erroneous

teachings. The teachings were going to be detrimental for the women as well as the church. Therefore Paul rhetorically uses the example of Eve to show that these elite women are also deceived. Should they not heed his correction, they will also end up transgressing as Eve did. Contrary to the classical reading of this passage, Paul does not imply that women are more prone to deception than men.

The example of gender paralleling in Luke and Acts supports this interpretation. Luke was a close disciple of Paul, therefore it is appropriate to assume that he would have been significantly influenced by Paul's views. Luke intentionally parallels women and men in his Luke and Acts corpus (see appendix B). These parallels indicate that males do not enjoy an ontological superiority over females. For example, the angel Gabriel appears to both Zechariah and to Mary. In these two angelic visitations, contrary to Greco-Roman assumptions and expectations, Zechariah, the elder priest, fails in the challenge of faith while Mary, the thirteen/fourteen-year-old girl, succeeds. When Joseph and Mary bring Jesus to the temple for his dedication, they are met by the righteous Simeon and the prophetess Anna. Both Simeon and Anna recognize the significance of the infant in the outworking of the redemptive plan of God. These and the other Lucan parallels demonstrate that there is no ontological difference between the sexes (see appendix B). H. Flender articulates it this way: "Luke expresses by this arrangement that man and woman stand together and side by side before God. They are equal in honour and grace, they are endowed with the same gifts and have the same responsibilities (cf. Gen 1:27; Gal 3:28)" (1967, 10).

21   In 1 Corinthians 11:3 Paul conceptualizes marriage within a cosmic hierarchy with God and Christ. By this connection with the divine, Paul elevates marriage from the status of a profane contract that could be broken to the level of the sacred.

22   With regard to a more contemporary example of the "cunning" of women, which could also be categorized as an "illegitimate" use of power , see Dubisch (1986, 17–18).

23   A struggle for power is an inherent aspect of large power distance (Hofstede 2001, 98).

24   I am indebted to John Elliott for this insight. He makes this observation about Peter's treatment of the household codes in his commentary on 1 Peter (2000, 509).

25 Paul's use of Greco-Roman forms is the practical outworking of the decision of the Jerusalem council in Acts 15 to release the faith from its Jewish cultural roots and enable it to spread throughout the world. "Appropriate Christianity would now change forms as it spread from one cultural context to another" (Whiteman 2005, 50).

26 Co-cultural theory states that one dominant cultural group formulates systems of communication in accordance with their perception of the world (Orbe 1998, 1–3). The complementarian analysis of the Pauline discourses reflects this dominant dimension in communication. Even though complementarians take great pains to avoid affirming male dominance, their emphasis on prescribed gender roles appears to be shaped more by their androcentric perspective of roles rather than by the biblical emphases of freedom and empowerment. Their definition of gender roles grants men power and prestige and places women in a disadvantaged position. Feminist discourses on the Pauline texts have raised awareness of this issue. However, being a co-cultural group and engaging in co-cultural practices (ibid., 17), feminists have labeled the texts misogynistic. Since the Greco-Roman urban world was patriarchal and male dominated, it could be argued that the communication system which Paul employed was not representative of the women's world. However, Paul's intent was not to affirm patriarchy or misogyny; his intent was to transform the system in which he was living. As we consider the contemporary global context, males still exercise a significant level of dominance in gender relations. Therefore Paul's instructions are as pertinent today as they were almost two thousand years ago.

27 It also ignores the foundation laid by the Jerusalem council in Acts 15.

28 For a synopsis of the assumptions and values that influence egalitarianism, see Kraft (1996, 322–24).

29 This concurs with Shaw and Van Engen: "There is no such thing as pure theology; all theologies are local theologies" (2003, 47).

30 Though Paul acknowledges that some women are susceptible to being beguiled by cunning, predatorial males (2 Tim 3:6), this is in no way a disparaging remark about females being inherently more easily deceived than men. Paul states that men are also capable of being deceived (2 Cor 11:3; Gal 1:6,7; 2:13). Since Paul claims that both sexes are susceptible to being deceived, one cannot assert that women's nature is somehow prone to being more easily deceived. As we have seen, this

deprecating assumption has been made throughout history and even by some engaged in the contemporary dialogue. However, this assumption has been read into the biblical texts, not developed from the texts. When Paul requires husbands and wives to jointly decide on how long they will remain sexually abstinent, he demonstrates the assumption that they are equal in ability to think and to make decisions.

14

Conceptualizing Transformational Involvement

PURDAH IS THE PASHTUN SOCIAL SYSTEM of managing sexuality. It is an integral part of Pashtun identity and society, even though it is experiencing a significant degree of change. Therefore Christian workers should accept purdah's vital role in Pashtun culture and adapt to it.

What makes adaptation difficult for many Western Christians is that they come from postindustrial societies. Shaw and Van Engen point out that these societies are characterized by "concerns about human rights, especially with respect to eliminating sexism" (2003, 134). Postindustrial concerns about justice can motivate Western Christians to denigrate cultural values and expressions that they perceive as unjust. In addition, purdah is built upon assumptions and values that conflict with their biblically influenced assumptions and values, raising the level of tension within postindustrial Christians in an Islamic context such as Peshawar.

In this context it could be easy for outsiders of the culture to view purdah as an oppressive system. However, purdah is the system that provides a framework of protection and order. Purdah also is the means by which trust is built between a husband and wife, and between the members of a family and their women. Where a reasonable level of trust exists, families will give women a greater range of movement and even the opportunity for employment. This creates a dialectic within the system. Though purdah can function as a system of control and oppression, it also can function as a system of liberation and empowerment. The caveat is that the liberation and empowerment have to find expression within acceptable limits.

The Christian worker who is struggling with purdah due to a biblically inspired sense of justice and who also seeks to facilitate transformational development has a solid rationale to work for organic change within the system of purdah. The presence of the aforementioned dialectic, the presence of other dialectics, and the Pauline model provide the rationale. Transformational development is possible through an intentional, incarnational, prophetic, dialogical process that treats a people and their society with dignity. In addition, due to internal cultural impacts, it is vital that change be perceived as coming from within the system and not as something that is being imposed from without.

Involvement and Intentionality

Christian involvement in the Pashtun region has primarily been in the realm of development work. Intentionality in addressing the cultural system has to be an integral aspect of Christian development. This is because the goal of transformational development is not development that simply increases efficiency or economic gain—the goal is enabling people to reach their fullest potential as having been made in God's image. Transformational development is renewal, releasing people at the personal and communal levels from destructive and limiting ideas and behaviors. Thus transformational development requires intentionally addressing issues that impact the cultural system.

Transformational development is multidimensional. It takes seriously the powerful influence cultural and social systems have on each other.[1] It recognizes that these are "semi-autonomous systems that reinforce each other" (Hiebert 1996, 143).

Therefore, since changes in one system do not guarantee changes in the other, the development worker seeking transformation has to be intentional in working toward positive change at both levels. However, from my experience in development work, unless concerted effort is directed at the cultural system, the bulk of one's efforts will only temporarily impact specific aspects of the social system.[2]

Prophetic Dialogue

Christian workers from postindustrial societies should allow their efforts to be shaped by a transcultural theological paradigm. Working for change that transforms is the heart and soul of Christian involvement. However, a culturally insensitive theology can be used to justify advocacy that may resemble cultural imperialism rather than the advancement of justice and human rights.[3]

Drawing from Bevans and Schroeder, a constructive theological paradigm for transformational involvement in the twenty-first century that rectifies "imperialism as advocacy" is "prophetic dialogue" (2005, 348).[4] Prophetic dialogue means that Christians should engage the world in a way that reflects the character of the Trinity (dialogue), while acknowledging and addressing the reality of sin[5] (prophetic). The dialogical nature of our involvement seeks to image the manner in which God interacts with the creation. God does not impose himself and his ways upon people. He created humankind and released them to exercise a limited dominion over the earth. God respects that freedom and responds to humanity's rebellion with patient persuasion. In this light, Bevans and Schroeder assert:

> Mission can no longer proceed in ways that neglect the freedom and dignity of human beings. Nor can a church that is rooted in a God that saves through self-emptying think of itself as culturally superior to the peoples among whom it works. Mission, as participation in the mission of the Triune God, can only proceed in dialogue and can only be carried out in humility. (Ibid.)

Unless the word "dialogue" is properly modified, the dialogue would not be a true reflection of God's manner of acting in the creation. This dialogue must be prophetic in nature, confronting injustice and sin. Furthermore, being prophetic, this dialogue must also include God's solution for sin: reconciliation and new creation through the Spirit.[6]

Involvement as Incarnation

The Trinitarian response to the creation includes the incarnation. The incarnation promotes a high view of culture and adds content in thinking about how prophetic dialogue should shape development.[7] Christ became a Jew to work among the Jews. Paul, modeling the incarnation, became a Gentile to work among Gentiles. The incarnation elevates the status of each host culture and authorizes the host culture to provide the framework for prophetic dialogue and change. Thus the incarnational dimension of transformational involvement compels Christian workers to submerge themselves into the world of the host culture and live God's word in that cultural context.[8] The prophetic nature of transformational involvement requires that the worker engage the culture with God's word. The dialogical nature of transformational involvement authorizes the members of the host culture to process God's word and determine the manner in which God's justice will be expressed.

Thus, intentional, incarnational, prophetic dialogue provides a theological framework by which workers can constructively engage their host cultures and focus on transforming cultural systems rather than focusing solely on social systems. As the members of a host culture process the workers' engagement with them, and as the Spirit of God transforms their worldview, beliefs, assumptions, and values, the members themselves can begin to independently shape their narratives and act upon their social structures to ensure that this transformation is fully actualized. This type of involvement treats host cultures with the dignity they deserve.

Conceptualizing Change within Pashtunistan

What can help Christian workers in authorizing host cultures to express change is to acknowledge that change is constantly occurring within these cultures. Cultures are dynamic, and some degree of change is always happening within them (Shaw and Van Engen 2003, 142).

With regard to Pashtunistan, this fact of constant change is a source of encouragement to the development worker. The reality that changes are always happening stands in marked contrast with the Pashtun cultural narrative, which places great value on tradition.[9] The strength of the Pashtun narrative caused me to question whether or not change was possible within Pashtunistan. I was surprised by the findings of my field research. The diversity of ways purdah is expressed among the urban Pashtuns demonstrates that a significant degree of change is ongoing within the society. Recognizing the reality of change and its dynamism inspired hope in me in envisioning constructive change and development within Pashtun culture.

Since change in the broad perspective is a constant within all cultures, and especially within Pashtunistan, the Christian worker's concern should focus on identifying the potential impediments to particular changes.

The Crisis of Trust

Some of these impediments to change are identifiable within the Pashtun context. First, there is the impact of the Pashtun use of bounded sets, which is the manner in which Pashtuns classify people as insiders or outsiders. Pashtuns view outsiders with a certain degree of suspicion due to the pessimistically inclined, relational trust paradigm. Though this suspicion is neutralized over time within the context of personal relationships, this inclination toward suspicion negatively impacts the ability of outsiders in introducing innovative ideas to the society and seeing such ideas diffused.

This context of suspicion is exacerbated when the ones with the innovative ideas are Christians. Due to the manner in which many Pashtuns merge their Islam with their bounded sets, many view Christians with a certain level of aversion. This aversion intensifies when the changes contradict assumptions and values that are sanctioned by Islamic sacred writ. The aversion also intensifies when the changes touch on a primary narrative theme: purdah. In the Pashtun narrative, a Pashtun has to protect his women and ensure their sanctity (*namus*). This is nonnegotiable. A Pashtun cannot feel threatened in this area. If threatened, a Pashtun may respond out of *ghairat*, which is an emotion that overrides the intellect and demands retaliatory action.

This interactive relationship of the suspicion of the outsider, the "Christian" influence behind potential changes, and the fact that these changes impact a cultural narrative cautions outsiders in thinking they can overtly advocate for changes in the cultural and social systems of purdah.[10]

Dialectic Tension

However, what does inspire working for change is that change is happening. The variations in the assumptions and values that men hold about women, as well as the variations in the way purdah is expressed, demonstrate that there is an ongoing internal dialogue about the cultural values and social expressions of purdah. This dialogue and these changes are the result of a number of dialectic tensions among urban Pashtuns. Dialectic tensions foster change (Papa, Singhal, and Papa 2006, 22).

One of these dialectic tensions is the dialectic between backwardness (being uneducated) and being progressive (being educated). Many view certain religious and cultural traditions as backward. The beard exemplifies this. It is a sign of a pious man to sport a beard in the tradition of the Prophet, yet I saw few urban Pashtuns wearing beards. Only two of the men interviewed had a beard. Some of the expressions of purdah that one sees in the city are seen as backward, such as the use of the *burqa* (shuttlecock-style covering). Many urban families prefer to have their women use a *chaddar* (long, rectangular sheet of cloth), because it fulfills the requirement of covering in purdah while avoiding the negative label of backwardness.

Second, there is a dialectic between the traditional, arranged marriage and love marriage. This dialectic intersects with the dialectic of backwardness and progressiveness, but it should be perceived as a dialectic of its own. One of the traditional customs of the arranged marriage is having the marriage arranged independently of the son's or daughter's consent. Nowadays this custom has lost most of its currency within the society.

I was surprised to hear men admit that the traditional marriages had failed, especially with the Pashtun allegiance to tradition. This admission draws our attention to some of the changes in assumptions that have been taking place in the culture. First, the admission is linked to a hope that marriage could be more than what it traditionally has been. From where did that hope come? Second, there are growing expectations that marriages can succeed if there is a foundation that facilitates the growth of love in the relationship. Why has "love" become so important for urban Pashtuns? This indicates that people are expecting more from life. From where do these hopes come? Why have these assumptions had such an impact? It appears that the urban Pashtuns have another assumption. They assume that love is attainable if both parties consent. One of the factors in facilitating this change is that parents are afraid that their sons will blame them if they have problems in their marriages. This is what some sons have been doing.[11] The increase in the incidence of love marriages and the desire for a meaningful understanding between the couple has also contributed to creating these trends in marriage.

There is the additional dialectic between living in a joint family setting and living separately from the extended family after marriage. With the growth of the local economy, living separately will probably gain more momentum.

The presence of these dialectics and the consequent changes in marriage customs, along with the dialectics connected to the change in attitudes toward female education and the growing incidence of women working, demonstrate that changes are occurring within the society and that change is possible within certain boundaries. The nature of these changes demonstrates that even these boundaries are fluid and will change with time.

The Direction of Change

The concern I have is in the direction of these changes. Change happens as a result of a dialectic struggle. How does one know if the struggle will result in the adoption of values that facilitate transformational development?[12]

If we look at the reason for the change from parental fiat in the choice of the spouse in marriage to getting the consent of the couple, we can see that it is twofold. First, it is because there is an admission that marriages have "failed."[13] Second, there are growing expectations that marriages could "succeed" if there were a foundation that facilitated the growth of an "understanding" in the relationship. Why has the quest for an understanding become so important for urban Pashtuns, important enough for them to change their customs? It appears that the urban Pashtuns have another assumption. They assume that this understanding is attainable if both parties consent to the marriage.

My concern is that the results are mixed regarding the success of these marriages of consent, as well as the success of love marriages, since success is defined as satisfaction with the marriage partner. If the marriages are not successful, in which direction will the culture turn? If marriages fail that are founded upon consent, or "love," and the Pashtun cultural narrative idealizes the past, will people be tempted to return to their previous traditions? Or will they simply stay with the present form and get consent without giving couples in the future the space and the social skills necessary for developing a satisfying relationship? Some of the wealthier and more educated couples are given the space to interact. However, their interaction demonstrates that the men's assumptions require submission from the wife-to-be even in this time of interaction. This does not bode well for the long-term success in developing a satisfying marriage relationship.

To facilitate the positive trend in change that is happening in urban Pashtunistan, Christian workers should help Pashtuns come to terms with some of the demeaning assumptions men hold about women and learn practical relational skills in how to build healthy female and male relationships prior to the engagement.

The Construction of Trust

Although there are many urban Pashtuns who have discontinued holding traditional, demeaning values about women, traditional values still exert significant influence upon the society. The fact that changes are occurring demonstrates that the values are being reevaluated. However, if the society feels threatened from the outside, this reflective process may be hampered. Those who are resistant to change may employ defensive-posturing rhetoric ("we are under attack") in order to discourage change.

The negatively inclined Pashtun disposition toward outsiders increases the risk of the society viewing development workers with suspicion. Therefore there is ample rationale for making the construction of trust through relationships the first step in any development work by outsiders.[14] With regard to the importance of trust-building in communication, Charles Kraft writes:

> Receptors may be pictured as encased in a kind of bubble which only they give permission to enter. When someone wants to transact or negotiate some form of communication, then, he/she needs to gain permission for the interaction from the one who can control access to that bubble. The transactional nature of communication requires that each participant gain the permission of the other in order to either initiate or continue the interaction.... Whether or not a receptor grants permission for a message to enter relates to what may be termed the "range of tolerance" of that receptor for the particular type of message presented and/or for the person presenting the message. A communicator needs to give high priority to winning the permission of his/her receptors. (2005, 158)

Building a platform of trust takes time; however, it is essential if the workers expect their ideas to gain acceptance in the community. This is especially true when ideas happen to touch upon the values and customs regarding women.

Paul's model of adopting forms of the culture provides a solid rationale for not contesting the system of purdah and encourages expatriates to adapt their lifestyles to the system. The incarnational model for development also reinforces the reason for respecting and adapting to the forms of purdah.

Since there are a variety of expressions of purdah within the city, I suggest that Christian workers adopt an expression suitable for their position in the society; however, they should adopt other varieties of expression when conformity to those expressions would facilitate trust-building. They do not want to appear to their communities as if they are challenging purdah. The appearance of challenge will impair their ability to build trust.

Conclusion

Paul's model of adoption of Greco-Roman forms provides a rationale for the postindustrial, justice-oriented Christian worker to accept a cultural and social system that appears unjust. The incarnation provides a solid rationale for honoring the many diverse expressions of culture. This does not mean that the Christian worker is obliged to accept the cultural values that conflict with metacultural biblical values. However, the model of the incarnation requires that the worker first enter the world of the host culture and understand that culture.

The cultural impacts of the outsider within Pashtun society require that Christian workers immerse themselves within the culture and build trust. When trust-building becomes the foundation of their involvement, it prepares the way for meaningful, prophetic dialogue. Even though the society functions on a pessimistically inclined, relational trust paradigm, the society has a built-in mechanism for trust-building. This is done through extended relationships. In addition, adapting to the system of purdah can facilitate one's acceptance within the community as it is a means of building trust. As we have seen, when women faithfully abide by the limits of purdah, they build trust within their families. As Christian outsiders adapt their lifestyles to purdah, they too can build trust in their communities.

As trust is built, the path is open for meaningful dialogue. Within that dialogue, Christian workers can be intentional and prophetic, respectfully addressing the cultural system and challenging it with the creational/biblical metacultural themes. Respectful, challenging, constructive dialogue can facilitate the community in adopting new ideas. It also authorizes them to experiment and formulate new ways of behaving, especially with regard to the issues relating to sexuality.

---

1   I am using Hiebert's model in my conceptualization of these systems (1996, 140–43), except I include Bruce Bradshaw's identification of cultural myths as cultural narratives (2002, 24–30), and I do not mention the personal dimension in Hiebert's model. (See appendix A for a description of these two systems.) I find Daniel Chirot's classification of society into four subsystems particularly helpful: the economic system (resources), the political system (power), social institutions (social relationships), and culture (1994, 117).

2   Daniel Chirot points out that it is in the economic and cultural spheres that change originates and the social and political institutions consistently resist these changes (1994, 120). Therefore, if social change is the goal of the development worker, it is imperative that both these areas be targeted.

3 Bruce Bradshaw proposes a postindustrial, culturally influenced, Western development model built upon a poor theological foundation. He posits a "biblical" view of the *kosmos* (world), which in his view is "the matrix of human cultures that people construct to provide order to their lives" (2002, 13). He never presents a rationale as to why his definition of *kosmos* can be justifiably classified as "biblical." However, he boldly asserts that *kosmos* in John 3:16 speaks not only of individuals but also of social structures. His view is sociologically based, and reflects postindustrial, Western thinking. However, his assertion does not develop exegetically from the text of John 3:1–21, which is particularly individualistic in terminology ("whoever believes"; John 3:16) but globally inclusive. This is an example of how a contemporary thinker uses Scripture to construct a local theology. I do not disagree with Bradshaw that redemption includes the transformation of social structures; I disagree with his interpretation of *kosmos* in John 3:16.

4 As an evangelical, I disagree with Bevans and Schroeder's religious pluralism; however, I wholeheartedly agree with their conceptualizing Christian engagement in the world as a reflection of how the Triune God interacts with creation.

5 In mentioning sin, I am not advocating a positivistic approach to knowledge; however, I affirm critical realism as a valid epistemological paradigm.

6 Johannes Nissen writes, "Dialogue with Christ brings two characteristics of all authentic dialogue to maximum intensity. The first characteristic is confrontation. The second one is change" (2002, 87)

7 The incarnation is one of the shaping principles for all mission and development work because Jesus said, "As the Father has sent me, even so I am sending you" (John 20:21 ESV).

8 With regard to the importance of congruence between the life and the words of the worker, see Guder (1985, 157).

9 For a definition of cultural narratives and an explanation of their function, see Bradshaw (2002, 20–30).

10 Kraft identifies a principle of receptor-oriented communication that is relevant here. He states, "Receptors, then, either *grant or withhold permission* for any given message to enter what might be termed the receptor's 'communicational space'" (2005, 158; italics in the original).

Without a platform of trust, the development worker will have no permission to enter this communicational space, removing any potential for meaningful dialogue.

11   I saw evidence of this blame in one participant observation. A Pashtun told his story of woe. He had been studying in Britain, and he wanted to get a job there after his graduation. His parents did not want him to settle down in Britain. So they feigned that his father was deathly ill after he graduated. The son immediately returned to Pakistan only to find that the sickness was a ploy to get him out of Britain and bring him back to Pakistan. To settle him down here, his parents had arranged his marriage. He consented to the marriage as a good son was expected to do and settled down to a life of marital stress (he did not like his wife) and financial hardship. He lamented his dismal fate.

12   Chirot states that the change in the economic or cultural spheres of the society "opens an ever increasing gap between material or ideological pressures and institutional reforms. This gap may become so large as to cause sudden and major breaks with the past as social institutions finally crack and either remold themselves to accommodate the pressures for change that have been building up or fail and drag down the entire society" (1994, 120–21).

13   A society's recognition of failure is a powerful motivation for change (see Chirot 1994, 124–25).

14   With regard to the importance of building trust, see Elmer (2002, 98–104).

APPENDIX A

Cultural and Social Systems

Relationships develop within a cultural milieu, with each milieu having its own particular mores. Context affects the nature and the parameters of the relationships, influencing the way people form their expectations of what should transpire in their relationships. Thus a process of identifying the assumptions and values of each cultural context must be carried out in order for one to understand the relational expectations, parameters, and dynamics. In addition, relationships are made and carried out by humans. Being individuals with unique personalities, humans are going to produce significant variations in the way relationships are conducted within the parameters of the culture. This is why no single description of human relationships can exhaustively include all the variances that occur. However, many of the assumptions, values, and expectations within any given culture that people carry into their relationships are shared. This is what makes generalization possible, because similarities exist in spite of the diversity within any given cultural context (Moreau 1995, 121–22).

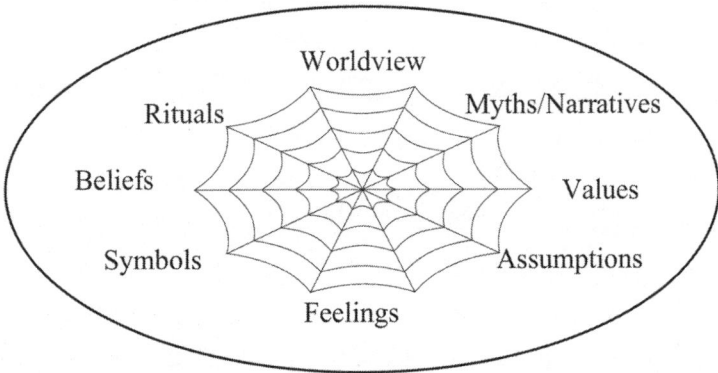

Fig. 5. Dimensions of a Cultural System

The shared assumptions and values governing relationships are found within the cultural system of any given ethnic group. A cultural system is an integrated amalgamation of the culture's worldview, myths/narratives, beliefs, assumptions, values, symbols, and rituals, and the resulting emotional attachment an insider has to all these (Hiebert 1996, 141; see fig. 5).

Social systems are the ways in which a society constructs and uses social relationships, resources, power, and legitimacy (ibid., 140–41). (See fig. 6.)

With regard to social relationships, societies have varying ways they express family relationships. In the USA we primarily live as nuclear families. In Pakistan people live primarily in virilocal, extended family settings, where a man resides with his mother, father, sisters, and brothers, and with his brothers' wives and their children. In addition, people may relate with others outside their immediate family context in clubs (such as the Rotary Club) or in professional associations (legal, academic, etc.).

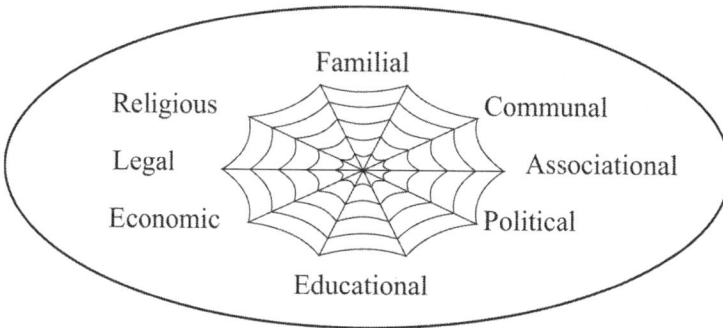

Fig. 6. Institutional Expressions of a Social System
(adapted from Moreau 2001)

These systems are semiautonomous. Therefore, a change that occurs in one system does not necessarily guarantee that a corresponding change will happen in the other. In addition, if the social system does not change, it can counteract and nullify any significant change in the cultural system (Hiebert 1996, 143).

APPENDIX B

Gender Parallelism in Luke and Acts

LUKE

Zechariah and Mary:

    The angelic annunciation.....................................Luke 1:10–20,26–38

    Glory to God..Luke 1:46–55,67–79

Simeon and Anna..Luke 2:25–38

Widow of Zarephath, and Naaman ....Luke 4:25–38

Healing of Peter's mother-in-law and demoniac ....Luke 4:31

Centurion of Capernaum and widow of Nain......................Luke 7:1–17

Simon the Pharisee and the sinner woman........................Luke 7:36–50

Good Samaritan and Mary/Martha....................................Luke 10:29–42

Man with mustard seed and woman with leaven ....Luke 13:18–21

Man with one hundred sheep, and woman
    with ten pieces of silver.....................................Luke 15:4–10

Sleeping man and woman at the mill in the
    last judgment ....Luke 17:34,35

Importunate widow and the publican...............................Luke 18:1–14

Women at the tomb and the Emmaus disciples ....Luke 23:55–24:35

ACTS

Ananias and Sapphira..Acts 5:1–11

Aeneas and Tabitha ....Acts 9:32–42

Lydia and the Philippian jailor ....Acts 16:13–34

Dionysius and Damaris ....Acts 17:34

(adapted from Witherington 1988, 129)

REFERENCES

Abu Dawud, Sulaiman ibn Ash'ath Sijistani. 2004. *Sunan Abu Dawud*. Trans. A. Hasan. 3 vols. Lahore, Pakistan: Sh. Muhammad Ashraf.

Ahmed, Akbar S. 1980. *Pukhtun economy and society: Traditional structure and economic development in a tribal society*. Ed. A. Kuper. International Library of Anthropology. London: Routledge & Kegan Paul.

Ahmed, Leila. 1992. *Women and gender in Islam: Historical roots of a modern debate*. London: Yale University Press.

Alföldy, Géza. 1988. *The social history of Rome*. Trans. D. Braund and F. Pollock. Baltimore: Johns Hopkins University Press.

Alter, Robert. 1981. *The art of biblical narrative*. New York: Basic Books.

Antonelli, Judith S. 1997. *In the image of God: A feminist commentary on the Torah*. Softcover ed. Northvale, NJ: Aronson.

Aristophanes. 2000. *"Birds," "Lysistrata," "Women at the* Thesmophoria.*"* Ed. and trans. Jeffrey Henderson. Vol. 3 of *Aristophanes*. Loeb Classical Library. Cambridge, MA: Harvard University Press.

Arlandson, James Malcolm. 1997. *Women, class, and society in early Christianity: Models from Luke-Acts*. Peabody, MA: Hendrickson.

Augustinus, Aurelius. 1961. *St. Augustine's confessions*. Trans. W. Watts. Ed. T. E. Page, E. Capps, I. A. Post, W. H. D. Rouse, and E. H. Warmington. Vol. 2. Loeb Classical Library. Cambridge, MA: Harvard University Press.

_____. 1982. *St. Augustine: The literal meaning of Genesis*. Trans. J. H. Taylor. Ed. J. Quasten, W. J. Burghardt, and T. C. Lawler. Vol. 2 of *Ancient Christian writers: The works of the fathers in translation*. New York: Newman.

_____. 1990. *The Trinity*. Trans. E. Hill. Ed. J. E. Rotelle. Vol. 5 of *The works of Saint Augustine: A translation for the 21st century*. Brooklyn: New City Press.

Bailey, Kenneth E. 1998. Women in the New Testament: A Middle Eastern cultural view. *Evangelical Review of Theology* 22, no. 3: 208–26.

_____. 2011. *Paul through Mediterranean Eyes: Cultural studies in 1 Corinthians*. Downers Grove, IL: InterVarsity Press Academic.

Baker, Cynthia, Judith Wuest, and Phyllis Noerager Stern. 1995. Method slurring: The grounded theory / phenomenology example. In *Grounded theory 1984–1994*, ed. B. G. Glasser. Mill Valley, CA: Sociology Press.

Balswick, Jack O., and Judith K. Balswick. 1995. Gender relations and marital power. In *Families in multicultural perspective*, ed. B. B. Ingoldsby and S. Smith. New York: Guilford.

Bamyeh, Mohammed A. 1999. *The social origins of Islam: Mind, economy, discourse*. Minneapolis: University of Minnesota Press.

Banerjee, Mukulika. 2000. *The Pathan unarmed: Opposition and memory in the North West Frontier*. Ed. W. James and N. J. Allen. World Anthropology. Oxford: James Currey.

Barlas, Asma. 2002. *"Believing women" in Islam: Unreading patriarchal interpretations of the Qur'an*. Austin: University of Texas Press.

Barrett, C. K. 1968. *The First Epistle to the Corinthians*. Ed. H. Chadwick. Vol. 7 of *Harper's New Testament commentaries*. New York: Harper & Row.

Barth, Fredrik. 1965. *Political leadership among Swat Pathans*. Ed. A. Forge. Vol. 19 of *Monographs on social anthropology*. London: Athlone.

_____. 1981. *Features of person and society in Swat: Collected essays on Pathans*. Vol. 2 of *Selected essays of Fredrik Barth*. London: Routledge and Kegan Paul.

Barth, Karl. 1958. *Church dogmatics: The doctrine of creation*. Trans. J. W. Edwards, O. Bussey, and H. Knight. Ed. G. W. Bromiley and T. F. Torrance. Vol. 3, part 1. Edinburgh: Clark.

Bartlotti, Leonard N. 2000. Negotiating Pakhto: Proverbs, Islam and the construction of identity among Pashtuns. PhD diss., University of Wales.

Barton, Stephen C. 1986. Paul's sense of place: An anthropological approach to community formation in Corinth. *New Testament Studies* 32: 225–46.

_____. 1997. Christian community in the light of 1 Corinthians. *Studies in Christian Ethics* 10: 1–15.

Baumert, Norbert. 1996. *Woman and man in Paul: Overcoming a misunderstanding*. Trans. P. Madigan and L. M. Maloney. Collegeville, MN: Liturgical Press.

BBC News. 2000. Licence to kill. September 4. http://news.bbc.co.uk/2/hi/programmes/correspondent/909948.stm.

Beattie, Gillian. 2005. *Women and marriage in Paul and his early interpreters*. Ed. M. Goodacre. Vol. 296 of *Journal for the study of the New Testament supplement series*. London: Clark.

BeDuhn, Jason David. 1999. "Because of the angels": Unveiling Paul's anthropology in 1 Corinthians 11. *Journal of Biblical Literature* 118 (Summer): 295–320.

Bell, Richard. 1937. *The Qur'an: Translated with a critical re-arrangement of the surahs.* Vol. 1. Edinburgh: Clark.

Belleville, Linda L. 2001. Women in ministry. In *Two views on women in ministry,* ed. J. R. Beck and C. L. Blomberg. Grand Rapids: Zondervan.

Best, Ernest. 1998. *A critical and exegetical commentary on Ephesians.* Ed. J. A. Emerton, C. E. B. Cranfield, and G. N. Stanton. The International Critical Commentary on the Holy Scriptures of the Old and New Testaments. Edinburgh: Clark.

Beuken, Willem A. M. 1999. The human person in the vision of Genesis 1–3: A synthesis of contemporary insights. *Louvain Studies* 24, no. 1: 3–20.

Bevans, Stephen B., and Roger P. Schroeder. 2005. *Constants in context: A theology of mission for today.* The American Society of Missiology Series #30. Maryknoll, NY: Orbis Books.

Biblia Hebraica Stuttgartensia: With Westminster Hebrew morphology. 1996. Electronic ed. Stuttgart: German Bible Society; Glenside, PA: Westminster Seminary.

Birch, Bruce C., Walter Brueggemann, Terence E. Frethheim, and David L. Petersen. 1999. *A theological introduction to the Old Testament.* Nashville: Abingdon.

Bird, Phyllis A. 1981. "Male and female he created them": Gen 1:27b in the context of the priestly account of creation. *Harvard Theological Review* 74, no. 2: 129–59.

———. 1994. Bone of my bone and flesh of my flesh. *Theology Today* 50, no. 4: 521–34.

Blocher, Henri. 1984. *In the beginning: The opening chapters of Genesis.* Trans. D. G. Preston. Downers Grove, IL: InterVarsity Press.

Blomberg, Craig. 1995. *1 Corinthians.* Ed. T. Muck. The NIV Application Commentary: From Biblical Text to Contemporary Life. Grand Rapids: Zondervan.

Bock, Darrell L. 2006. Opening questions: Definition and philosophy of exegesis. In *Interpreting the New Testament text: Introduction to the art and science of exegesis,* ed. D. L. Bock and B. M. Fanning, 23–32. Wheaton: Crossway Books.

Bonhoeffer, Dietrich. 1965. *No rusty swords: Letters, lectures, and notes 1928–36.* Trans. E. H. Robertson and J. Bowden. Vol. 1. London: Collin's.

Bordwine, James E. 1996. *The Pauline doctrine of male headship: The apostle versus biblical feminists.* Vancouver, WA: Westminster Institute.

Bouhdiba, Abdelwahab. 1998. *Sexuality in Islam*. Trans. A. Sheridan. London: Saqi Books.

Boyarin, Daniel. 2004. Paul and the genealogy of gender. In *A feminist companion to Paul*, ed. A.-J. Levine and M. Blickenstaff, 13–41. Cleveland: Pilgrim Press.

Bradley, Keith R. 1991. *Discovering the Roman family: Studies in Roman social history*. New York: Oxford University Press.

Bradshaw, Bruce. 2002. *Change across cultures: A narrative approach to social transformation*. Grand Rapids: Baker Academic.

Brownson, James V. 1996. Speaking the truth in love: Elements of a missional hermeneutic. In *The church between gospel and culture: The emerging mission in North America*, ed. G. R. Hunsberger and C. Van Gelder, 228–59. Grand Rapids: Eerdmans.

Bruce, F. F. 1971. *1 and 2 Corinthians*. Ed. R. E. Clements and M. Black. Vol. 46–47 of *New Century Bible: Based on the Revised Standard Version*. London: Oliphants.

Brueggemann, Walter. 1982. *Genesis: A Bible commentary for teaching and preaching*. Ed. J. L. Mays. Interpretation: A Bible Commentary for Teaching and Preaching. Atlanta: John Knox.

_____. 1997. *Theology of the Old Testament: Testimony, dispute, advocacy*. Minneapolis: Fortress.

Brümmer, Vincent. 1993. *The model of love: A study in philosophical theology*. Cambridge: Cambridge University Press.

Bucholtz, Mary. 2003. Theories of discourse as theories of gender: Discourse analysis in language and gender studies. In *The handbook of language and gender*, ed. J. Holmes and M. Meyerhoff, 43–68. Malden, MA: Blackwell.

Bukhari, Abu 'Abdullah Muhammad ibn Isma'il al. 1997. *The translation of the meanings of "Sahih al-Bukhari."* Trans. M. M. Khan. 9 vols. Riyadh: Darussalam.

Bultmann, R. 1983. *aidos* [shame/modesty]. In *Theological dictionary of the New Testament*, ed. G. Kittel, Vol. 1, 169-171. Grand Rapids: Eerdmans.

Cairns, Douglas L. 2002. The meaning of the veil in ancient Greek culture. In *Women's dress in the ancient Greek world*, ed. L. Llewellyn-Jones, 73–93. London: Duckworth and Classical Press of Wales.

Calvin, John. 1847. *Commentaries on the first book of Moses called Genesis*. Trans. J. King. Vol. 1. Edinburgh: Calvin Translation Society.

Cantarella, Eva. 1987. *Pandora's daughters: The role and status of women in Greek and Roman antiquity*. Trans. M. B. Fant. Baltimore: Johns Hopkins University Press.

_____. 2002. Marriage and sexuality in republican Rome: A Roman conjugal love story. In *The sleep of reason: Erotic experience and sexual ethics in ancient Greece and Rome*, ed. M. C. Nussbaum and J. Sihvola, 269–82. Chicago: University of Chicago Press.

Caragounis, Chrys C. 1996. "Fornication" and "concession"? Interpreting 1 Cor. 7,1–7. In *The Corinthian correspondence*, ed. R. Bieringer, 543–60. Leuven, Belgium: Leuven University Press.

Carson, D. A. 1991. "Silent in the churches": On the role of women in 1 Corinthians 14:33b–36. In *Recovering biblical manhood and womanhood*, ed. J. Piper and W. A. Grudem, 140–53. Wheaton: Crossway Books.

Cassuto, Umberto. 1961. *A commentary on the book of Genesis*. Trans. I. Abrahams. Vol. 1. Jerusalem: Magnes Press.

Castelli, Elizabeth A. 1999. Disciplines of difference: Asceticism and history in Paul. In *Asceticism and the New Testament*, ed. L. E. Vaage and V. L. Wimbush, 171–85. New York: Routledge.

Cato, Marcus Porcius, and Marcus Terentius Varro. 1954. *On Agriculture and On Agriculture*. Trans. W. D. Hooper and H. B. Ash. Ed. T. E. Page, E. Capps, I. A. Post, W. H. D. Rouse, and E. H. Warmington. Loeb Classical Library. Cambridge, MA: Harvard University Press.

Charmaz, Kathy. 2006. *Constructing grounded theory: A practical guide through qualitative analysis*. Thousand Oaks, CA: SAGE.

Chaudhry, Muhammad Sharif. 1991. *Women's rights in Islam*. Lahore, Pakistan: Sh. Muhammad Ashraf.

Chirot, Daniel. 1994. *How societies change*. Ed. C. Ragin, W. Griswold, and L. Griffin. Sociology for a New Century. Thousand Oaks, CA: Pine Forge.

Chow, John K. 1997. Patronage in Roman Corinth. In *Paul and empire: Religion and power in Roman imperial society*, ed. R. A. Horsley, 104–25. Harrisburg, PA: Trinity Press.

Chrysostom, Dio. 1985. *Dio Chrysostom*. Trans. H. L. Crosby. Ed. G. P. Goold. Vol. 5. Loeb Classical Library. Cambridge, MA: Harvard University Press.

Chrysostom, John. 1956a. *Saint Chrysostom: Homilies on the Epistles of Paul to the Corinthians*. Trans. T. W. Chambers. Ed. P. Schaff. Vol. 12 of *A select library of the Nicene and post-Nicene fathers of the Christian church*. Grand Rapids: Eerdmans.

_____. 1956b. *Saint Chrysostom: Homiles on Galatians, Ephesians, Philippians, Colossians, Thessalonians, Timothy, Titus, and Philemon*. Trans. T. W. Chambers. Ed. P. Schaff. Vol. 13 of *A select library of the Nicene and post-Nicene fathers of the Christian church*. Grand Rapids: Eerdmans.

———. 1983. *On virginity and against remarriage.* Trans. S. R. Shore. Vol. 9 of *Studies in women and religion.* New York: Mellen.

Clark, Elizabeth A. 1999. *Reading renunciation: Asceticism and Scripture in early Christianity.* Princeton, NJ: Princeton University Press.

Clark, Gillian. 1996. Roman women. In *Women in antiquity,* ed. I. McAuslan and P. Walcot. New York: Oxford University Press.

Clarke, John R. 2003. *Art in the lives of ordinary Romans: Visual representation and non-elite viewers in Italy, 100 B.C.–A.D. 315.* Berkeley: University of California Press.

Cohick, Lynn H. 2009. *Women in the World of the Earliest Christians: Illuminating Ancient Ways of Life.* Grand Rapids, MI: Baker Academic.

Collins, Jack. 1999. Discourse analysis and the interpretation of Gen. 2:4–7. *Westminster Theological Journal* 61, no. 2: 269–76.

Collins, Raymond F. 1999. *First Corinthians.* Ed. D. J. Harrington. Vol. 7 of *Sacra pagina.* Collegeville, MN: Liturgical Press.

———. 2002. *1 and 2 Timothy and Titus: A commentary.* Ed. C. C. Black, J. T. Carroll, and B. R. Gaventa. The New Testament Library. Louisville: Westminster John Knox.

Conzelmann, Hans. 1975. *1 Corinthians: A commentary on the First Epistle to the Corinthians.* Trans. J. W. Leitch. Ed. H. Koester, J. E. Epp, R. W. Funk, G. W. S. J. MacRae, and J. M. Robinson. *Hermeneia:* A Critical and Historical Commentary on the Bible. Philadelphia: Fortress.

Cope, Lamar. 1980. 1 Cor. 11:2–16: One step further. *Journal of Biblical Literature* 97: 435–36.

Corbier, Mireille. 2001. Child exposure and abandonment. In *Childhood, class and kin in the Roman world,* ed. S. Dixon, 52–73. New York: Routledge.

Crook, J. A. 1986. Feminine inadequacy and the *senatusconsultum Velleianum.* In *The family in ancient Rome: New perspectives,* ed. B. Rawson, 83–92. Ithaca, NY: Cornell University Press.

Croom, A. T. 2000. *Roman clothing and fashion.* Charleston, SC: Tempus.

Davies, Glenys. 2005. What made the Roman toga *virilis?* In *The clothed body in the ancient world,* ed. L. Cleland, M. Harlow, and L. Llewellyn-Jones, 121–30. Oxford: Oxbow Books.

Davies, Maximos. 2002. Celibacy in context. *First Things* 128 (December): 13–15.

Dawes, Gregory W. 1998. *The body in question: Metaphor and meaning in the interpretation of Ephesians 5:21–33.* Ed. A. Culpepper and R. Rendtorff. Biblical Interpretation Series. Leiden: Brill.

Delitzsch, Franz Julius. 1888. *A new commentary on Genesis.* Trans. S. Taylor. Vol. 1. Edinburgh: Clark.

Delobel, Joel. 1986. 1 Cor 11:2–16: Toward a coherent interpretation. In *L' Apôtre Paul: Personnalité, style, et conception du ministère,* ed. A. Vanhoye, 369–89. Leuven, Belgium: Leuven University Press.

Deming, Will. 2004. *Paul on marriage and celibacy: The Hellenistic background of 1 Corinthians 7.* 2nd ed. Grand Rapids: Eerdmans.

deSilva, David A. 2000. *Honor, patronage, kinship and purity: Unlocking New Testament culture.* Downers Grove, IL: InterVarsity Press.

Dionysius of Halicarnassus. 1948. *The Roman antiquities of Dionysius of Halicarnassus.* Trans. E. Spelman. Ed. T. E. Page, E. Capps, and W. H. D. Rouse. Vol. 1. Loeb Classical Library. Cambridge, MA: Harvard University Press.

Dixon, Suzanne. 1992. *The Roman family.* Baltimore: Johns Hopkins University Press.

Doriani, Daniel. 1995. Appendix 1: A history of the interpretation of 1 Timothy 2. In *Women in the church: A fresh analysis of 1 Timothy 2:9–15,* ed. A. J. Köstenberger, T. R. Schreiner, and H. S. Baldwin, 209–67. Grand Rapids: Baker Books.

Douglas, J. D., ed. 1993. *The new Greek-English interlinear New Testament: A new interlinear translation of the Greek New Testament; United Bible Societies' fourth, corrected edition with the New Revised Standard Version, New Testament.* Wheaton: Tyndale House.

Driver, Samuel Rolles. 1909. *The book of Genesis.* Ed. W. Lock. 7th ed. Westminster Commentaries. London: Methuen.

Dubisch, Jill. 1986. Introd. to *Gender and power in rural Greece,* ed. J. Dubisch. Princeton, NJ: Princeton University Press.

Dumbrell, William J. 1989. Creation, covenant and work. *Evangelical Review of Theology* 13, no. 2: 137–56.

Dunn, James D. G. 1996. *The Epistles to the Colossians and to Philemon: A commentary on the Greek text.* Ed. I. H. Marshall. The New International Greek Testament Commentary. Grand Rapids: Eerdmans.

———. 2000. The First and Second Letters to Timothy and the Letter to Titus: Introduction, commentary, and reflections. Vol. 11 of *The new interpreter's Bible: General articles and introduction, commentary, and reflections for each book of the Bible including the Apocryphal/Deuterocanonical books in twelve volumes,* ed. L. E. Keck, 773–880. Nashville: Abingdon.

Durham, John I. 1987. *Exodus.* Ed. D. A. Hubbard, G. W. Barker, and J. D. W. Watts. Word Biblical Commentary. Waco: Word Books.

Edwards, David B. 1996. *Heroes of the age: Moral fault lines on the Afghan frontier.* Ed. B. D. Metcalf. Vol. 21 of *Comparative studies on Muslim societies.* Berkeley: University of California Press.

El Fadl, Khaled Abou. 2001. *Speaking in God's name: Islamic law, authority, and women.* Oxford: Oneworld.

Elliott, John H. 2000. *1 Peter: A new translation with introduction and commentary.* Ed. W. F. Albright and D. N. Freedman. The Anchor Bible. New York: Doubleday.

Ellis, E. Earle. 1981. The silenced wives of Corinth (1 Cor. 14: 34–35). In *New Testament textual criticism: Its significance for exegesis,* ed. E. J. Epp and G. D. Fee, 213–220. Oxford: Oxford University Press.

Elmer, Duane. 2002. *Cross-cultural connections: Stepping out and fitting in around the world.* Downers Grove, IL: InterVarsity Press.

Esposito, John L., and Natana J. DeLong-Bas. 2001. *Women in Muslim family law.* 2nd ed. Contemporary Issues in the Middle East. Syracuse, NY: Syracuse University Press.

Eyben, Emiel. 1991. Fathers and sons. In *Marriage, divorce, and children in ancient Rome,* ed. B. Rawson, 114–43. Oxford: Oxford University Press.

Fatum, Lone. 1991. Image of God and glory of man: Women in the Pauline congregations. In *Image of God and gender models in Judaeo-Christian tradition,* ed. K. E. Børresen, 56–137. Oslo: Solum Forlag.

Fee, Gordon D. 1987. *The First Epistle to the Corinthians.* Ed. F. F. Bruce. The New International Commentary on the New Testament. Grand Rapids: Eerdmans.

———. 1988. *1 and 2 Timothy, Titus.* Ed. W. W. Gasque. Rev. ed. Vol. 13 of *New international biblical commentary.* Peabody, MA: Hendrickson.

———. 1994. *God's Empowering Presence: The Holy Spirit in the Letters of Paul.* Peabody, MA: Hendrickson.

———. 2005a. Male and female in the new creation: Galatians 3:26–29. In *Discovering biblical equality: Complementarity without hierarchy,* ed. R. W. Pierce and R. M. Groothuis, 172–85. 2nd ed. Downers Grove, IL: InterVarsity Press.

———. 2005b. Praying and prophesying in the assemblies: 1 Corinthians 11:2–16. In *Discovering biblical equality: Complementarity without hierarchy,* ed. R. W. Pierce and R. M. Groothuis, 142–60. 2nd ed. Downers Grove, IL: InterVarsity Press.

Fiorenza, Elisabeth Schüssler. 1983. *In memory of her: A feminist theological reconstruction of Christian origins.* New York: Crossroad.

Fitzmeyer, Joseph A. 1957–58. A feature of Qumran angelology and the angels of 1 Cor. XI:10. *New Testament Studies* 4: 48–58.

_____. 1989. Another look at *kephale* in 1 Corinthians 11.3. *New Testament Studies* 35: 503–11.

Flemming, Dean. 2005. *Contextualization in the New Testament: Patterns for theology and mission.* Downers Grove, IL: InterVarsity Press.

Flender, Helmut. 1967. *St. Luke: Theologian of redemptive history.* Trans. R. H. Fuller and I. Fuller. London: SPCK.

Foh, Susan T. 1974. What is the woman's desire? *Westminster Theological Journal* 37: 376–83.

Foster, George McClelland. 1967a. The dyadic contract: A model for the social structure of a Mexican peasant village. In *Peasant society: A reader,* ed. J. M. Potter, M. M. Diaz, and G. M. Foster. Boston: Little, Brown and Company.

_____. 1967b. Introd. to *Peasant society: A reader,* ed. J. M. Potter, M. M. Diaz, and G. M. Foster. Boston: Little, Brown and Company.

Fox, Everett. 1989. Can Genesis be read as a book? *Semeia* 46: 31–40.

Fretheim, Terence E. 1994. The book of Genesis: Introduction, commentary, and reflections. Vol. 1 of *The new interpreter's Bible,* ed. L. E. Keck, G. T. Long, B. C. Birch, K. P. Darr, W. L. Lane, G. R. O'Day, D. L. Petersen, J. J. Collins, J. A. Keller, J. E. Massy, and M. L. Soards, 319–674. Nashville: Abingdon.

Friedmann, Yohanan. 2003. *Tolerance and coercion in Islam: Interfaith relations in the Muslim tradition.* Ed. D. Morgan, V. Aksan, M. Brett, M. Cook, P. Jackson, T. Khalidi, and C. Robinson. Cambridge Studies in Islamic Civilization. Cambridge, MA: Cambridge University Press.

Galen. 1982. *Galen's commentary on the Hippocratic Treatise: Airs, waters, places in the Hebrew translation of Solomon Ha-Me'ati.* Trans. A. Wasserstein. Vol. 6, no. 3 of *The Israel Academy of Sciences and Humanities proceedings.* Jerusalem: Israel Academy of Sciences and Humanities.

Gallagher, Maggie. 2004. Reflections on headship. In *Does Christianity teach male headship? The equal-regard marriage and its critics,* ed. D. Blankenhorn, D. Browning, and M. S. Van Leeuwen, 111–25. Grand Rapids: Eerdmans.

Garland, David E. 2003. *1 Corinthians.* Ed. R. W. Yarbrough and R. H. Stein. Baker Exegetical Commentary on the New Testament. Grand Rapids: Baker Academic.

Garnsey, Peter, and Richard Saller. 1987. *The Roman Empire: Economy, society and culture.* London: Duckworth.

Gibbs, Eddie. 2005. *Leadership next: Changing leaders in a changing culture*. Downers Grove, IL: InterVarsity Press.

Giles, Kevin. 2002. *The Trinity and subordinationism: The doctrine of God and the contemporary gender debate*. Downers Grove, IL: InterVarsity Press.

Gill, David W. J. 1990. The importance of Roman portraiture for head-coverings in 1 Corinthians 11:2–16. *Tyndale Bulletin* 41, no. 2: 245–60.

Gillingham, S. E. 1994. *The poems and psalms of the Hebrew Bible*. Ed. P. R. Ackroyd and G. N. Stanton. Oxford Bible Series. Oxford: Oxford University Press.

Goldingay, John. 2003. *Old Testament theology: Israel's gospel*. Vol. 1. Downers Grove: InterVarsity Press.

Greenleaf, Robert K. 2003. *Servant leadership: A journey into the nature of legitimate power and greatness*. 25th anniv. ed. Mumbai: Magna Publishing.

Grenz, Stanley J. 2001. *The social God and the relational self: A Trinitarian theology of the imago Dei*. Louisville: Westminster John Knox.

Gritz, Sharon Hodgin. 1991. *Paul, women teachers, and the mother goddess at Ephesus: A study of 1 Timothy 2:9–15 in light of the religious and cultural milieu of the first century*. Lanham, MA: University Press of America.

Grudem, Wayne A. 1985. Does ΚΕΦΑΛΗ ("head") mean "source" or "authority over" in Greek literature? A survey of 2,336 examples. *Trinity Journal* 6, no. 1: 38–59.

———. 2002. The meaning of *kephale* ("head"): An evaluation of new evidence, real and alleged. In *Biblical foundations for manhood and womanhood*, ed. W. A. Grudem. Wheaton: Crossway Books.

———. 2006. *Countering the claims of evangelical feminism*. Colorado Springs: Multnomah Publishers.

Guder, Darrell L. 1985. *Be my witnesses*. Grand Rapids: Eerdmans.

Gundry-Volf, Judith M. 1994. Male and female in creation and new creation: Interpretations of Galatians 3:28c in 1 Corinthians 7. In *To tell the mystery: Essays on New Testament eschatology in honor of Robert H. Gundry*, ed. T. E. Schmidt and M. Silva, 95–121. Sheffield, UK: Sheffield Academic.

———. 1996. Controlling the bodies: A theological profile of the Corinthian sexual ascetics (1 Cor. 7). In *The Corinthian correspondence*, ed. R. Bieringer, 519–41. Leuven, Belgium: Leuven University Press.

———. 1997. Gender and creation in 1 Corinthians 11:2–16: A study in Paul's theological method. In *Evangelium schriftauslegung kriche: Festschrift für Peter Stuhlmacher zum 65 geburtstag*, ed. J. Ådna, S. J. Hafemann, and O. Hofius, 151–71. Göttingen, Germany: Vandenhoeck and Ruprecht.

Gunkel, Hermann. 1997. *Genesis: Translated and interpreted by Hermann Gunkel.* Trans. M. E. Biddle. Mercer Library of Biblical Studies. Macon, GA: Mercer University Press.

Gunton, Colin E. 1997. *The promise of Trinitarian theology.* 2nd ed. Edinburgh: Clark.

_____. 2002. *The Christian faith: An introduction to Christian doctrine.* Oxford: Blackwell.

_____. 2003. *Act and being: Toward a theology of the divine attributes.* Grand Rapids: Eerdmans.

Hales, Shelley. 2003. *The Roman house and social identity.* New York: Cambridge University Press.

Hall, David R. 2003. *The unity of the Corinthian correspondence.* Ed. S. E. Porter. Vol. 251 *Journal for the study of the New Testament supplement series.* London: Clark.

Hall, Kevin. 2001. The theology of Genesis 1–11. *Southwestern Journal of Theology* 44, no. 1: 56–75.

Hanson, Ann E. 1999. The Roman family. In *Life, death, and entertainment in the Roman empire,* ed. D. S. Potter and D. J. Mattingly, 19–66. Ann Arbor: University of Michigan Press.

Harlow, Mary. 2005. Dress in the *Historia Augusta:* The role of dress in historical narrative. In *The clothed body in the ancient world,* ed. L. Cleland, M. Harlow, and L. Llewellyn-Jones, 143–53. Oxford: Oxbow Books.

Harman, Allan M. 1997. 'ezer [helper]. In *New international dictionary of Old Testament theology and exegesis,* ed. W. A. Van Gemeren, Vol. 3 of 5, 378–79. Grand Rapids: Zondervan.

Hasel, Gerhard F. 1982. The Sabbath in the Pentateuch. In *The Sabbath in Scripture and history,* ed. K. A. Strand, 21–43. Washington, DC: Review and Herald Publishing.

Hatch, Evelyn. 1992. *Discourse and language education.* Cambridge Language Teaching Library. Cambridge: Cambridge University Press.

Hays, Richard B. 1996. *The moral vision of the New Testament: Community, cross, new creation; A contemporary introduction to New Testament ethics.* New York: HarperCollins.

_____. 1997. *First Corinthians.* Ed. J. R. Mays. Interpretation: A Bible Commentary for Teaching and Preaching. Louisville: John Knox.

_____. 2004. Paul on the relation between men and women. In *A feminist companion to Paul,* ed. A.-J. Levine and M. Blickenstaff, 137–47. Cleveland: Pilgrim.

Heschel, Abraham. 1962. *The prophets*. Vol. 2. New York: HarperCollins.

Hess, Richard S. 2005. Equality with and without innocence: Genesis 1–3. In *Discovering biblical equality: Complementarity without hierarchy*, ed. R. W. Pierce and R. M. Groothuis, 79–95. 2nd ed. Downers Grove, IL: InterVarsity Press.

Hiebert, Paul G. 1996. The gospel in our culture: Methods of social and cultural analysis. In *The church between gospel and culture: The emerging mission in North America*, ed. G. R. Hunsberger and C. Van Gelder, 139–57. Grand Rapids: Eerdmans.

———, and Eloise Hiebert Meneses. 1995. *Incarnational ministry: Planting churches in band, tribal, peasant and urban societies*. Grand Rapids: Baker Books.

———, R. Daniel Shaw, and Tite Tienou. 1999. *Understanding folk religion: A Christian response to popular beliefs and practices*. Grand Rapids: Baker Books.

Hirshfelder, Umm Abdur Rahman, and Umm Yasmeen Rahmaan. 2003. *From monogamy to polygyny: A way through*. Riyadh: Darussalam.

Hoehner, Harold W. 2002. *Ephesians: An exegetical study*. Grand Rapids: Baker Academic.

Hofstede, Geert. 2001. *Culture's consequences: Comparing values, behaviors, institutions, and organizations across nations*. 2nd ed. Thousand Oaks, CA: SAGE.

———, and Gert Jan Hofstede. 2005. *Cultures and organizations: Software of the mind*. 2nd ed. New York: McGraw-Hill.

Holmyard, Harold R., III. 1997. Does 1 Corinthians 11:2–16 refer to women praying and prophesying in church? *Bibliotheca Sacra* 154, no. 616: 461–72.

Holstein, James A., and Jaber F. Gubrium. 1995. *The active interview*. Ed. J. Van Maanen, P. K. Manning, and M. L. Miller. Vol. 37 of *Qualitative research methods*. Thousand Oaks, CA: SAGE.

Hooker, Morna D. 1964. Authority on her head: An examination of 1 Cor. 11:10. *New Testament Studies* 10: 410–16.

Horatius Flaccus, Quintus. 2004. *Odes and epodes*. Trans. N. Rudd. Ed. J. Henderson. Loeb Classical Library. Cambridge, MA: Harvard University Press.

Horrell, David G. 1996. *The social ethos of the Corinthian correspondence: Interests and ideology from 1 Corinthians to 1 Clement*. Edinburgh: Clark.

Horsley, Richard A. 1998. *1 Corinthians*. Ed. V. P. Furnish. Abingdon New Testament Commentaries. Nashville: Abingdon.

Houghton, Leslie William. 1976. The concept of woman in the Pauline corpus in light of the social and religious environment of the first century. PhD diss., Northwestern University.

House, Paul R. 1998. *Old Testament theology*. Downers Grove, IL: InterVarsity Press.

Hurd, John Coolidge. 1963. *The origin of 1 Corinthians*. New York: Seabury.

Hurley, James B. 1981. *Man and woman in biblical perspective*. Grand Rapids: Zondervan.

Ibn Anas, Malik. 1989. *Al-Muwatta of Imam Malik ibn Anas: The first formulation of Islamic law*. Trans. A. A. Bewley. London: Kegan Paul.

Ibn Hisham, Abu Muhammad 'Abd al-Malik bin Hisham. 1936. *Al-Sirah al-Nabawiyah / li-ibn Hisham; Haqqaqaha wa-dabataha wa-sharahaha wa-wada'a faharisaha Mustafa al-Saqqa, Ibrahim al-Ibyari, 'Abd al-Hafiz*. Vol. 4. Cairo: Maṭba'at Muṣṭafá al-Bābī al-Ḥalabī.

Ibn Kathir, Abu al-Fida 'Imad Ad-Din Ismai'il bin Umar. 2003. *Tafsir ibn Kathir* (abridged). Trans. J. Abualrub, N. Khitab, H. Khitab, A. Walker, M. al-Jibali, and S. Ayoub. 2nd ed. Vol. 1. Riyadh: Darussalam.

Instone-Brewer, David. 2001. 1 Corinthians 7 in the light of the Jewish Greek and Aramaic marriage and divorce papyri. *Tyndale Bulletin* 52, no. 2: 225–43.

Jerome. 1984. *Novum Testamentum Latine: Novam Vulgatam Bibliorum Sacrorum Editionem secuti apparatibus titulisque additis ediderunt Kurt Aland et Barbara Aland una cum Instituto studiorum textus Novi Testamenti Monasteriensi (Westphalia)*. Stuttgart, Germany: Deutsche Bibelgesellschaft.

Jervis, L. Ann. 1995. 1 Corinthians 14:34–35: A reconsideration of Paul's limitation of the free speech of some Corinthian women. *Journal for the Study of the New Testament* 58 (June): 51–74.

Johnston, Alan. 2006. Women ponder future under Hamas. BBC News. March 3. http://news.bbc.co.uk/go/pr/fr/-/1/hi/world/middle_east/4767634.stm.

Jorgensen, Danny L. 1989. *Participant observation: A methodology for human studies*. Ed. L. Bickman and D. J. Rog. Vol. 15 of *Applied social research methods series*. Thousand Oaks, CA: SAGE.

Josephus. 1961. *Josephus*. Translated by H. S. J. Thackeray. Edited by T. E. Page, E. Capps, W. H. D. Rouse, L. A. Post and E. H. Warmington. 9 vols. Vol. 4, *The Loeb Classical Library*. Cambridge, MA: Harvard University Press.

Justinianus, Caesar Flavius. 1985. Digesta: *English and Latin*. Trans. A. Watson. Vol. 1. Philadelphia: University of Pensylvania Press.

Juvenalis, Decimus Junius. 2004. *Juvenal and Persius*. Trans. S. M. Braund. Ed. J. Henderson. Loeb Classical Library. Cambridge, MA: Harvard University Press.

Karim, al-Haj Maulana Fazlul. 1998. *Al-Hadis: An English translation and commentary with Arabic text of Mishkat-ul-Masabih*. Vol. 2. Lahore, Pakistan: Islamic Education Center.

Karmi, Ghada. 1996. Women, Islam, and patriarchalism. In *Feminism and Islam: Legal and literary perspectives*, ed. M. Yamani, 69–86. New York: New York University Press.

Keener, Craig S. 1992. *Paul, women and wives: Marriage and women's ministry in the letters of Paul*. Peabody, MA: Hendrickson.

———. 1995. *The NIV application commentary: 1 Corinthians; From biblical text to contemporary life*. Ed. T. Muck. The NIV Application Commentary Series. Grand Rapids: Zondervan.

———. 2001. Women in ministry. In *Two views on women in ministry*, ed. J. R. Beck and C. L. Blomberg. Grand Rapids: Zondervan.

Klein, George L. 2001. Reading Genesis 1. *Southwestern Journal of Theology* 44, no. 1: 22–38.

Klein, Laura F. 2004. *Women and men in world cultures*. New York: McGraw-Hill.

Knight, George W., III. 1991. The family and the church: How should biblical manhood and womanhood work out in practice? In *Recovering biblical manhood and womanhood: A response to evangelical feminism*, ed. J. Piper and W. A. Grudem, 345–57. Wheaton: Crossway Books.

———. 1992. *The Pastoral Epistles: A commentary on the Greek text*. Ed. I. H. Marshall and W. W. Gasque. The New International Greek Testament Commentary. Grand Rapids: Eerdmans.

Kraft, Charles H. 1996. *Anthropology for Christian witness*. Maryknoll, NY: Orbis Books.

———. 2005. Meaning equivalence contextualization. In *Appropriate Christianity*, ed. C. H. Kraft, 155–68. Pasadena: William Carey Library.

Kümmel, Werner Georg. 1975. *Introduction to the New Testament*. Trans. H. C. Kee. 17th ed. Nashville: Abingdon.

Kvale, Steinar. 1996. *Interviews: An introduction to qualitative research interviewing*. Thousand Oaks, CA: SAGE.

Lacey, W. K. 1986. *Patria potestas*. In *The family in ancient Rome: New perspectives*, ed. B. Rawson, 121–44. Ithaca, NY: Cornell University Press.

Lenski, Gerhard Emmanuel. 1984. *Power and privilege: A theory of social stratification*. Chapel Hill: University of North Carolina Press.

Lerner, Gerda. 1986. *The creation of patriarchy*. New York: Oxford University Press.

Levine, A., ed. 1951. *The early Syrian fathers on Genesis: From a Syriac ms. on the Pentateuch in the Mingana Collection.* Trans. A. Levine. London: Taylor's Foreign Press.

Lewins, Ann, and Christina Silver. 2007. *Using software in qualitative research: A step-by-step guide.* Los Angeles: SAGE.

Lieber, David, ed. 2001. Etz hayim: *Torah and commentary.* Vol. 1. New York: Jewish Publication Society.

Lietzmann, Hans. 1953. *A history of the early church: The beginnings of the early church.* Trans. B. L. Woolf. 3rd ed. Vol. 1. London: Lutterworth.

Lincoln, Andrew T. 1990. *Ephesians.* Ed. D. A. Hubbard, G. W. Barker, and R. P. Martin. Vol. 42 of *Word biblical commentary.* Dallas: Word Books.

———, and A. J. M. Wedderburn. 1993. *The theology of the later Pauline Letters.* Ed. J. D. G. Dunn. New Testament Theology. Cambridge: Cambridge University Press.

Lindholm, Charles. 1982. *Generosity and jealousy.* New York: Columbia University Press.

Litke, Wayne. 1995. Beyond creation: Galatians 3:28, Genesis and the Hermaphrodite myth. *Studies in Religion* 24, no. 2: 173–78.

Livius, Titus. 1953. *Livy.* Trans. E. T. Sage. Ed. T. E. Page, E. Capps, L. A. Post, W. H. D. Rouse, and E. H. Warmington. Vol. 9. Loeb Classical Library. Cambridge, MA: Harvard University Press.

———. 1957. *Livy.* Trans. B. O. Foster. Ed. T. E. Page, E. Capps, I. A. Post, W. H. D. Rouse, and E. H. Warmington. Vol. 1. Loeb Classical Library. Cambridge: Harvard University Press.

Loader, William. 2004. *The Septuagint, sexuality, and the New Testament: Case studies on the impact of the LXX in Philo and the New Testament.* Grand Rapids: Eerdmans.

———. 2005. *Sexuality and the Jesus tradition.* Grand Rapids: Eerdmans.

Lock, Walter. 1924. *A critical and exegetical commentary on the Pastoral Epistles (I and II Timothy and Titus).* The International Critical Commentary on the Holy Scriptures of the Old and New Testaments. Edinburgh: Clark.

Lohse, Eduard. 1971. *Colossians and Philemon.* Trans. W. R. Poehlmann and H. Karris. Ed. H. Koestner, E. J. Epp, R. W. Funk, G. W. MacRae, and J. M. Robinson. *Hermeneia:* A Critical and Historical Commentary on the Bible. Philadelphia: Fortress.

Longenecker, Richard N. 1986. Authority, hierarchy and leadership patterns in the Bible. In *Women, authority and the Bible*, ed. A. Mickelsen, 66–85. Downers Grove, IL: InterVarsity Press.

Lowery, David K. 1986. The head covering and Lord's Supper in 1 Cor 11:2–34. *Bibliotheca Sacra* 143 (April–June): 155–63.

Lucretius Carus, Titus. 1997. *On the nature of the universe*. Trans. S. R. Melville. Oxford: Oxford University Press.

Lukens-Bull, Ronald A. 2007. Between text and practice: Considerations in the anthropological study of Islam. In *Defining Islam: A reader*, ed. A. Rippin, 37–57. London: Equinox.

MacDonald, Dennis Ronald. 1987. *There is no male and female: The fate of a dominical saying in Paul and gnosticism*. Ed. M. R. Miles and B. J. Brooten. Vol. 20 of *Harvard dissertations in religion*. Philadelphia: Fortress.

MacDonald, Margaret Y. 1990. Women holy in body and spirit: The social setting of 1 Corinthians 7. *New Testament Studies* 36: 161–81.

_____. 1996. *Early Christian women and pagan opinion: The power of the hysterical woman*. Cambridge: Cambridge University Press.

_____. 2000. *Colossians and Ephesians*. Ed. D. J. Harrington. Vol. 17 of *Sacra pagina*. Collegeville, MN: Liturgical Press.

_____. 2004. Virgins, widows, and wives: The women of 1 Corinthians 7. In *A feminist companion to Paul*, ed. A.-J. Levine and M. Blickenstaff. Cleveland: Pilgrim.

Madani, Aiysha. 2005. *A review of contemporary thought in women rights with reference to Amina Wadud and others*. Islamabad, Pakistan: Poorab Academy.

Madani, Mohammad Ismail Memon. 2000. *Hijab: The Islamic commandments of hijab*. Trans. M. Sadiq. Karachi, Pakistan: Darul Ishaat.

Magonet, Jonathan. 1992. The themes of Genesis 2–3. In *A walk in the garden: Biblical, iconographical and literary images of Eden*, ed. P. Morris and D. Sawyer, 39–46. Sheffield, UK: JSOT.

Maier, Walter A. 1991. An exegetical study of 1 Corinthians 14:33b–38. *Concordia Theological Quarterly* 55, nos. 2–3: 81–104.

Malina, Bruce J. 2001. *The New Testament world: Insights from cultural anthropology*. 3rd ed. Louisville: Westminster John Knox.

_____, and Jerome H. Neyrey. 1996. *Portraits of Paul: An archaeology of ancient personality*. Louisville: Westminster John Knox.

Marshall, I. Howard. 2005. Mutual love and submission in marriage: Colossians 3:18–19 and Ephesians 5:21–33. In *Discovering biblical equality: Complementarity without hierarchy*, ed. R. W. Pierce and R. M. Groothuis, 186–204. 2nd ed. Downers Grove, IL: InterVarsity Press.

Martialis, Marcus Valerius. 1993. *Martial: Epigrams*. Trans. D. R. S. Bailey. Ed. G. P. Goold. 3 vols. Loeb Classical Library. Cambridge, MA: Harvard University Press.

Martin, Dale B. 1995. *The Corinthian body*. New Haven, CT: Yale University Press.

Martin, Francis. 1993. Male and female he created them: A summary of the teaching of Genesis chapter one. *Communio: International Catholic Review* 20 (Summer): 240–65.

Matthews, Kenneth A. 1996. *Genesis 1–11:26*. Ed. E. R. Clendenen. Vol. 1a of *The new American commentary*. Nashville: Broadman and Holman.

Maududi, Abul A'la. 2004. *Purdah and the status of women in Islam*. Trans. al-Ahs'ari. 18th ed. Lahore, Pakistan: Islamic Publications.

Maximus, Valerius. 2000. *Memorable doings and sayings*. Trans. D. R. S. Bailey. Ed. J. Henderson. 2 vols. Loeb Classical Library. Cambridge, MA: Harvard University Press.

McComiskey, Thomas E. 1980. ['a â]. In *Theological wordbook of the Old Testament*, ed. M. J. Harris, G. L. J. Archer, and B. K. Waltke. Vol. 2, 701–702. Chicago: Moody Press.

Meeks, Wayne A. 1973. The image of the androgyne: Some uses of a symbol in earliest Christianity. *History of Religions* 13, no. 1: 165–208.

————. 2001. Corinthian Christians as artificial aliens. In *Paul beyond the Judaism/Hellenism divide*, ed. T. Engberg-Pedersen, 129–38. Louisville: Westminster John Knox.

Meier, John P. 1978. On the veiling of hermeneutics (1 Cor 11:2–16). *Catholic Biblical Quarterly* 40: 212–26.

Mernissi, Fatima. 1991. *The veil and the male elite: A feminist interpretation of women's rights in Islam*. Trans. M. J. Lakeland. Reading, MA: Addison-Wesley. Original edition, *Le harem politique*.

Meyers, Carol L. 1983. Gender roles and Genesis 3:16 revisited. In *The word of the Lord shall go forth*, ed. C. L. Meyers and M. O'Connor, 337–54. Winona Lake, IN: Eisenbrauns.

Mickelsen, Berkeley, and Alvera Mickelsen. 1986. What does *kephale* mean in the New Testament? In *Women, authority and the Bible*, ed. A. Mickelsen, 97–110. Downers Grove, IL: InterVarsity Press.

Miles, Matthew B., and A. Michael Huberman. 1994. *Qualitative data analysis: An expanded sourcebook*. 2nd ed. Thousand Oaks, CA: SAGE.

Miletic, Stephen Francis. 1988. *"One flesh": Eph. 5.22–24, 5.31; Marriage and the new creation*. Vol. 115 of *Analecta biblica: Investigationes scientificae in res biblicas*. Rome: Editrice Pontificio Istituto Biblico.

Miller, Barbara Diane. 1993. The anthropology of sex and gender hierarchies. In *Sex and gender hierarchies*, ed. B. D. Miller, 3–31. Cambridge, MA: Cambridge University Press.

Molnar, Paul D. 2002. *Divine freedom and the doctrine of the immanent Trinity: In dialogue with Karl Barth and contemporary theology*. London: Clark.

Moo, Douglas. 1991. What does it mean not to teach or have authority over men? 1 Timothy 2:11–15. In *Recovering biblical manhood and womanhood*, ed. J. Piper and W. A. Grudem, 179–93. Wheaton: Crossway Books.

Moody, Dwight A. 1995. On the road again. *Review and Expositor* 92, no. 1: 95–101.

Moreau, A. Scott. 1995. The human universals of culture: Implications for contextualization. *International Journal of Frontier Missions* 12, no. 3: 121–25.

_____. 2001. INTR 532: Case study worksheet. http://www.wheaton.edu/intr/Moreau/532/cswork.pdf (accessed June 9, 2007).

Mounce, William D. 2000. *Pastoral Epistles*. Ed. B. M. Metzger, D. A. Hubbard, and G. W. Barker. Vol. 46 of *Word biblical commentary*. Nashville: Thomas Nelson.

Muddiman, John. 2001. *A commentary on the Epistle to the Ephesians*. Ed. M. D. Hooker. Black's New Testament Commentaries. New York: Continuum.

Murphy-O'Connor, Jerome. 1976. The non-Pauline character of 1 Corinthians 11:2–6? *Journal of Biblical Literature* 95, no. 4: 615–21.

_____. 1979. *1 Corinthians*. Ed. H. Wilfred and D. Senior. Vol. 10 of *New Testament message*. Wilmington, DE: Glazier.

_____. 1980. Sex and logic in 1 Corinthians 11:2–16. *Catholic Biblical Quarterly* 42: 482–500.

_____. 1986. Interpolations in 1 Corinthians. *Catholic Biblical Quarterly* 48, no. 1: 81–94.

_____. 1988. 1 Corinthians 11:2–16 once again. *Catholic Biblical Quarterly* 50, no. 2: 265–74.

_____. 1996. *Paul: A critical life*. Oxford: Clarendon.

Muslim, Abdu'l-Hussain 'Asakir-ud-Din. 1998a. *Sahih Muslim.* Trans. M. Matraji. Vol. 2B. Karachi, Pakistan: Darul-Ishaat.

_____. 1998b. *Sahih Muslim.* Trans. M. Matraji. Vol. 3B. Karachi, Pakistan: Darul-Ishaat.

_____. 1998c. *Sahih Muslim.* Trans. M. Matraji. Vol. 4B. Karachi, Pakistan: Darul-Ishaat.

Muzaffar-ud-din, Syed. 2000. *A comparative study of Islam and other religions.* Lahore, Pakistan: Sh. Muhammad Ashraf.

Nadvi, Syed Muzaffar-ud-Din. 1992. *Human rights and obligations: In the light of the Quran and Hadith.* Lahore, Pakistan: Sh. Muhammad Ashraf.

Nelson, Haydn D. 2005. A Trinitarian perspective on the destiny of the unevangelized. In *Text and task: Scripture and mission,* ed. M. Parsons, 157–171. Waynesboro, GA: Paternoster.

The News International. 2007. Punjab minister Zill-e-Huma shot dead. October 27. http://www.thenews.com.pk/top_story_detail.asp?Id=6000 (accessed October 27, 2007).

Niccum, Curt. 1997. The voice of the manuscripts on the silence of women. *New Testament Studies* 43 (April): 242–55.

Nissen, Johannes. 2002. *New Testament and mission: Historical and hermeneutical perspectives.* 2nd ed. Frankfurt: Peter Lang GmbH.

O'Brien, Peter T. 1999. *The Letter to the Ephesians.* Ed. D. A. Carson. The Pillar New Testament Commentary. Grand Rapids: Eerdmans.

Odell-Scott, David W. 2005. Patriarchy and heterosexual eroticism: The question in Romans and Corinthians. In *Gender, tradition and Romans: Shared ground, uncertain borders,* ed. C. Grenholm and D. Patte, 209–26. New York: Clark.

O'Donovan, Oliver. 1986. *Resurrection and moral order: An outline for evangelical ethics.* Leicester, UK: InterVarsity Press.

Ogden, Graham S. 1985. A fresh look at the "curses" of Genesis 3:14–19. *Taiwan Journal of Theology* 7: 129–40.

Økland, Jorunn. 2004. *Women in their place: Paul and the Corinthian discourse of gender and sanctuary space.* Ed. M. Goodacre. Vol. 269 of *Journal for the study of the New Testament supplement series.* London: Clark.

Orbe, Mark P. 1998. *Constructing co-cultural theory: An explication of culture, power, and communication.* Thousand Oaks, CA: SAGE.

Ortland, Raymond C., Jr. 1991. Male-female equality and male headship: Genesis 1–3. In *Recovering biblical manhood and womanhood: A response to evangelical feminism*, ed. J. Piper and W. Grudem, 95–112. Wheaton: Crossway Books.

Osiek, Carolyn. 2003. Female slaves, *porneia*, and the limits of obedience. In *Early Christian families in context: An interdisciplinary dialogue*, ed. D. L. Balch and C. Osiek, 255–74. Grand Rapids: Eerdmans.

———, and David L. Balch. 1997. *Families in the New Testament world: Households and house churches*. Ed. D. S. Browning and I. S. Evison. The Family, Religion, and Culture. Louisville: Westminster John Knox.

Oster, Richard. 1988. When men wore veils to worship: The historical context of 1 Corinthians 11.4. *New Testament Studies* 34: 481–505.

Ovidius Naso, Publius. 1962. *Ovid: The art of love and other poems*. Trans. J. H. Mozley. Ed. T. E. Page, E. Capps, I. A. Post, W. H. D. Rouse, and E. H. Warmington. Loeb Classical Library. Cambridge, MA: Harvard University Press.

Padgett, Alan. 1984. Paul on women in the church: The contradictions of coiffure in 1 Corinthians 11:2–16. *Journal for the Study of the New Testament* 20, no. 1: 69–86.

Page, Franklin S. 1980. Toward a biblical ethic of women in ministry. PhD diss., Southwestern Baptist Theological Seminary.

Paige, Terrence. 2002. The social matrix of women's speech at Corinth: The context and meaning of the command to silence in 1 Corinthians 14:33b–36. *Bulletin for Biblical Research* 12, no. 2: 217–42.

Papa, Michael J., Arvind Singhal, and Wendy H. Papa. 2006. *Organizing for social change: A dialectic journey of theory and praxis*. New Delhi: SAGE.

Patton, Michael Quinn. 1990. *Qualitative evaluation and research methods*. 2nd ed. Newbury Park, CA: SAGE.

Peerbolte, L. J. Lietaert. 2000. Man, woman, and the angels in 1 Cor. 11:2–6. In *The creation of man and woman: Interpretations of the biblical narratives in Jewish and Christian traditions*, ed. G. P. Luttikhuizen, 76–92. Leiden: Brill.

Peterson, Steven A. 1991. Human ethology and political hierarchy: Is democracy feasible? In *Hierarchy and democracy*, ed. A. Somit and R. Wildenmann, 63–78. Carbondale: Southern Illinois University Press.

Philo Judaeus. 1929. Philo: with an English translation by F. H. Colson, M.A. and the Rev. G. H. Whitaker, M.A. Edited by T. E. Page, E. Capps and W. H. D. Rouse. Vol. 1 of 10, The Loeb Classical Library. New York, NY: G. P. Putnam's Sons.

_____. 1961. *Philo: Questions and answers on Genesis: Translated from the ancient Armenian Version of the Original Greek*. Translated by R. Marcus. Edited by T. E. Page, E. Capps, W. H. D. Rouse, L. A. Post and E. H. Warmington. Vol. Supplement 1, *The Loeb Classical Library*. Cambridge, MA: Harvard University Press.

Piper, John. 1991. A vision of biblical complementarity: Manhood and womanhood defined according to the Bible. In *Recovering biblical manhood and womanhood: A response to evangelical feminism*, ed. J. Piper and W. A. Grudem. Wheaton: Crossway Books.

_____, and Wayne A. Grudem. 1991. An overview of central concerns: Questions and answers. In *Recovering biblical manhood and womanhood: A response to evangelical feminism*, ed. J. Piper and W. A. Grudem, 60–92. Wheaton: Crossway Books.

Plautus, Maccius. 1966. *Plautus*. Trans. P. Nixon. Ed. T. E. Page, E. Capps, I. A. Post, W. H. D. Rouse, and E. H. Warmington. Vol. 1. Loeb Classical Library. Cambridge, MA: Harvard University Press.

Plinius Caecilius Secundus, Gaius. 1952. *Pliny: Natural history*. Trans. H. Rackham. Ed. T. E. Page, E. Capps, I. A. Post, W. H. D. Rouse, and E. H. Warmington. Vol. 4. Loeb Classical Library. Cambridge, MA: Harvard University Press.

_____. 1969. *Pliny: Letters and* Panegyricus. Trans. B. Radice. Ed. E. H. Warmington. Vol. 2. Loeb Classical Library. Cambridge, MA: Harvard University Press.

Plutarchus. 1931. *Plutarch's "Moralia."* Trans. F. C. Babbitt. Ed. T. E. Page, E. Capps, and W. H. D. Rouse. Vol. 3. Loeb Classical Library. New York: Putnam.

_____. 1950. *Plutarch's lives: Alcibiades and Coriolanus, Lysander and Sulla*. Trans. B. Perrin. Ed. T. E. Page, E. Capps, I. A. Post, W. H. D. Rouse, and E. H. Warmington. Vol. 4. Loeb Classical Library. Cambridge, MA: Harvard University Press.

_____. 1955. *Plutarch's lives: Agesilaus and Pompey, Pelopidas and Marcellus*. Trans. B. Perrin. Ed. T. E. Page, E. Capps, I. A. Post, W. H. D. Rouse, and E. H. Warmington. Vol. 5. Loeb Classical Library. Cambridge, MA: Harvard University Press.

_____. 1959. *Plutarch's lives: Sertorius and Eumenes, Phocion and Cato the Younger*. Trans. B. Perrin. Ed. T. E. Page, E. Capps, I. A. Post, W. H. D. Rouse, and E. H. Warmington. Vol. 8. Loeb Classical Library. Cambridge, MA: Harvard University Press.

_____. 1998. *Plutarch's "Moralia."* Trans. F. C. Babbitt. Ed. C. P. Goold. Vol. 2. Loeb Classical Library. Cambridge, MA: Harvard University Press.

Pomeroy, Sarah B. 1975. *Goddesses, whores, wives, and slaves: Women in classical antiquity*. New York: Schocken Books.

Propertius, Sextus Aurelius. 1952. *Propertius*. Trans. H. E. Butler. Ed. T. E. Page, E. Capps, I. A. Post, W. H. D. Rouse, and E. H. Warmington. Loeb Classical Library. Cambridge, MA: Harvard University Press.

Quinn, Jerome D., and William C. Wacker. 2000. *The First and Second Letters to Timothy: A new translation with notes and commentary*. Ed. D. N. Freedman and A. B. Beck. The Eerdmans Critical Commentary. Grand Rapids: Eerdmans.

Rahman, Mir Jamilur. 2007. Murder of a minister. *The News International*, February 24. http://www.thenews.com.pk/daily_detail.asp?id=44162 (accessed February 24, 2007).

Ramsey, George W. 1988. Is name-giving an act of domination in Genesis 2:23 and elsewhere? *Catholic Biblical Quarterly* 50: 24–35.

Rashi. 1985. *Chumash with Targum Onkelos, Haphtaroth and Rashi's commentary*. Trans. A. M. Silbermann and M. Rosenbaum. Vol. 1. Jerusalem: Silbermann Family.

Ratzinger, Joseph, and Angelo Amato. 2004. Letter to the bishops of the Catholic Church: On the collaboration of men and women in the church and in the world. May 31. Women for Faith and Family. http://www.wf-f.org/CDF-LetteronCollaboration.html.

Rawson, Beryl. 2001. Children as cultural symbols. In *Childhood, class and kin in the Roman world*, ed. S. Dixon, 21–42. New York: Routledge.

Rei, Annalisa. 1998. Villains, wives, and slaves in the comedies of Plautus. In *Women and slaves in Greco-Roman culture: Differential equations.*, ed. S. R. Joshel and S. Murnaghan, 92–108. New York: Routledge.

Roetzel, Calvin J. 1998. *Paul: The man and the myth*. Ed. D. M. Smith. Studies on Personalities of the New Testament. Columbia: University of South Carolina Press.

Rogers, Mary F. 1980. Goffman on power, hierarchy, and status. In *The view from Goffman*, ed. J. Ditton, 100–133. New York: St. Martin's.

Ronning, John L. 1997. The curse on the serpent (Genesis 3:15) in biblical theology and hermeneutics. PhD diss., Westminster Theological Seminary.

Rosen, Lawrence. 2002. *The culture of Islam: Changing aspects of contemporary Muslim life*. Chicago: University of Chicago Press.

Ross, Alan P. 1988. *Creation and blessing: A guide to the study and exposition of Genesis*. Grand Rapids: Baker Books.

Rousselle, Aline. 1992. Body politics in ancient Rome. In *A history of women in the West: From ancient goddesses to Christian saints*, ed. P. S. Pantel, 296–337. Cambridge, MA: Belknap Press of Harvard University Press.

Rufus, Musonius. 1947. *Musonius Rufus: "The Roman Socrates."* Trans. C. Lutz. Vol. 10 of *Yale classical studies*. New Haven, CT: Yale University Press.

Sailhamer, John. 1992. *The Pentateuch as narrative: A biblical-theological commentary*. Grand Rapids: Zondervan.

Saller, Richard P. 1987. Slavery and the Roman family. In *Classical slavery*, ed. M. I. Finley. London: Cass.

_____. 1994. *Patriarchy, property and death in the Roman family*. Ed. P. Laslett, R. Schofield, and E. A. Wrigley. Vol. 25 of *Cambridge studies in population, economy and society in past time*. Cambridge, MA: Cambridge University Press.

_____. 2003. Women, slaves, and the economy of the Roman household. In *Early Christian families in context: An interdisciplinary dialogue*, ed. D. L. Balch and C. Osiek, 185–204. Grand Rapids: Eerdmans.

Sawyer, John F. A. 1992. The image of God, the wisdom of the serpents and the knowledge of good and evil. In *A walk in the garden: Biblical, iconographical and literary images of Eden*, ed. P. Morris and D. Sawyer, 64–73. Sheffield, UK: Sheffield Academic.

Schmitt, John J. 1991. Like Eve, like Adam: *m l* in Gen. 3:16. *Biblica* 72, no. 1: 1–22.

Scholer, David M. 1990. Women in the church's ministry: Does 1 Timothy 2:9–15 help or hinder? *Daughters of Sarah* 16, no. 4: 7–12.

_____. 1993. Paul and sexuality: Reflections on "The Bible and human sexuality." *American Baptist Quarterly* 12, no. 4: 334–39.

_____. 1998. Galatians 3:28 and the ministry of women in the church. *Covenant Quarterly* 56, no. 3: 2–17.

_____. 2003. 1 Timothy 2:9–15 and the place of women in the church's ministry. In *A feminist companion to the Deutero-Pauline Epistles*, ed. A.-J. Levine and M. Blickenstaff, 98–121. Cleveland: Pilgrim.

Schreiner, Thomas R. 1991. Head coverings, prophecies and the Trinity: 1 Corinthians 11:2–16. In *Recovering biblical manhood and womanhood*, ed. J. Piper and W. A. Grudem, 124–39. Wheaton: Crossway Books.

_____. 1995. An interpretation of 1 Timothy 2:9–15: A dialogue with scholarship. In *Women in the church: A fresh analysis of 1 Timothy 2:9–15*, ed. A. J. Köstenberger, T. R. Schreiner, and H. S. Baldwin, 105–54. Grand Rapids: Baker Books.

_____. 2005. An interpretation of 1 Timothy 2:9–15: A dialogue with scholarship. In *Women in the church: An analysis and application of 1 Timothy 2:9–15*, ed. A. J. Köstenberger and T. R. Schreiner, 85–120. 2nd ed. Grand Rapids: Baker Academic.

Scott, T. Lynn. 1998. Symbolic healing and the body at Corinth: An anthropological analysis of Paul's rhetoric. PhD diss., Vanderbilt University.

Scroggs, Robin. 1972. Paul and the eschatological woman. *Journal of the American Academy of Religion* 40, no. 3: 283–303.

Sebesta, Judith Lynn. 2001. Symbolism in the costume of the Roman woman. In *The world of Roman costume*, ed. J. L. Sebesta and L. Bonfante, 46–53. Madison: University of Wisconsin Press.

Seneca, Lucius Annaeus. 1928. *Moral essays*. Trans. J. W. Basore. Ed. T. E. Page, E. Capps, I. A. Post, W. H. D. Rouse, and E. H. Warmington. Vol. 1. Loeb Classical Library. Cambridge, MA: Harvard University Press.

_____. 1951. *Moral essays*. Trans. J. W. Basore. Ed. T. E. Page, E. Capps, I. A. Post, W. H. D. Rouse, and E. H. Warmington. Vol. 2. Loeb Classical Library. Cambridge, MA: Harvard University Press.

Shahri, Mohammad Aashiq Ilahi Buland. 2001. *The book of clothing and hijab*. Trans. R. A. Rahman. Karachi, Pakistan: Darul Isha'at.

Shaw, R. Daniel, and Charles E. Van Engen. 2003. *Communicating God's word in a complex world: God's truth or hocus pocus?* Lanham, MD: Rowman and Littlefield.

Sherif, Mostafa Hashem. 1987. What is hijab? *Muslim World* 77, nos. 3–4: 151–63.

Siddiqi, Muhammad Iqbal. 1992. *Islam forbids free mixing of men and women*. Delhi: Adam Publishers.

Snodgrass, Klyne R. 1986. Galatians 3:28: Conundrum or solution? In *Women, authority and the Bible*, ed. A. Mickelsen, 161–81. Downers Grove, IL: InterVarsity Press.

Soggin, Alberto. 1997. The equality of humankind from the perspective of the creation stories in Genesis 1:26–30 and 2:9, 15, 18–24. *Journal of Northwest Semitic Languages* 23, no. 2: 21–33.

Somit, Albert. 1991. Democratic philosophy: An endangered species? In *Hierarchy and democracy*, ed. A. Somit and R. Wildenmann, 23–43. Carbondale: Southern Illinois University Press.

Soranus of Ephesus. 1991. *Soranus' gynecology*. Trans. T. Owsei, N. J. Eastman, L. Edelstein, and A. F. Guttmacher. Baltimore: Johns Hopkins University Press.

Speiser, E. A. 1964. *Genesis: Introduction, translation, and notes*. Ed. W. F. Albright and D. N. Freedman. The Anchor Bible. Garden City, NJ: Doubleday.

Stegemann, Ekkehard W., and Wolfgang Stegemann. 1999. *The Jesus movement: A social history of its first century*. Trans. O. C. Dean Jr. Minneapolis: Fortress. Original edition, Urchristliche Sozialgeschichte: Die Anfänge im Judentum und die Christusgemeinden in der mediterranen Welt.

Stendahl, Krister. 1966. *The Bible and the role of women: A case study in hermeneutics*. Trans. E. T. Sander. Ed. J. H. P. Reumann. Vol. 15 of *Facet books: Biblical series*. Philadelphia: Fortress.

Stitzinger, Michael F. 1981. Genesis 1–3 and the male/female role relationship. *Grace Theological Journal* 2, no. 1: 23–44.

Stowasser, Barbara Freyer. 1994. *Women in the Qur'an, Traditions, and interpretation*. Oxford: Oxford University Press.

———. 1998. Gender issues and contemporary Quran interpretation. In *Islam, gender, and social change*, ed. Y. Y. Haddad and J. L. Esposito, 30–44. New York: Oxford University Press.

Strabo. 1949. *The geography of Strabo*. Trans. H. L. Jones. Ed. T. E. Page, E. Capps, I. A. Post, W. H. D. Rouse, and E. H. Warmington. Vol. 8. Loeb Classical Library. Cambridge, MA: Harvard University Press.

Strauss, Anselm, and Juliet Corbin. 1998. Grounded theory methodology: An overview. In *Strategies of qualitative inquiry*, ed. N. K. Denzin and Y. S. Lincoln. Thousand Oaks, CA: SAGE.

Suetonius Tranquillus, Gaius. 1960. *Suetonius*. Trans. J. C. Rolfe. Ed. T. E. Page, E. Capps, I. A. Post, W. H. D. Rouse, and E. H. Warmington. Vol. 1. Loeb Classical Library. Cambridge, MA: Harvard University Press.

Swartley, Willard M. 1986. Response. In *Women, authority and the Bible*, ed. A. Mickelsen, 85–91. Downers Grove, IL: InterVarsity Press.

Tacitus, Cornelius. 1943. *Tacitus: The histories and the annals*. Trans. C. H. Moore and J. Jackson. Ed. T. E. Page, E. Capps, I. A. Post, W. H. D. Rouse, and E. H. Warmington. Vol. 2. Loeb Classical Library. Cambridge, MA: Harvard University Press.

Talbert, Charles H. 2002. *Reading Corinthians: A literary and theological commentary*. Rev. ed. Macon, GA: Smyth and Helwys.

Talbot, Mary. 2003. Gender stereotypes: Reproduction and challenge. In *The handbook of language and gender*, ed. J. Holmes and M. Meyerhoff, 468–86. Malden, MA: Blackwell.

Thiselton, Anthony C. 1978. Realized eschatology at Corinth. *New Testament Studies* 24: 510–26.

_____. 2000. *The First Epistle to the Corinthians: A commentary on the Greek text.* Ed. I. H. Marshall and D. A. Hagner. The New International Greek Testament Commentary. Grand Rapids: Eerdmans.

Thomason, Dana Andrew. 1987. Transcending sexual distinctions: 1 Corinthians 11:2–16 and Corinthian worship practices. PhD diss., Iliff School of Theology.

Thompson, Cynthia L. 1988. Hairstyles, head-coverings, and St. Paul: Portraits from Roman Corinth. *Biblical Archaeologist* 51, no. 2: 99–115.

Tirmidhi, Abu Isa Muhammad ibn Isa ibn Surat ibn Musa ibn ad-Dahhak as-Sulami at-. 2006. Sunan at-Tirmidhi. In *The Alim.* CD-ROM. Version 6.0.11.1. Silver Spring, MD: ISL Software.

Towner, Philip H. 2006. *The Letters to Timothy and Titus.* Ed. G. D. Fee. The New International Commentary on the New Testament. Grand Rapids: Eerdmans.

Tracy, Thomas F. 1994. Divine action, created causes, and human freedom. In *The God who acts: Philosophical and theological explorations,* ed. T. F. Tracy, 77–102. University Park: Pennsylvania State University Press.

Treggiari, Susan. 1991. *Roman marriage: Iusti coniuges from the time of Cicero to the time of Ulpian.* Oxford: Oxford University Press.

Trible, Phyllis. 1973. Depatriarchalizing in biblical interpretation. *Journal of the American Academy of Religion* 41 (March): 30–48.

_____. 1978. *God and the rhetoric of sexuality.* Ed. W. Brueggemann and J. R. Donahue. Overtures to Biblical Theology. Philadelphia: Fortress.

Trompf, G. W. 1980. On attitudes toward women in Paul and Paulinist literature: 1 Corinthians 11:3–6 and its context. *Catholic Biblical Quarterly* 42: 196–215.

Van Beek, Walter E. A. 1987. *The Kapsiki of the Mandara Hills.* Prospect Heights, IL: Waveland.

Van Leeuwen, Mary Stewart. 2004. Is equal regard in the Bible? In *Does Christianity teach male headship? The equal-regard marriage and its critics,* ed. D. Blankenhorn, D. Browning, and M. S. Van Leeuwen, 13–22. Grand Rapids: Eerdmans.

Van Seters, John. 1992. *Prologue to history: The Yahwist as historian in Genesis.* Louisville: Westminster John Knox.

Van Wolde, Ellen J. 1994. *Words become worlds: Semantic studies of Genesis 1–11.* Ed. R. A. Culpepper and R. Rendtorff. Vol. 6 of *Biblical interpretation series.* Leiden: Brill.

Vasholz, Robert I. 1994. "He will rule over you": A thought on Genesis 3:16. *Presbyterion* 20, no. 1: 51–52.

Velleius Paterculus, C. 1955. *Res gestae divi Augusti.* Trans. F. W. Shipley. Ed. T. E. Page, E. Capps, I. A. Post, W. H. D. Rouse, and E. H. Warmington. Loeb Classical Library. Cambridge, MA: Harvard University Press.

Vervenne, Marc. 2001. Genesis 1:1–2,4: The compositional texture of the priestly overture to the Pentateuch. In *Studies in the book of Genesis: Literature, redaction and history,* ed. A. Wenin, 35–79. Leuven, Belgium: Leuven University Press.

Veyne, Paul. 1987. The Roman empire. In *A history of private life: From pagan Rome to Byzantium,* ed. P. Veyne, 4 –233. Cambridge, MA: Belknap Press of Harvard University Press.

von Rad, Gerhard. 1961. *Genesis: A commentary.* Trans. J. H. Marks. Ed. G. E. Wright, J. Bright, J. Barr, and P. Ackroyd. The Old Testament Library. Philadelphia: Westminster Press.

Wadud, Amina. 1999. *Qur'an and woman: Rereading the sacred text from a woman's perspective.* New York: Oxford University Press.

Walker, William. O., Jr. 1975. 1 Corinthians 11:2–6 and Paul's views regarding women. *Journal of Biblical Literature* 94: 94–110.

Wallace-Hadrill, Andrew. 1996. Engendering the Roman house. In *I Claudia: Women in ancient Rome,* ed. D. E. E. Kleiner and S. B. Matheson, 104–15. New Haven, CT: Yale University Art Gallery.

Walsh, Jerome. 1977. Genesis 2:4b–3:24: A synchronic approach. *Journal of Biblical Literature* 96, no. 2: 161–77.

Waltke, Bruce K. 1975. The creation account in Genesis 1:1–3. Part 4: The theology of Genesis one. *Bibliotheca Sacra* 132, no. 528: 327–42.

Ward, Roy Bowen. 1990. Musonius and Paul on marriage. *New Testament Studies* 36: 281–89.

Ware, Bruce A. 2002. Male and female complementarity and the image of God. In *Biblical foundations for manhood and womanhood,* ed. W. A. Grudem, 71–92. Wheaton: Crossway Books.

Warmington, Eric Herbert, trans. 1967. *Remains of Old Latin.* Ed. T. E. Page, E. Capps, I. A. Post, W. H. D. Rouse, and E. H. Warmington. Vol. 3. Loeb Classical Library. Cambridge, MA: Harvard University Press.

Watt, W. Montgomery. 1956. *Muhammad at Medina.* Oxford: Oxford University Press.

Webb, William J. 2001. *Slaves, women, and homosexuals: Exploring the hermeneutics of cultural analysis*. Downers Grove, IL: InterVarsity Press.

Welker, Michael. 1991. What is creation? Rereading Genesis 1 and 2. *Theology Today* 48, no. 1: 56–71.

Wenham, Gordon J. 1979. *The book of Leviticus*. Ed. R. K. Harrison. The New International Commentary on the Old Testament. Grand Rapids: Eerdmans.

———. 1987. *Genesis 1–15*. Ed. D. A. Hubbard, G. W. Barker, and J. D. W. Watts. Vol. 1 of *Word biblical commentary*. Waco: Word Books.

Westermann, Claus. 1984. *Genesis 1–11: A commentary*. Trans. J. J. Scullion. Minneapolis: Augsburg.

Wevers, John William. 1993. *Notes on the Greek text of Genesis*. Ed. L. L. Greenspoon. Vol. 35 of *Society of Biblical Literature: Septuagint and cognate studies*. Atlanta: Scholars Press.

Wherry, E. M. 1975. *A comprehensive commentary on the Quran: Comprising Sale's translation and preliminary discourse, with additional notes and emendations*. Vol. 1. New York: AMS Press. (Orig. pub. 1896.)

Whiteman, Darrell L. 2005. The function of appropriate contextualization in mission. In *Appropriate Christianity*, ed. C. H. Kraft, 49–65. Pasadena: William Carey Library.

Wilson, Ian. 1995. *Out of the midst of the fire: Divine presence in Deuteronomy*. Ed. M. Fox and P. Perkins. Vol. 151 of *Society of Biblical Literature: Dissertation series*. Atlanta: Scholars Press.

Wilson, R. M. 2005. *A critical and exegetical commentary on Colossians and Philemon*. Ed. G. I. Davies, G. N. Stanton, J. A. Emerton, and C. E. B. Cranfield. The International Critical Commentary on the Holy Scriptures of the Old and New Testaments. London: Clark.

Wimbush, Vincent L., ed. 1990. *Ascetic behavior in Greco-Roman antiquity: A sourcebook*. Ed. J. M. Robinson. Studies in Antiquity and Christianity. Minneapolis: Fortress.

Winter, Bruce W. 2001. *After Paul left Corinth: The influence of secular ethics and social change*. Grand Rapids: Eerdmans.

———. 2003. *Roman wives, Roman widows: The appearance of new women and the Pauline communities*. Grand Rapids: Eerdmans.

Wire, Antoinette Clark. 1990. *The Corinthian women prophets: A reconstruction through Paul's rhetoric*. Minneapolis: Fortress.

Witherington, Ben, III. 1981. Rites and rights for women: Galatians 3:28. *New Testament Studies* 27: 593–604.

_____. 1988. *Women in the earliest churches*. Ed. G. N. Stanton. Society for New Testament Studies Monograph Series. Cambridge, MA: Cambridge University Press.

_____. 1995. *Conflict and community in Corinth: A socio-rhetorical commentary on 1 and 2 Corinthians*. Grand Rapids: Eerdmans.

_____. 1998. *The Paul quest: The renewed search for the Jew of Tarsus*. Downers Grove, IL: InterVarsity Press.

_____. 2006. *Letters and homilies for Hellenized Christians: A socio-rhetorical commentary on Titus, 1–2 Timothy and 1–3 John*. Vol. 1. Downers Grove, IL: InterVarsity Press.

Wright, Christopher J. H. 1995. *Walking in the ways of the Lord: The ethical authority of the Old Testament*. Downers Grove, IL: InterVarsity Press.

_____. 2004. *Old Testament ethics for the people of God*. Downers Grove, IL: InterVarsity Press.

_____. 2006. *The mission of God: Unlocking the Bible's grand narrative*. Downers Grove, IL: InterVarsity Press.

Wright, Nicholas Thomas. 1992. *The New Testament and the people of God*. Vol. 1 of *Christian origins and the question of God*. Minneapolis: Fortress.

_____. 2005. *Paul: In fresh perspective*. Minneapolis: Fortress.

Xenophon. 1997. *"Memorabilia," "Oeconomicus," "Symposium," "Apology."* Trans. E. C. Marchant and O. J. Todd. Ed. C. P. Goold. Vol. 4. Loeb Classical Library. Cambridge, MA: Harvard University Press.

Yarbrough, O. Larry. 1985. *Not like the Gentiles: Marriage rules in the Letters of Paul*. Ed. C. H. Talbert. Vol. 80 of *Society of Biblical Literature: Dissertation series*. Atlanta: Scholars Press.

Young, Frances M. 1994. *The theology of the Pastoral Letters*. Ed. J. D. G. Dunn. New Testament Theology. Cambridge, MA: Cambridge University Press.

Yusufzai, Mushtaq. 2006. Handbill warns NGOs to quit Bajaur Agency. *The News International*, August 25. http://www.thenews.com.pk/TodaysPrintDetail.asp x?ID=21301&Cat=7&dt=8/25/2006.

INDEX